KING OF THE WORLD

راى لصور بادشاه

اى لا رو ى اگر بو نو ر بدى ى جهان را ٭ مهر نور افرو ز خرب ز من را و ز مان را

The Emperor Shah Alam by courtesy of the British Museum

KING OF
THE WORLD

*The Life and Times of Shah Alam
Emperor of Hindustan*

MICHAEL EDWARDES

TAPLINGER PUBLISHING COMPANY
NEW YORK

First published in the United States in 1971 by
Taplinger Publishing Co., Inc.
New York, New York

ISBN 0-8008-4465-3

Library of Congress Catalog Card Number 72-131025

Printed in Great Britain

Contents

Frontispiece: Portrait of Shah Alam, from a manuscript of the emperor's own Persian poem, Diwani-i-Aftāb, dated Shawwal 1209 (April 1795). Originally in the library of the Kings of Oudh, Lucknow. Reproduced by courtesy of the Trustees of the British Museum, London.

PART ONE

A Wanderer Without a Home

The throne of the Moguls was the sport of servants and strangers, and he who was entitled to occupy it was a wanderer without a home.

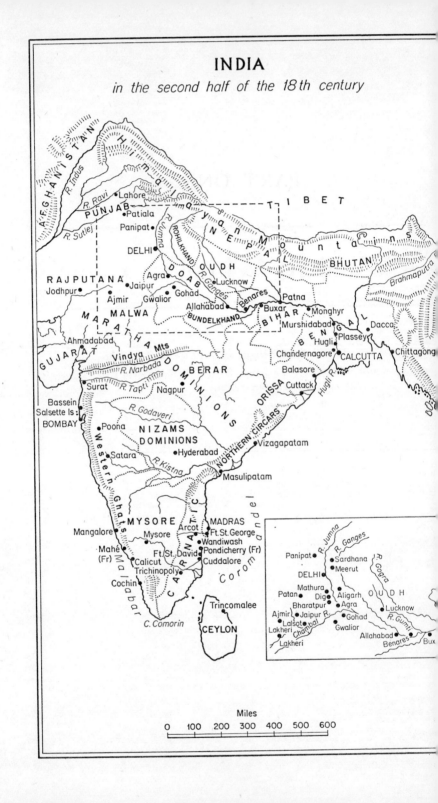

INDIA
in the second half of the 18th century

AFGHANISTAN

Himalaya Mts

R. Indus

R. Ravi · Lahore

PUNJAB

R. Sutlej

· Patiala

Panipat ·

DELHI ●

TIBET

NEPAL

Mountains

BHUTAN

Brahmaputra

RAJPUTANA

Jodhpur ·

Agra ·

Ajmir · · Jaipur

Gwalior ·

· Gohad

DOAB

ROHILKHAND

OUDH

· Lucknow

R. Ganges

Allahabad · · Benares

BUNDELKHAND

· Patna

· Buxar · Monghyr

BIHAR

Murshidabad ●

Dacca ●

BENGAL

Hugli ● · Plassey

Chandernagore ● CALCUTTA

● Chittagong

MALWA

MARATHA

Ahmadabad ·

GUJARAT

Vindya Mts

R. Narbada

R. Tapti

Surat ·

Nagpur ·

DOMINIONS

BERAR

Balasore ·

ORISSA

Cuttack ·

Hugli R.

Bassein
Salsette Is ·
BOMBAY

· Poona

Western Ghats

R. Godaveri

NIZAMS
DOMINIONS

· Hyderabad

· Satara

R. Kistna

NORTHERN CIRCARS

· Vizagapatam

● Masulipatam

MYSORE

Mangalore ·

· Mysore

Arcot ·

Ft. St. George

MADRAS

Malabar

Mahé
(Fr)

Calicut ·

Trichinopoly ·

Ft. St. David

Wandiwash ·

Pondicherry (Fr)

Cuddalore ·

CARNATIC

Coromandel

Cochin ·

· Trincomalee

C. Comorin

CEYLON

R. Jumna

R. Ganges

Panipat ·

· Sardhana

R. Gogra

DELHI ·

· Meerut

Mathura ·

Patan · · Dig

· Aligarh

OUDH

Bharatpur ·

· Agra

· Lucknow

R. Gumti

Ajmir · · Jaipur R.

· Gohad

Lalsot ·

Chambal

· Gwalior

Allahabad ·

Lakheri ·

· Benares

· Bux

· Lakheri

Miles

0   100   200   300   400   500   600

1
King of the world

THE CEREMONIES were just as they would have been if they had taken place in a palace, instead of in an armed camp. There was the prince on his throne, the symbolic royal umbrella over his head; before him, the great men of his empire.

A herald proclaimed the new emperor's titles, and they rolled around the pavilion like a prayer or a magic spell—both of which the empire stood much in need of. 'Great king', 'King of the world', 'Sword of the faith', 'Asylum of the universe'.

Then the great men made their offerings of gold, and the superintendent of the royal kitchens brought in sweetmeats on a golden tray. Mounting his state elephant, the new emperor Shah Alam tossed to his cheering soldiers a few coins and jewels—silver coins, not gold; and flawed pearls and semi-precious stones where once there would have been dark red rubies and shining pale green zircons.

The elephant and its escort, a handful of richly clothed courtiers and officers of state lost amid the armed horsemen, battle-ready, moved towards the house of God to give thanks to God. As the throne room had been of cloth and not of marble, so the mosque had none of the great majesty of an imperial capital. It was small, simple, of brick and stucco, as befitted a village in southern Bihar hundreds of miles from the palaces and mosques of Delhi. But the emperor made the customary prayer, and the roll of his glorious ancestors was read aloud—from Tamerlane the Conqueror, all the way down through the centuries to the new emperor's father, ingloriously murdered by his own chief minister.

It was 24 December 1759.

2
A city drowned in blood

TWENTY YEARS before, as a boy of ten, Shah Alam had listened while a city drowned in blood. Though he was a prince of the Mughal imperial house which had once ruled all India, he was a state prisoner in the fortress at Delhi. He was not alone, for his family was imprisoned too, as were hundreds of those dependants known as 'emperors' grandsons', descendants of past rulers by the numerous women of the imperial harems. All these were of the blood royal and therefore dangerous, a possible focus for rebellion, puppets to be manoeuvred by any ambitious minister or strong man who might materialize out of nowhere with an army at his back.

During the empire's two centuries of existence, there had been many threats to its rulers. Perhaps its founder had been the only one not to suffer from the intrigues and ambitions of his relatives. Instead, Babur had had to face treachery, like all conquerors, though he had not been as great a conqueror as his ancestor Tamerlane, who had spread his hand across the heartland of Asia and died on his way to conquer China. A century after Tamerlane's death, Babur had turned to northern India after failing to take his ancestral kingdom of Samarkand. After two invasions, he had defeated the sultan of Delhi in a great battle in 1526. Babur lived for only four more years, dying—according to the chronicler—because he had offered his life in exchange for that of his son, Humayun, then gravely ill.

To Humayun, Babur left the task of consolidating his conquests. For ten years, Humayun did so, but his campaigns were separated by long periods of indolence. While he took his pleasure in Delhi, the leaderless chiefs of northern India had time to recover their shattered nerve. This process threw up a challenger to the new Mughal power in the person of Sher Shah Sur, an Afghan who had supported Babur in 1526 but had subsequently set himself up as an independent ruler in southern Bihar. From this base he began to challenge Humayun. Finally, after two desperate defeats, he drove the Mughal from Delhi in 1540. Sixteen years of exile for Humayun were the result; his own brother turned against him and he was forced to take refuge in Persia. But he returned and took Delhi again, only to die six months later from the effects of a fall on the marble steps of his library.

It was a barbed heritage that Humayun left to his thirteen-year-old son, Akbar. Northern India was in confusion and disorder. There were many opponents willing and anxious to shatter the frail new regime, and there was little loyalty to draw upon. Members of the royal family had their own ambitions, and their partisans. The great nobles would change sides at any moment, if there was a prospect of profit in the change. Fortunately for Akbar, his guardian was a man to be trusted, a good general and a sound politician. He gave Akbar four years of personal security and, at the same time, defeated enemies and extended the empire. At eighteen, Akbar was himself ready to take over the control of his dominions.

During the reign of Akbar, the Mughals became naturalized. Akbar was no longer a conqueror from the north, his eyes focused longingly on the high hills and the central Asian wastes from which his ancestors had emerged. Nor was he a conqueror imposing the will of a minority on the majority of different race and religion. For the forty years which followed his assumption of personal rule, Akbar consciously set about coming to terms not only with India but with the Indian rulers who still exercised power. His tactics were partly those of conquest, partly those of persuasion. One by one, the great Hindu princes of the Rajputana were won over. Akbar married a Rajput princess who was to become the mother of the next Mughal emperor. He pushed forward the boundaries of the empire until more than half of India came under his control. Akbar's politics were the politics of symbiosis, the coming together of different groups for their mutual benefit. Hindu nobles became great officers of state. The expanding bureaucracy was staffed by Hindu clerks. A burgeoning trade and industry were left to the skill of Hindu entrepreneurs.

The empire of Akbar was Akbar's own creation. Though he could neither read nor write, his mind was alive with ideas and sparkling with intellectual curiosity. To his court were invited representatives of many religions—the sects of the religion he was born into, Islám, as well as Hindus, Zoroastrians and Christians. Even subtle Jesuits, sent with the approval of the Portuguese, who had settled themselves into little pockets of India when Babur was only considering his own invasion, were made welcome and invited to dispute. Akbar accepted none of the established religions for himself but created a new faith out of what he regarded as the virtues of many. It did not survive his death.

The unorthodoxy and tolerance of the emperor invited rebellion. The ruling minority had, with some reluctance, accepted the association of Hindu rulers in what was essentially a Muslim conquest because it was a matter of politics. It made good sense in terms of power. But that the emperor should desert the Muslim faith—should become, in effect, a heretic—was another matter. In 1580 the orthodox rebelled, using the emperor's brother as a figurehead. Though the revolt was suppressed, opposition remained. Akbar's eldest son turned on him in 1600 and, with the support of the orthodox party, held out for three years before finally submitting. He had not much longer to wait. Akbar died in 1605, and his son succeeded as the emperor Jahangir.

Though he owed his throne to the orthodox, and though he in turn had to suppress a rebellion led by his own son before he could feel secure on it, Jahangir was no bigot. He too was interested in other religions, though not as much as in painting and in music. A man of taste, he was also addicted to drugs and liquor. His palace was partly an atelier and partly an opium den. During Jahangir's reign, the first English ambassador appeared, begging for commercial privileges; ways were found to use the English against the Portuguese.

Jahangir had to deal with the revolt of another of his sons, and when he died in 1627 there was a fight for the succession. The victorious son was Shah Jahan, who was to build the great palace fort of Delhi. Shah Jahan tried to expand the empire to its natural limits before he too was overthrown by *his* son. He was allowed, however, to see out his remaining years at Agra where, seated in a marble pavilion, he could look across the river to the elegant poetry of his wife's tomb, the Taj Mahal—a constant reminder of the transience of power.

Shah Jahan's attempts to expand the empire had shown that, to the south, there were a number of Muslim rulers who would have to be destroyed. His son and successor, Aurangzeb, had already begun the campaign in the south before seizing power in 1658, and he continued the battle, with success, from 1681 until his death. But the confusion caused by an expanding empire had allowed new rulers to emerge and take advantage of the chaos. One of these was Sivaji, whose father had been in the employ of the sultan of Bijapur.

Sivaji was a Hindu by faith and a Maratha by race. The Marathas were a tough, low-caste people, cultivators from the west coast of India. Until they suddenly emerged into the glare of late seventeenth-century Indian politics, they seem to have had no history. Their land was poor, and many of their chiefs took military service with Muslim rulers. Sivaji had taken advantage of the disintegration of the state of Bijapur under the pressure of Mughal expansion to make himself an independent ruler. He defeated a general sent against him and then, with his own hands—to which had been attached claws of sharpened steel—killed him. From that episode in 1659 until his death in 1680 Sivaji built up and consolidated a well-organized Hindu kingdom.

7

The Mughals tried to make him an ally, but Sivaji would have none of it. When on one occasion he was captured and taken to Aurangzeb, he managed a romantic escape to add to his legend.

But Sivaji's kingdom did not long survive his death. As Aurangzeb conquered to the south, Sivaji's state was slowly broken up. The Marathas turned to the guerrilla tactics which Sivaji had used so successfully, and though Aurangzeb could not suppress them neither could they sustain an orderly administration. Though the campaign was inconclusive, it was disastrous for the Maratha character. It was as if the loss of Sivaji's kingdom, the symbol of Maratha nationalism and Maratha Hinduism, made them sour and changed them, in a single generation, from patriotic guerrillas to ruthless bandits.

Aurangzeb died in 1707, leaving the Marathas uncrushed and other Hindu leaders in a state of unease. The empire, however, was substantially larger than it had been when he seized the throne. His successor, Bahadur Shah, made an agreement with the Marathas, calmed the Rajputs—who were also feeling their way towards revolt—and decisively defeated the Sikhs of the Punjab, who were in open rebellion. But the vigour was an illusion. After a reign of no more than five years, Bahadur Shah died, the last of the great emperors. Seven years of wars of succession followed.

Bahadur Shah was succeeded by Shah Alam's grandfather, who was strangled in 1713 by a prince who belonged to another branch of the imperial family. The murderer reigned, a puppet of stronger men, for six years before he too suffered the same fate. 1719 was a year of kings. Four reigned, and three of them were murdered. The survivor, Muhammad Shah, was thought by the kingmakers to be docile. But he had a talent for intrigue. Within two years he had disposed of them.

Outside the palace, the empire had begun to tear at the seams. The great officers of state had begun to make themselves independent in the territories they governed. To the south, the Deccan was in the hands of Asaf Jah, who had retired there in 1723 because of opposition at court. With his going, the empire was virtually divided in two. Not into rival empires, however. Asaf Jah remained an officer of state and returned to the north to help his emperor when Delhi was threatened.

Early in 1738 the Marathas appeared outside the imperial capital and plundered the suburbs. To them, the empire's troubles had brought little but profit. The weakness of the central government had meant that they had been left alone. In 1713, Sivaji's descendant, the nominal head of the Marathas, delegated authority to an official known as the Peshwa, who had his capital at Poona. The Marathas began to take on the appearance of an organized state, though they formed in fact a confederation of individual chiefs who, as the Maratha conquests spread, set themselves up as independent rulers. In 1723, the Peshwa decided that the Marathas' future lay in the north. By attacking the empire at its centre, he believed, it would be possible to take control of the parts. 'Let us strike at the trunk of the withering tree', he is reported to have said in council, 'and the branches will fall by themselves'.

The Maratha campaigns to the north were slow but successful. The threat to the imperial capital appeared particularly grave and the emperor was forced to cede to the Marathas the province of Malwa, which lay between Delhi and the south. Muhammad Shah had maintained himself on the throne by playing off one faction against another, buying one here, inciting another there. To him the Marathas were no more than another, greedier, faction in the imperial game.

But in 1739, after twenty years of keeping his opponents divided, Muhammad Shah was at last faced by an enemy who could neither be outmanoeuvred nor bought off. One reason for this, perhaps, was that the enemy came not from inside India but from Persia.

Persia had been conquered by the Afghans in 1722 and it had taken five years for the Persians to recover sufficiently to drive them out. The victorious Persian general was a man of genius who, in 1736, assumed the throne for himself. His name was Nadir Shah.

In the process of consolidating his new kingdom, Nadir Shah attacked the Afghans of Kandahar. Some of them fled into an area of Afghanistan which was then part of the empire of Hindustan, and Nadir Shah sent ambassadors to Delhi asking for the Mughal emperor's help in capturing them.

Muhammad Shah replied with promises and nothing more. There was, in fact, little he could do. The marches of his empire were policed by ill-fed, badly armed, rarely paid troops; his governor at Kabul passed the time either in hunting or praying. The gate from Afghanistan to India stood open. So, too, did that of the Punjab, the gate that led to Delhi.

Through both came Nadir Shah. On 10 May 1738 he crossed the imperial frontier and slowly moved down into India, flicking aside the imperial generals and their feeble attempts at defence. In Delhi, the emperor still pretended to a power he did not have and refused to answer Nadir Shah's communications. One of Nadir Shah's couriers was murdered and the Persian advance became even more determined, but the emperor—a victim of the factions whose balance maintained his own position, and of advisers who were both ill-informed and partisan—still made no preparations to resist.

By the middle of January 1739, Nadir Shah had captured the great city of Lahore, 270 miles from Delhi. The imperial governor, viewing resistance as worthless, delivered the keys of the fort to the Persian king and was rewarded with a robe of honour, an Arab horse with a gold-embroidered saddle, a jewelled sword and dagger, and reinstatement in office. At Lahore, Nadir learned that the emperor had at last decided on war and was determined to fight—although Nadir insisted that his own intentions were friendly and warned Muhammad Shah of the consequences of war.

The imperial preparations had at last got under way in December 1738, but so slowly that the army, the great officers of state, and the emperor himself had progressed no further than Karnal, seventy-six miles north of Delhi. There the Mughal forces surrounded themselves with a mud wall, placed their guns in position, dug trenches, and waited for Nadir Shah.

The Mughal emperor's army was no small compact fighting force. It was more like a swarm of locusts, for, though the number of combatants was only about 75,000, the camp housed closer to a million people, as well as thousands of horses, elephants and bullocks. The emperor and his officers had brought their women with them, and vast bodies of retainers. Carriers, coolies, and a wide variety of hangers-on (complete with families) made up the rest. It was said that the surrounding mud wall stretched for twelve miles.

In contrast to this clumsy encampment, cluttered with useless men, Nadir Shah commanded a force of about 160,000, about a third of whom were servants. But they, too, were mounted and armed. Over six thousand women, dressed in long padded coats of crimson cloth and, at a distance, indistinguishable from the men, added an exotic note to the Persian army.

Nadir's tactics were simple—to invest the imperial camp as if it were a fortress, preventing fodder and food from being taken in, making famine and disease into powerful allies. The Persian cavalry raided the Mughal grass and fuel stores, while the main body of the army bypassed the imperial entrenchment and cut its communications with Delhi. It seemed that the emperor was now faced with a choice between coming out and fighting, or staying in—and starving. But reinforcement, in the shape of thirty thousand cavalry, with stores, reached the Mughal camp under the command of one of Muhammad Shah's officers of state.

The emperor now seemed anxious for battle and the imperial forces moved out. They had no pre-arranged plan, and no action had been decided upon. One section of the army—the largest—with the emperor and his chief minister at its head, settled down on the edge of a canal and remained detached from the conflict. The Persian forces, on the other hand, consisted entirely of cavalry and were highly mobile. Even the artillery—long swivel-guns firing a two-pound ball—was mounted on camels which were trained to lie down so that the guns might be fired from their backs.

The battle began a little after one o'clock on the afternoon of 13 February, and by sunset two of the commanders were out of action—one, the Mughal commander-in-chief, mortally wounded, and the other a prisoner. With what remained of his army, the emperor retired to his camp. Many of his soldiers had fled, and many were wounded. Close on 15,000 were dead. The night was given up to looting and to fear, the imperial army no more than a rabble listening to the thumping of its own heart.

But the next step was negotiation. On the advice of the captured commander, one of the emperor's remaining ministers, Asaf Jah, was sent to Nadir Shah under safe conduct to discuss terms. These were simple. Nadir wanted an indemnity of five million rupees, two million to be paid at once and the balance in three instalments as the Persian forces retired. The terms seemed not only reasonable but possible, and the minister returned to the emperor carrying an invitation for the emperor to dine with Nadir Shah at the Persian camp on the following day.

The emperor was welcomed by Nadir's son. As they approached the king's tent, Nadir himself came to the entrance and, taking the emperor by the hand, led him on to the royal carpet. It was, said one official historian (who was not present at the meeting), 'as if two suns had risen in the east, or as if two bright moons shed their light at one time'. But the emperor still feared that he might be poisoned. Claiming that open war, not assassination, was his method, Nadir Shah exchanged his dish with that of the emperor just as they were about to eat. A few hours later, the emperor was able to return to his camp and his anxious—perhaps surprised—family.

Yet the courtesies could not conceal that the emperor's

camp was still surrounded by Persian troops, and the camp itself was full of tensions. The wounded commander-in-chief had died, after trying to prevent the emperor from meeting Nadir Shah. His office devolved on Asaf Jah—which alienated the Mughal emperor's second commander, Saadat Khan, then a prisoner in Nadir Shah's camp. In an audience with Nadir Shah, Saadat Khan pointed out that five million rupees need be no more than an appetiser. Delhi, he said, was bursting with bullion and precious stones. All the Persian king needed to do was lay a trap for the new commander-in-chief, and the emperor would do whatever he wanted. Saadat Khan also volunteered to withdraw his own troops from the imperial camp and transfer them to the Persian service.

Nadir Shah accepted the offer. After allowing the conspiracy to mature a little, he made his first demand. This proved unacceptable. Nadir Shah therefore placed a close embargo on the emperor's camp, permitting no supplies to enter and no persons to leave. After a week, he summoned the Mughal commander-in-chief and told him that two million rupees must be paid immediately and twenty thousand troopers transferred to the Persian forces. Asaf Jah pleaded that such a sum could not be raised. He was promptly arrested. When this news reached the emperor, his younger nobles tried to persuade him to fight but he decided instead to pay another visit to Nadir Shah.

This time his reception was frigid. For a while he was left alone and unattended, then, when night fell, he was taken to Nadir Shah and told that he was a prisoner. Next day, his harem, his personal servants, and his tents were moved over to the Persian encampment. The courtesies were observed, but they were even emptier of meaning than before. Other captive nobles were instructed to transfer their families and retainers from the imperial camp, which now stood vast and uneasy behind its useless mud walls. Those who remained were told contemptuously that they might stay there or make their own way back to Delhi, or even to their own homes. But their way was strewn with dangers. The Persian cavalry controlled the roads to Delhi, free to plunder and destroy as they chose, while the ordinary people of the countryside, smarting from the expropriations of the imperial army, had armed themselves and were eager to extort compensation from any travellers weaker than themselves.

The great imperial camp broke up. One of the ambassadors who had accompanied the emperor, a representative of one of the rising Hindu powers—the Marathas—feared for his own life and that of his family. Plucking up courage—making, as he put it in a report to his master, 'a fort of his breast'—he set off along the imperial highway to Delhi, accompanied by an escort of foot soldiers, elephants, camels, and baggage. After taking a circuitous route through the jungle at one point, he reached the capital only to leave again the same day. Delhi was not a comfortable place when the hand of the Mughal was not there to restrain its citizens. Reaching safety at last, the ambassador breathed a sigh of relief. 'God has averted a great danger from me and has helped me to escape with honour', he said. And added : 'The Mughal empire is at an end and the Persian has begun'.

It must have seemed so to even the least—or most—percipient of men. The emperor was a prisoner, and so were the great nobles of the empire. The imperial capital lay open to the conqueror. The discipline of empire had gone. Law and order, those fingers of the hand of power, had lost their grip and the countryside and even the streets of the capital were in chaos. The people of Delhi had been as confident of victory as their rulers as they had watched the vast imperial army, polychromed with magnificent display, leave to teach the invader a lesson. Even the state prisoners in the fortress—the young Shah Alam and all the 'emperor's grandsons'—had seen little prospect of an imperial defeat, however much they might hope for the release which such a defeat might bring.

At first, when news of the defeat reached the city and various elements prepared for plunder, the chief of police contrived to maintain a strict watch on the streets. The entries to the city were strictly controlled, and private citizens were encouraged to fortify their houses, hire guards, and prepare for the worst.

To begin with, it seemed as if the worst was not to come. The governor of Delhi prepared to defend the city, but Saadat Khan, enmeshed in his conspiracy with the Persian king, warned him that it would be useless to resist. Letters from the emperor and from Nadir Shah reinforced this advice. The emperor ordered the governor to hand over the keys of the palaces and of the imperial treasuries and store-houses, and added that he should 'guard the princes care-fully'—an instruction, presumably, that no pretender to the throne should be permitted to escape. Nadir Shah's letter contained no orders, only compliments on the governor's honesty and devotion, and confirmation of his office.

Outside the city, the conqueror and the conquered stopped in the bird-haunted gardens of the Shalimar, in the shadow of whose tall trees one of the greatest of Mughal emperors, Aurangzeb, had crowned himself. From there, his defeated successor went on alone to prepare his palace for the arrival of the victor.

Muhammad Shah travelled on a portable throne. No band played. No banners fluttered gaily in the breeze. A silence suitable to mourning accompanied him, and the only sound was the shuffle of the palanquin-bearers and the faint snuffling of the horses of his escort.

On the following day, Friday 9 March, Nadir Shah entered the city on a grey horse. Persian troops lined the route from the gardens to the palace, where the ground was spread with carpets of cloth of gold and the emperor waited to welcome him to the marble pavilions of Shah Jahan. The Persian army pitched camp around the palace, the lights of its camp fires glistening menacingly in the waters of the river.

It was a time of reckoning. The conspirator Saadat Khan was called upon to produce the treasure he had sworn was in the palace. Failing, he was soon convinced, as a court diarist laconically reported, that 'so long as he was alive the Shah would not give up his demands. So he took poison and died'.

It was the emperor's turn next. Again, there were no open threats. But though an elegant cloud of diplomatic courtesies might obscure the position, they hardly altered it. Nadir Shah called upon the emperor in his own quarters and told him that he might keep his throne and enjoy the support and friendship of the Persian ruler, for they were brothers, 'of the same Turcoman stock'. Bowing low, the emperor thanked the victor for his generosity. 'He had received', said the Shah's secretary, 'no small favour. It was a gift of a crown added to the gift of life'. Gratitude could ask no less than that the emperor should offer the Shah all the treasures of his capital. Courtesy insisted that the Shah should refuse—even though 'the piled-up wealth of all the other kings of the world did not amount to a tenth part of a tenth part of this immense hoard'. At last the Shah was constrained to 'yield to the importunity' of the emperor by appointing 'trustworthy officers to take delivery of the money and other property'.

While this charade was taking place within the walls of the palace, the city outside was trembling with rumours. The streets were full of Nadir Shah's soldiers and camp followers, men from the harsh wastes of central Asia, Turks, Mongols and Kurds. Delhi, 'the navel of the world', was a city of palaces and mosques, a place of wonders, and Nadir's men went sightseeing—carelessly, as conquerors should— swaggering through the streets and bazaars in ones and twos. It was Saturday 10 March, a Muslim feast day commemorating Abraham's intended sacrifice of his son Ishmael.

About four o'clock in the afternoon, someone shouted the news that Nadir Shah had been assassinated, on the emperor's orders, by one of the Amazon guard. Suitably embroidered, the rumour spread swiftly all over the city. A Persian soldier was stabbed in one of the bazaars. Others were chased down the narrow alleys, cornered, and killed. Sensible men took no action, but the dregs of the city turned on the conquerors, and the riot spread. The police administration had broken down.

The Mughal nobles, fearing for themselves, remained immured in their houses behind their barriers of iron grilles and muskets, hoping that the rumour was true. It was not, but no one tested it by going to the palace to find out. When early reports of the murders reached Nadir Shah, he refused to believe them. Some of his soldiers, he thought, had invented the tale so that he might be induced to allow them to plunder the city in revenge. But when two agents sent to investigate were killed by the mob at the very gate of the palace, Nadir ordered troops into the streets to disperse the crowds. The dark night made it dangerous for troops unacquainted with the byways of the city, and musketeers were placed at strategic points in order to prevent the mobs from joining up. Soon the city quietened down—but it was only a respite.

The situation was out of control. Next day was the beginning of another festival, this time the Hindu Bacchanal of sex and drink, *holi*. At dawn the mobs came out in the streets again.

Nadir Shah, dressed in armour and surrounded by spearmen, rode to the Golden Mosque which stood in the centre of the principal avenue of the city. There, having decided which parts of the city the mobs had come from, he raised his sword as a signal to his men that they could take their revenge. In the condemned areas, houses were stormed, looted, and set on fire. Every man was killed, whatever his age, and the women were dragged out, raped, and carried off to the camp. In some houses, the head of the family chose to kill his wives and daughters before cutting his own throat or running out into the street to be hacked down by the Persian troops. In others, the women threw themselves down the well. Their screams were added to the cries of those who were burning to death. In one area, men were dragged off to the river bank and there beheaded. Soon, the narrow alleys were filled with corpses, and the smell of death, of burning, and of blood filled the air. Twenty thousand people were massacred in five short and terrible hours.

In the palace, the emperor finally sent his two principal

ministers to the Shah to beg him to stop the killing. Convinced at last, perhaps, that he was not faced with a general rising, the Shah sent a herald and the chief of police through the city ordering the troops to stop the burning and killing. The granaries were sealed, the gates of the city closed, and the walls guarded by patrols.

Disease and hunger now took over. It was days before permission was given to clear the streets of bodies and burn them in the open spaces. With the granaries closed and no food coming into the city, some of its desperate inhabitants tried to break out. Those who were caught had their ears and noses cut off and were sent back into the city. The villages surrounding the imperial capital were in no happier situation. For thirty or forty miles around the Persian forces were intent on plunder, and anyone foolish enough to resist was killed out of hand.

At last some kind of normality returned. The granaries were opened and food began to come in. Nadir Shah remained in the palace while his men gathered together the loot he intended to take back with him to Persia. With considerable display, his younger son was married to an imperial princess. The walls of the palace were illuminated. Combats between elephants and tigers were held every day. The best dancers and singers performed before the Shah. For two months Nadir Shah relaxed in Delhi while the storerooms were stripped of jewels and gold, furniture, fine cloth, cannon, and everything else of value. The crown jewels were packed up carefully, and the Peacock Throne dismantled. This throne, one of the wonders of Delhi, was rather like a couch—six feet long by four feet wide—whose twelve pillars, covered with pearls and gems, supported a golden canopy. At the back, two peacocks spread their tails of rubies, sapphires, emeralds and pearls. Between them was a parrot which is said to have been carved from a single great emerald.

It was not only the emperor and the imperial families that were being squeezed. Such citizens of Delhi as had survived the massacres were ordered to give up one half of their property. The whole affair was carried out with great efficiency. A census was taken, lists prepared, the unwilling were tortured, and the floors of houses dug up in the search for buried treasure. Suicides became common. Whole families took poison. The heart, as well as the pocket, of the city was emptied.

Even then, the humiliations were not over. The emperor was deprived of his title, 'king of kings', and coinage was struck bearing the cypher of Nadir Shah. Provincial governors were required to declare the Persian king their suzerain.

Soon, news of the sack of Delhi was known throughout India. Its barbarities were emphasized and enlarged. When Nadir announced that he was considering making a pilgrimage to the shrine of a Muslim saint at Ajmir in the Rajputana, the local ruler hustled his family off to a mountain fortress and himself prepared for battle. But Nadir was anxious to return to Persia. His army had had enough of India and wanted to enjoy their plunder in the comfort of their native lands. In May, after reinstating the emperor in his tormented empire, Nadir Shah and his army left Delhi. As well as the loot, they took with them hundreds of masons, carpenters and stone-cutters who were to build in Persia a city greater than Delhi itself. As the vast army laden with plunder moved off, the countryside behind it rose up and cut off the stragglers. In retaliation there were massacres. But the Persians at last reached their homeland, and there, eight years later, the Shah was assassinated. The treasures of Hindustan were dispersed, some, like the Peacock Throne, never to be seen again.

As the tide of Nadir Shah's conquest receded, new men emerged to continue the dismemberment of the Mughal empire. Afghanistan and the north-west, now part of the Persian dominion, formed a powerhouse for invasions to come. The passes of India lay unguarded. The Punjab—retaining wall of the empire—was a scene of utter desolation and disorder. Robbers roamed the countryside, while the nobles fought one another for control of the towns. In the south the Marathas, now in control of former provinces of the empire, prepared to move outwards on their own quest for dominion.

In Delhi, the shattered emperor found himself deserted by his principal advisers and officers of state, anxious to ensure their bases of power and to confirm the reality of their independence behind its loose mask of deference to the imperial name.

3

The puppet and the strings

DESPITE the blows of Nadir Shah, despite the undermining by the Marathas and others of the foundations of the empire, despite even the ambitions of the great Mughal nobles, the empire of Muhammad Shah soon seemed to acquire a new hold on life. The tree might be withering— but it could still put out a leaf.

The Imperial forces began to reassert themselves and, when a new invasion threatened from the north-west, were even able to repel it. This invasion was a direct consequence of the assassination of Nadir Shah in 1747. The Afghans threw off Persian rule, and one of them, Ahmad Shah Abdali, seized Kandahar and Kabul. In the following year he moved into India and reached Lahore without opposition. But at a place near Ambala, an imperial army nominally commanded by the heir-apparent barred the way and, by a combination of courage, good luck, and the fact that the invaders were more anxious to return home with their plunder than they were to fight, succeeded in repelling the Afghans.

In one of the engagements the Mughal commander-in-chief was killed. It was said that, when the news reached Delhi, the emperor suffered a heart attack. 'The staff of my old age is broken', he is reported to have murmured. 'No such faithful servant can I ever find again'. Whatever the proximate cause, the emperor Muhammad Shah died on 15 April 1748, in the thirty-first year of his reign. He was forty-six years old.

The heir-apparent was away from the capital at the time, and it was thought better to conceal the emperor's death until his successor arrived in case some ambitious nobleman should decide to release one of the 'emperors' grandsons' from confinement and place him on the throne. The emperor's body, wrapped in a tablecloth, was therefore placed in the long wooden case of an English clock and buried in one of the inner gardens of the palace. Letters were sent to the heir-apparent telling him that the emperor was dangerously ill and that he should return to Delhi with all possible speed.

The prince, hastening back, was met by a procession which had been sent by Safdar Jang, one of the imperial ministers, bearing emblems of royalty. Though he was reluctant to assume the title of emperor until he had proof that his father was dead, the prince was forced to issue a proclamation declaring his accession under the name of Ahmad Shah. The minister hailed the new monarch with : 'I congratulate your majesty on becoming emperor', and Ahmad Shah duly replied : 'I congratulate you on becoming my wazir [chief minister]'. As Asaf Jah, chief minister to the late Muhammad Shah, was still in power in Delhi, the appointment of Safdar Jang was kept secret.

Asaf Jah was the same man who had negotiated on Muhammad Shah's behalf with the Perisan invader ten years before. He had made himself an almost independent ruler in the area later to become known as Hyderabad, where—though his pretensions were challenged by the Marathas—he had managed to retain not only his dominions but, through a combination of his own real talent and the mediocrity of his enemies, an important place in the hierarchy of the empire. Unfortunately, he was old—over eighty, in fact—and by June 1748 he was dead and his sons were competing, in the classic tradition, for his legacy. To his imperial office now openly succeeded Safdar Jang, who was the nephew of that Saadat Khan who had taken poison rather than face torture by the Persians.

The stage was being set for an encounter which was to deal another savage blow at the empire. The new emperor had spent most of his life in enforced seclusion, as his father had not trusted him. He had no experience of running an administration and no inclination to learn. His father had survived by astutely playing off one faction against another and allowing none to dominate, but Ahmad Shah, instead of following his example or of at least giving his full support to the new chief minister, retired by choice into a seclusion that could now be made more variously enjoyable than before. There was no point in being an emperor if a man could not use the power to enjoy his vices.

The characters in the melodrama of imperial collapse prepared to play their roles. The central plot concerned the struggle to become the puppet-master who controlled the emperor. To this all the subsidiary plots—and there were many—were subordinate. In one sense, the least important figure was the emperor himself, for it was not he but what he represented that counted. For twenty-one years before his accession he had been kept among the women of the harem in comparative poverty, with nothing to occupy him but enjoyment of the senses. On his accession, he was encouraged to enlarge the harem, to expand his choice of wines and drugs. An area of about four square miles was turned into a *parc des cerfs* where no male but the emperor was permitted access.

The business of the state was dominated by the emperor's mother, a former Hindu dancing-girl who had caught Muhammad Shah's fancy. She had an immense and uncritical love for her son, and an equally immense hatred for those of the imperial family who had looked down upon her for her low birth and doubtful profession. Now in power, she was able to make them suffer. As a counterbalance, however, the members of the imperial family who had long been neglected in the state prison found their poverty considerably eased by her charity, though they were not released. From behind the marble screens of the harem, she pretended to administer the state, passing orders and appointing officials. But the real ruler was Javed Khan, once assistant superintendent of the harem servants and, though supposedly a eunuch, the queen mother's lover. After Ahmad Shah's accession, titles were conferred on Javed Khan that raised him above the highest nobles of the empire and he was appointed head of the privy council, which meant that he controlled all access to the emperor.

Under Javed Khan and the queen mother, profit for the few and neglect for the many became a substitute for government. The principal nobles and officers of state were ignored. The imperial army was—foolishly—left unpaid. Even the royal guards were starving. The imperial revenues declined as provincial governors kept the taxes for themselves. Lesser officials appropriated the income from a number of towns. The customs dues on the movement of goods disappeared into the pockets of minor functionaries. The superintendent of canals kept the canal dues for himself. The grain markets of the cities became a comfortable monopoly for the hangers-on of Javed Khan.

With the troops unpaid and mutinous, and no money available for weapons or ammunition, the central authority was unable to move against those who expropriated state property. The rich province of Bengal had long ago stopped paying revenue to the emperor. Safdar Jang who, as well as being chief minister, was governor of the province of Oudh, used the Oudh revenues to sustain his followers.

Soon the emperor found himself without resources. An inventory of the palace was made, and furniture, books, paintings, even the *batteries de cuisine* were sold off to shopkeepers in the city. The household troops took to plundering shops and houses. Imperial opulence turned into grinding distress, the imperial capital into a shambles.

The heart of the problem was the indifference of the great nobles to the state of the empire. Those who were anxious to control it nevertheless seemed unwilling to help preserve its dignity and prestige. Instead, they were divided amongst themselves.

The wazir Safdar Jang was a Persian who attracted to his banner men of his own race, such as ex-soldiers of Nadir Shah and members of the imperial civil service, which was almost entirely dominated by Persians. The old Mughal nobility looked upon him as an upstart. Most of them—and particularly those bound by kinship to the family of his predecessor, Asaf Jah—fed their antipathy on racial hatred, for they were Turks from central Asia and still recruited their retainers from there. To race was added religion, since the Persians were adherents of a Muslim sect which had very few followers in India. This racial, cultural and religious isolation was to contribute to Safdar Jang's failure to gain control of the empire.

The wazir's position was weak. He could not exert his authority without the aid of Javed Khan, whose sympathies lay elsewhere. Javed Khan wrote a secret letter to Nasir Jang, the son of the late Asaf Jah, asking him to come to the capital and dispose of the wazir by force. But Nasir Jang could not start immediately—his relatives had designs on his dominions—and when after several months he was at last ready to move he received a letter from the emperor ordering him back. This was the result of an unsuccessful attempt to assassinate Safdar Jang and its consequences.

The attempt had been made in November 1748 as Safdar Jang was returning from prayers to his mansion, which stood by a canal in the northern quarter of the city. A crowd brought his cortege to a halt for a moment, and a rocket and carbine were fired from a nearby shop, killing some of his guards but merely throwing the wazir, uninjured from his horse. The assailant could not be found. Houses and shops in the area were afterwards torn down, leaving a clear space in front of the wazir's house. Even a group of Hindu monks were forced to leave a spot that had been a sanctuary for centuries.

The wazir left his mansion and withdrew to the opposite side of the river from the imperial palace, where he set up tents and surrounded himself with armed retainers, complete with artillery. Not unnaturally, he refused to attend the emperor's court and so run the risk of another attempt on his life.

Following the break between the emperor and his nominal chief minister, the conspiracy to overthrow him with the aid of Nasir Jang came to light. To reassure Safdar Jang, Nasir had sent him a letter asking for his support in persuading the emperor to confirm him in his governorship of the Deccan, a post which he already held by right of possession. 'You and I', Nasir went on, 'shall turn with one heart to the regulation of the state'. His letter ended with the suggestion that, when he arrived in Delhi, Nasir would unite with the wazir to crush the Marathas. Safdar Jang showed the letter to the Maratha envoy in Delhi. In return, he was given to read a copy of a letter from Nasir to his younger brother in the capital, saying that he intended to crush Safdar Jang.

When Nasir was finally ready to start for Delhi, the wazir, supported by Maratha troops, moved to stop him. Safdar Jang's preparations for battle—he had some fifty thousand troops of his own—were made so ostentatiously that Javed Khan took fright and sent both the emperor and the queen mother to see him and try to pacify him. One of the terms of the reconciliation was the emperor's letter to Nasir Jang ordering him back to the Deccan. The order was softened by the formal appointment as governor.

But Safdar Jang's triumph was short-lived. His province of Oudh was threatened by the Rohillas, a group of Afghan chiefs and their followers who had settled on the borders of Oudh after having been driven east by the force of Nadir Shah's invasion. Safdar Jang found them difficult to subdue and was forced to call on the Marathas for help. On two occasions he was absent from the imperial capital for as much as a year. During the last of his absences, one of his allies—who had returned from a campaign against the Rajputs financially ruined by having to pay his troops out of his own resources—was deprived of the office of paymaster-general (an appointment which was virtually equivalent to commander-in-chief) and had his estates confiscated on the trumped-up charge that he was proposing to overthrow the emperor and place another prince on the throne. The appointment was given instead to Nasir Jang's brother. The post of governor of Ajmir was awarded to Intazim-ud-daula. Two of the greatest offices of state were now in the hands of enemies of Safdar Jang.

But an enemy who threatened *all* the factions at the imperial court had reappeared; Ahmad Shah Abdali was on the march again. The Afghan adventurer had penetrated to the Punjab in 1749 but had been temporarily bought off with a few slices of territory. In 1751, taking advantage of the chaotic conditions in the Punjab, where the rising power of the Sikhs was threatening the tenuous Mughal hold, the Afghans came again, moved upon the city of Lahore, and in March 1752, after a series of battles, defeated the Mughal governor. When an envoy from the Afghan leader reached Delhi with demands for the cession of the province, the demands were granted. Safdar Jang returned to Delhi too late to prevent this abject capitulation, having chosen to settle his own affairs before he concerned himself with those of the empire.

Once he had settled with the Rohillas on his borders, Safdar Jang had gone on into Oudh where the administration had fallen to pieces after the death of his deputy. When he had finished re-imposing his rule, he at last responded to a peremptory appeal from the emperor that he should return and bring with him a force of Marathas, whatever such an alliance might cost. Safdar Jang concluded a treaty with the Marathas which included a substantial subsidy, a lien on the revenues of a number of provinces, the appointment of the Maratha leader as governor of Ajmir, and the right for the Maratha generals to attend the imperial court as officers of state. The emperor accepted these terms, but threw away the advantages of the treaty by his capitulation to the demands of Ahmad Shah Abdali.

Unaware of this, Safdar Jang dawdled along the road to Delhi, taking thirty-four days to cover a journey that might have been completed in seven. He hoped perhaps to see his enemies' credit destroyed by their cowardice, and to enter the capital as the saviour of the state.

When he arrived, Javed Khan went to visit him with news of the cession of the Punjab.

With Safdar Jang were fifty thousand Marathas, whose leaders were looking forward to receiving their subsidy.

It was not forthcoming, and the Maratha soldiers began to plunder the countryside around Delhi. Unknown to Safdar Jang, Javed Khan began to negotiate with the commander of the Maratha force. The circumstances were ripe for such discussions, as the Marathas—a loose federation of chiefs owing a variable allegiance to the single leader known as the Peshwa—had begun to quarrel among themselves. Unfortunately for the Peshwa, his principal, and at one time only, supporter was the commander of the Maratha troops at Delhi. The commander and his troops were therefore happy to leave Delhi and return to the support of the Peshwa, accepting a sum in cash for the time being and the promise of more to come.

This occasion was only one of many on which Safdar Jang's position was flouted by Javed Khan, and the wazir finally decided that Javed Khan should be eliminated. To Delhi, he called one of his allies, Suraj Mal. With him came an agent of one of the Rajput princes, as well as the representative of a man who had once supported Safdar Jang but had in fact been bought by Javed Khan. All were accompanied by troops.

Javed Khan assumed that the new arrivals should visit him, as he held the key to the emperor's presence, but Suraj Mal and the agent of the Rajput prince would transact their business only through the wazir, they said. It was therefore arranged that Javed Khan should go to the wazir's mansion, where they would give audience together. On the morning of 27 August 1752, Javed Khan and his entourage of lancers and musketeers approached the mansion and were welcomed at the door, with a great show of cordiality, by the wazir himself. The two men took breakfast together. Suraj Mal joined them later, and discussions took place. Afterwards, the wazir took Javed Khan into an alcove—where he was stabbed in the back by a soldier.

Javed Khan's head was cut off and hurled amongst his waiting retainers, who sensibly fled before they met the same fate. The body was tossed out on the river bank.

When news of Javed Khan's death reached the emperor, it was sugared by protestations of loyalty from the wazir. The court historian reported that the emperor 'said not a word'. The queen mother put on white garments and conducted herself like a widow—though not for long, as she immediately set about trying to find supporters against Safdar Jang.

For seven months, the wazir's position was not challenged. There was even something like peace on the marches of the empire. But instead of taking the opportunity to reorganize the administration and the imperial army, the wazir spent the revenues on his own forces. When he would have been wise to practise conciliation, he antagonized the nobles by appointing men of his own race to positions of power and profit. His ally, Suraj Mal, was permitted to plunder the old city of Delhi with such thoroughness that his activities introduced a new phrase, meaning destruction, into the language of ordinary people.

Despite his success in gaining control of the strings that activated the emperor, Safdar Jang's position was essentially weak. He was neither a soldier nor a capable administrator. The majority of his private army consisted of mercenaries and, even worse, mercenaries of the same race as his enemies. All that was needed to entice them from him was an offer of higher reward. He was, too, a bad judge of men—a failing usually fatal to ambition. He permitted a boy of sixteen, a grandson of Asaf Jah, to take up the appointment of head of the army. This youth, known later by the title of Imad-ul-mulk, had no experience of war. He had been brought up with puritan severity, forbidden to mix with boys of his own age or to watch a performance by dancing girls. He had turned into a prodigy, a scholar and a linguist, and with immense ambitions. When Nasir Jang had been murdered, the boy's father had succeeded to the governorship of the Deccan. When he too died, the young Imad-ul-mulk went to Safdar Jang's house and sat at the door weeping and refusing to accept food or drink until the wazir agreed to persuade the emperor to permit the boy to inherit his father's titles as well as his estate. As a result, he was appointed commander-in-chief—a meaningless appointment, the minister thought, but one which was to prove of great significance both to himself and to the empire.

The conspiracy against Safdar Jang originated with the queen mother and fed upon the ambition and hatred of the Turkish nobles. Among these was Imad-ul-mulk. The court bought partisans with promises. By a trick, Safdar Jang's men were ejected from the palace and replaced by other troops. Artillery on the walls was trained on the wazir's house. On 18 March 1753, Safdar Jang offered the emperor what was virtually his resignation. To his surprise it was accepted. The appointment was given to a member of the old nobility, Intazim-ud-daula.

What followed was a story of indecision. A civil war began which left Safdar Jang and his allies in control of the old city of Delhi while the emperor's supporters held the palace and its surroundings. Failing to overawe the emperor, Safdar Jang set up his own emperor, allegedly a handsome boy who had recently joined the household of Safdar Jang's son. The emperor now despatched letters far and wide demanding support against the man who had rebelled against the throne. Agents moved among Safdar Jang's troops, offering bribes. Religious leaders thundered against his heretical beliefs, and a holy war was proclaimed. As an added incentive for Safdar Jang's troops, their property in Delhi was seized and their women turned out into the streets. This unsubtle combination of bribery and brutality had the desired effect. Within a few weeks, over twenty thousand men deserted. The Rohillas, anxious to take revenge on the man who had defeated them, came in strength to join his enemies. Every bandit in northern India, smelling loot and plunder, arrived at the gates of the imperial capital. Imad-ul-mulk spent the fortune which had been left by his puritan and parsimonious father on buying weapons and men. Even the queen mother discovered a talent for organization which she had never shown when she controlled the empire. Every supporter of Safdar Jang found his house plundered and his women absorbed into the harems of the plunderers.

But Safdar Jang was not prepared to give in without a fight. Towards the end of May he opened an assault on the imperial defences, but was driven back, mainly by Rohilla mercenaries. One of his generals, a Hindu monk whose reasons for supporting Safdar Jang are obscure, was killed, probably by the inefficiency of his own men. The monk had been regarded as a magician, whom neither sword nor bullet could destroy, and Safdar Jang suspended the fighting for ten days after his death. Though there was more fighting, Safdar Jang was actually in retreat. The emperor tried to open negotiations, but Safdar Jang had had enough. He retired to his province of Oudh and left the empire to tear itself to pieces.

Though Safdar Jang was defeated, the emperor was not victorious. The treasury was exhausted. The mercenaries demanded their reward—and there was nothing to pay them with. The two greatest ministers in the state, now that their common enemy had departed, honed their jealousy into a cutting edge. The Marathas harassed the margins of the empire and were wooed by the opposing ministers. Imad-ul-mulk, who had spent all he had on the battle with Safdar Jang, tried to persuade the emperor to join his troops and take the field against those who now threatened the security of the state. The emperor refused, and he and Imad moved steadily towards open conflict. To pay his troops, Imad seized the crown lands, and his deputy (and one-time tutor) descended on Delhi with a force of Marathas and began to pillage it.

The emperor and the chief minister who had succeeded Safdar Jang looked round for allies against Imad and the Marathas. These were easy enough to find, as the Marathas had a history of cruelty and oppression which united the opposition against them. Imad's deputy found himself forced out of the imperial capital. The chief minister tried to form a coalition against Imad and the Marathas. Rajput princes, Suraj Mal, even the defeated Safdar Jang, were all invited to join. To bring the coalition together it was necessary to arrange a meeting at some place other than Delhi, where the emperor was under the surveillance of his own soldiers, always on the verge of mutiny because of arrears of pay. On the pretence of a hunting expedition, the emperor left the city accompanied by an artillery train and a large number of retainers.

It was a journey into despair. Suraj Mal made his own terms with Imad, and the imperial camp was attacked by Marathas, who captured the women of the harem. The emperor, with his mother and his principal wife, escaped to Delhi with little more than their personal jewellery and a small escort.

Imad's Maratha allies were the real victors, but it was Imad who was to make the profit. The helpless emperor was persuaded to appoint him chief minister. On the following day, 2 June 1754, an envoy from Imad appeared in the quarters occupied by the 'emperors' grandsons' and demanded to see one Muhammad Aiz-ud-din. When this prince was brought into the presence of Imad-ul-mulk, the new wazir bowed and led him to the throne in the audience hall of the palace. The royal umbrella was held over his head and he was declared emperor as Alamgir II. Lost in the crowd of courtiers stood his son, a tall young man—the future emperor, Shah Alam.

4
A time of troubles

THE EMPEROR Alamgir II came out of the shadows of the state prison, but remained a shadow even in the bright sun of the imperial court, owing his throne to a boy of seventeen. After fifty-five years of neglect he was unprepared for power. His interests were scholarly and his passions histori-cal. He admired the great emperor Aurangzeb, whose title of Alamgir—'the world shaker'—he took as his own. Unlike his namesake, he had no interest in war, but he supported Imad's policy of persecuting those Muslims who belonged to the same sect as the late wazir, Safdar Jang. Alamgir II played at being an emperor, stocked his harem with young and nubile girls, and often declared in public, with humiliating honesty, that he was merely a puppet in the hands of his chief minister.

But the puppet-master himself was not altogether secure. He was wazir, but not unchallenged in the position, though the challenge was as yet a silent one—silent, and potentially bloody. The deposed emperor's wazir, Intazim-ud-daula, was still in the city, his mansion fortified with light artillery and with a garrison of six hundred men to defend it. It was always possible, in the atmosphere of ever-shifting alliances, that Intazim might overthrow Imad. Though Safdar Jang died in October 1754, his son inherited his father's ambitions. Suraj Mal had been antagonized by Imad's attempts to crush him in revenge for his earlier support of Safdar Jang. The Marathas, who could not be paid from an empty treasury, seemed likely to desert Imad at any time, while the leader of his Rohilla supporters, Najib Khan, though he had received land grants in exchange for his help in the recent civil war, would not bow to

Imad's authority and devoted himself to expanding his territories.

In Imad's search for money, everyone was squeezed. The ex-emperor had been blinded, on the orders of his successor, and his family was now driven out of the palace. Their possessions were confiscated, and the gold and jewels were paid over to the Marathas, who still haunted the imperial capital with their demands. No one was safe. Ordinary citizens and merchants were forced to pay a levy, and responded by rioting in the streets. Only the emperor's threat that he would starve himself to death saved them. The imperial forces remained unpaid. They filled Delhi and the surrounding villages with terror as they searched for food. One group occupied two of the principal mosques of the city and, from them, looted the adjoining shops. They were dislodged only when artillery opened up on them from the walls of the palace. The wazir's own mansion was sacked and food stolen.

The emperor himself was treated with no greater courtesy. The palace was at one point invested by mutinous troops, so that no food could be sent in. The emperor's personal guard deserted, as did the imperial band. On the rare occasions when he held a public audience, the emperor sat upon a wooden dais, its surface painted to represent gold and jewels, in imitation of the Peacock Throne looted by Nadir Shah.

Famine clutched the vast palace, and many died. The countryside was like a battlefield constantly harassed by guerrillas. Refugees hid in the forests and jungles. When they reached the imperial capital, they occupied the open spaces, the prayer grounds, and the royal parks.

In 1755 the Marathas were finally persuaded to retire. They had constantly pressed for their reward—frequently increasing their demands—but received very little. Even after everyone had been squeezed, there was still not enough. Ultimately they were bought off by having the revenues from certain provinces assigned to them, although they never received these revenues as there was no way for the imperial government to collect them.

Once the Marathas had gone, Intazim-du-daula became less dangerous. He had tried to induce the Marathas to support him against Imad, but they, knowing the state of the imperial treasury, could anticipate no profit from such an alliance. They refused. Negotiations were opened up between Intazim and Imad and a truce was agreed. Intazim was an intriguer, not a man of action, and the climate was temporarily unfavourable to conspiracy.

With two threats neutralized for the time being, Imad-ul-mulk decided to take the field against a rebel Afghan chief to the north of Delhi. It was a decision which was sound in theory and insane in practice. The troops were unpaid and badly armed. The cavalry horses were weak for lack of fodder.

The wazir despatched a force against the Afghan, who, with the aid of a sandstorm, defeated it. The victorious rebel, acting with a moderation alien to the imperial forces, began merely to occupy some towns and villages in the Punjab. Imad persuaded the emperor to accompany him on an expedition against the rebel. Even when he heard that the rebel had been defeated by another Afghan chief, Imad insisted on going on to Panipat despite his lack of stores and even of a suitable tent for the emperor. There, at least, there were houses. There were also mutinous troops.

In May 1755 these troops attacked Imad's house and dragged him half-dressed from his harem. After parading him through the town, the soldiers took him to their camp where he was stripped and beaten. Only after two hours of torment was he allowed to return to his house. There he dressed and, with the aid of the Rohilla, Najib Khan, attacked and routed the mutineers. By doing so, and then by confiscating all the mutineers' property in Delhi, Imad destroyed the army which, properly paid and handled, might have been the prop of the empire and Imad's own bulwark against such dangerous men as Najib Khan was to prove to be.

By the end of 1755, a kind of peace reigned around the imperial capital. A conspiracy against Imad had been quickly scotched. An attempted attack by Suraj Mal had been prevented. Imad had even mounted a successful campaign; with him had been the emperor's heir, Shah Alam.

But the peace was a mirage. That old enemy of the state, Ahmad Shah Abdali, was on the march again. By the end of 1756 the Punjab had been occupied by the Afghan king. Imad could find no friends, and had no money with which to buy allies. Though he was advised to march against the invader, the one effective force left in Delhi was that commanded by Najib Khan, who was believed to be a partisan of his fellow-Afghan.

Without the means of resistance, deserted not only by the nobles but by the citizenry of Delhi, who fled the city, Imad-ul-mulk was forced to capitulate. He had made some attempt to fortify the city but no one could be found to man the guns, and Najib Khan had gone over to the enemy. Secretly one morning, accompanied by four troopers, Imad left the city and arrived some hours later at the camp of Ahmad Shah Abdali. There he was stripped of his appointment as wazir, which was given to his old enemy Intazim-ud-daula, and detained as a prisoner in case he tried to escape and raise the Marathas.

At the end of January 1757 the Afghan forces occupied Delhi. Some of its citizens, anxious to ingratiate themselves with the new conqueror, had Ahmad Shah's titles proclaimed in the city mosques in place of those of the emperor. The pavilions of the palace echoed with the footsteps of men changing sides. The news reached the emperor at prayer, and he ordered his family to leave the imperial apartments and take refuge in another part of the palace. Two days later he himself was told to take up his quarters again in those rooms from which he had first emerged to become emperor. But he was not deposed. He was invited to visit the conqueror. Riding an elephant, and accompanied only by a horseman carrying drums, he went to Ahmad Shah's camp and was welcomed as emperor.

The next stage was the occupation of the palace, which had been cleaned and refurnished to receive the Afghan king. Then it was time for the reckoning. Rumours of the bankruptcy of the empire must have reached Ahmad Shah, but he did not believe them. Poverty seemed a likely disguise for treasure concealed under the floors. The Afghans wasted no time on finesse. They were anxious to pick the city clean and retire as quickly as possible before the harsh summer descended on the plains around Delhi. Nor did they forget the probability that the Marathas, whose hatred of the Afghans almost overcame their inter-necine jealousies, might have time to assemble their forces for an attack on the capital.

The deposed wazir, Imad-ul-mulk, was ordered to disgorge all the profits he had made during two-and-a-half years as chief minister of the empire. When he said that all his property had already been seized, he and his servants were ruthlessly beaten. Intazim-ud-daula, who had been foolish enough to promise a large sum in return for his appointment as wazir, was now commanded to pay up. To encourage him, he was shown a triangle of wood to which he would be tied for a beating if he did not produce an immediate payment on account. When the Afghans heard that Intazim's mother knew where the treasure was to be found, a party was sent off to intimidate her. The treasure was disclosed, and carried away. The soldiers even entered Intazim's harem and searched the women.

Ahmad Shah had his informers at the highest levels. No man was safe, nor any woman either. 'Wherever handsome Hindu women were reported', wrote a Maratha spy, 'Ahmad Shah sent his men and had them brought to his quarters'. He married off one of his sons to a daughter of the emperor. Then Intazim was deprived of office and the appointment was given instead to—Shah Alam. Intazim was made his deputy. Imad was given the empty title of regent, and the real power was invested in Najib Khan, who was created commander-in-chief. A number of other appointments were given to partisans of the Afghan king.

Ahmad Shah now decided to leave Delhi. He went accompanied by Imad-ul-mulk—who in March was re-appointed wazir—and the Afghan forces began to make a sweep of the countryside south of the imperial city, plundering, raping and burning as they went. Protecting its flank were the troops of Najib Khan, who made their own contribution to the violence. Heads were collected in great bundles, to be transported by captives, for every enemy head was rewarded with a payment of five rupees. Girls were tied to the men's saddles, to be enjoyed at leisure. But cholera broke out in the Afghan camp and, under its threat, Ahmad Shah's soldiers began to demand a return home to the cool heights of Afghanistan.

The army moved back through the shattered countryside. At Delhi, there was a brief halt while the Afghan king was married to a princess of the imperial family.

Ahmad Shah's political aims were simple. He had no intention of staying on in northern India, a country which he found unpleasantly hot and distasteful. He merely wanted acknowledgement of his sovereignty and a suitable sum in feudal dues. The emperor was not deposed; Ahmad Shah had a plan to regain the imperial provinces from the men who had seized them, so that the empire might be turned into a profitable undertaking once again. In this he was not to be successful, for the opposition was powerful and his own troops were just as tired of India as he was. He marched them away to recuperate, leaving behind him as his agent the Rohilla, Najib Khan.

With Ahmad Shah out of the way, Imad patched up his quarrel with the Marathas and, with them, marched on Delhi. Najib stormed Imad's mansion in the capital, stripped the women of his harem, and drove them into the streets. This violation of a harem, the insulting of women—especially those of a great noble—was the worst of all crimes in Indian eyes. Between the violator and the violated there was no possibility of reconciliation. But Imad's vengeance had to wait. Though the Marathas were able to invest the city and to force Najib out, they were able to achieve this only by cutting off food supplies. Najib's men were undefeated; they marched out of the city protected by an agreement with the Maratha general.

The city itself was once more a shambles, torn by disease and food shortage. Armed bands roamed the streets, and each house was a fortress. In November, the anarchy was compounded when a severe earthquake struck the city. It was, as the court historian mourned, 'a time of troubles'.

There seemed no end. The Marathas moved on from Delhi to the Punjab, captured Lahore, and then returned to the south. Their profits had proved small. There had been little of value left to plunder. The vast subsidies owing to them had not been paid. Their attack on the Punjab more or less ensured that, in the cold weather, Ahmad Shah Abdali would descend again. Najib Khan was still active and only awaited the return of his master.

During all this, Shah Alam had not been idle. He had troops, and he had begun a campaign to liberate some of the imperial sources of revenue. But he was unable to prevent his unpaid troops from plundering the countryside and, in an engagement with the forces of the raja of Jaipur, he was defeated. Though he managed to regroup his men, he was recalled to Delhi and his orders to collect revenue were countermanded. His recall had been instigated by Imad-ul-mulk, who was afraid that Shah Alam—who had shown considerable courage and initiative—might become a focus for opposition. This fear was reinforced when the prince came to an arrangement with one of the Maratha commanders and began, with him, to move towards the capital. Imad sent a force to seize the prince. When it was defeated, he accused the emperor of encouraging his son, confined the other princes to the palace, and prepared for the worst.

As usual, Imad tried to buy off Shah Alam's Maratha ally. At the same time he forced the emperor to write to his son asking him to return to visit him. At first the prince ignored these peaceable requests but, after a number of Imad's envoys had taken a variety of oaths and dispensed promises of safe conducts, Shah Alam entered Delhi. Instead of going to the palace, however, he took up residence in one of the houses in the city and surrounded himself with two thousand armed men. Imad neutralized the Maratha

KING OF THE WORLD

ally who was following the prince with a cash bribe, and prepared to attack.

On 19 May 1758 artillery opened up on the prince's house and troops began the assault. The defenders inflicted heavy casualties on the attackers but, though they held out through the night, numbers soon began to count. Early in the morning, as the wazir's men broke through the defences, Shah Alam and a hundred of his men fought clear and managed to cut their way through to the Maratha camp. There the Maratha commander's 'neutrality' faded and his troops covered Shah Alam's escape. Next day, under threat of attack, Imad paid his promised bribe to the Maratha commander in full. Shah Alam left the city, accompanied by the Marathas and followed by the puppet emperor's declaration that he was, officially, a rebel.

Shah Alam had lost everything when his house was besieged. A few days later he also lost the support of the Maratha contingent. In the middle of June, orders reached the Maratha commander that he was to cease helping Shah Alam collect supplies and revenue, and that he was to return to Delhi—*with* Shah Alam. Yet another 'arrangement' had been made, and the Maratha leaders were now disposed to help Imad against Shah Alam. But the Maratha commander left the prince with a small escort, headed by his son, and told him he was free to go. When the Maratha force had vanished, Shah Alam told his followers they could follow him or leave him as they wished. Most of them left him.

The prince, now a declared rebel against the state, 'turned his face to the path of the wilderness in sole reliance on God'.

5
The path of the wilderness

SHAH ALAM, pursued in a somewhat desultory manner by Imad with the emperor in his train, picked up military adventurers wherever he went but very little active support from people of consequence. It was characteristic of the times that, at one place, he was met by Najib Khan with royal honours and supplies for his troops—but a refusal to help him against the wazir. As Shah Alam moved first into the Rajputana and then turned east, Imad found the pursuit hampered by a hostile populace and at last gave up, returning to Delhi with the emperor.

Shah Alam continued towards Oudh, his army of hopeful mercenaries and soldiers of fortune steadily increasing in number. There was nothing more attractive than an exiled heir to a throne, when the circumstances were so changeable that he might succeed at any time. The prince's intention was to try to regain the province of Bihar, which had been lost to the empire when its governor rebelled many years earlier.

At Lucknow, Safdar Jang's son, Shuja-ud-daula, came out twelve miles beyond the city to meet the prince. Presents were offered, and—more important—cash. Shuja advised the prince to go on to Allahabad, where the governor was preparing for an attack on Bihar, and said that he himself would join the prince as soon as he had collected his forces.

Ahead of the prince went letters to the governors of Bihar and Bengal, demanding their immediate submission. It was, however, not merely a matter of bringing refractory officials to heel. Bengal, like Bihar, had been independent for years; even in ordinary circumstances, its ruler would have been unlikely to give in without a fight. And the circumstances were by no means ordinary. Behind the rulers of the two provinces was a new power on the Indian scene, not yet fully established, and the menace which it posed not yet fully recognized. Nearly two years previously, the then ruler of Bengal had been overthrown by the army of the English East India Company, and its general, Robert Clive, was now the real force in the province. The nominal ruler (known as 'the nawab') was his creature, though not wholly submissive. The English were unlikely to allow their puppet to respond to the demands of a rebel prince.

The position in Bihar was not quite the same. The governor, a Hindu, was not on friendly terms with the Muslim nawab of Bengal, and at one time the nawab had decided—encouraged by Clive—to march out against him. But Clive had changed his mind and insisted on a reconciliation between the two men. The governor of Bihar, however, did not feel himself altogether safe, and there were rumours that he had opened negotiations with Shuja-ud-daula even before Shah Alam appeared on the scene.

The real and physical dangers of the situation were compounded by questions of legality. The Mughal empire at its zenith had so dominated India that the emperor had become almost the sole source of legitimacy. His office—though not the man who occupied it—had semi-divine status; even after the blows that had been struck at it during the preceding half-century, it still remained a symbol of special potency. The men who were engaged on dismembering the empire continued to seek, from its nominal ruler, titles which legitimized their possession of what they had plundered. The British in Bengal had asked for, and received from, the puppet emperor Alamgir confirmation of the right to rule of the nawab they had placed on the throne of Bengal, while Robert Clive himself received a Mughal title which had done nothing but enhance his personal prestige in Indian eyes. The problem that faced both Clive and the nawab was whether it would be *right* for the nawab, holding the imperial authority, and a foreigner with a Mughal title to resist the entry into what was still supposedly a province of the Mughal empire of an army commanded by the Mughal heir-apparent—even though it was said that he had been declared a rebel.

Neither Clive nor the nawab would have allowed such a dilemma to influence them unduly, but they were saved from having to make the decision by the issue of a proclamation from Delhi stating that Shah Alam was indeed a rebel.

Clive instructed the governor of Bihar to resist Shah Alam and promised English support against the rebel. Unfortunately for the governor, Shah Alam was already at the gates of his capital of Patna. Though Clive had promised aid, no force had yet set out, and the English agent had left Patna, advising the governor to hold out as long as possible. It did not look as if this would be very long. Shah Alam was said to have an army of Rohillas and other tough mercenaries as well as a force of mainly French troops, under the command of Jean Law, a French agent who had left Bengal after the British triumph there.

Having no news of Clive, the governor decided to play for time by visiting the prince's camp. He was not impressed by what he saw. The prince's army looked a rabble, held loosely together by hope. The governor promised to raise a large sum of money but said he would have to return to Patna himself to arrange it. He then shut himself up in the fort and closed the city gates. Safe behind his fortifications, he sent an abusive and insolent letter to one of Shah Alam's generals and then waited for the attack to come. When it did, it was easily repulsed.

News that an English army was on the way convinced the prince that it would be best to leave while he still could, as the reputation of the English had been greatly enlarged by rumour and his own men were beginning to desert.

An air of farce was added to the situation by an exchange of letters between Clive and the prince. Before Clive left on his way to Patna, two emissaries from Shah Alam visited him. They offered him, Clive told the nawab of Bengal, 'provinces upon provinces' to turn against the nawab. 'It is the custom of the English', Clive went on, 'to treat the persons of ambassadors as sacred, and I told the prince's agents as much; but at the same time warned them never to come near me again, for if they did I would take their heads for their pains'. The letters that were exchanged, however, were neither so crude nor so outspoken. The prince's letter hailed Clive as 'the Most High and Mighty, Protector of the Great', and suggested that 'you should make it your business to pay your respect to me like a faithful servant, which will be great and happy for you'. Clive replied that he had received no notice from the emperor or his wazir to expect the prince. and that he regretted that, in the absence of such, 'I cannot pay that due regard to your Highness's orders which I would otherwise wish to do'. Furthermore, he informed the prince, 'I beg leave to inform you that I am under the strictest engagements with the nawab [of Bengal] to assist him at all times'.

When Clive reached Patna, he found that the prince had retired. He also heard that one of Shah Alam's principal supporters, the governor of Allahabad, had left him because, in his absence, Shuja-ud-daula had occupied his city. As Clive followed after the prince he received another letter from him which seemed, behind its flowery phrases, to contain a request for British protection. Clive replied that the emperor had asked him to take Shah Alam prisoner. He had, he said, no intention of doing so, but neither did he intend to aid him. His letter ended with a touch of homely philosophy, and a threat. 'It is better', he said, 'that one should suffer, however great, than that so many thousands should be rendered unhappy. I have only to recommend your Highness to the Almighty's protection. I am now on my march to the Karamnassa [river] and earnestly recommend you to withdraw before I arrive there'.

When the news reached Delhi that Shah Alam had taken Clive's advice, Imad wrote congratulating the Englishman on 'the faithful services you have performed' and expressing the hope that Clive would 'seize the rebel and send him to court'. But Clive had no intention of pursuing the prince beyond the borders of Bihar, especially as the rainy season was about to break.

While Shah Alam had been attacking Patna and retreating before the British, the situation at Delhi had remained as confused and violent as ever. Imad had encouraged a Maratha force to harass Najib Khan, though not very successfully. Rumours that Shuja-ud-daula was on his way from Oudh with a large army turned out to be true, and Imad's troops began to break and scatter. Worse still, Ahmad Shah Abdali entered the Punjab once more. The Maratha governor of Lahore fled the city, now in a dangerous position. Ahmad Shah's deputy being Najib Khan, it seemed likely that the Afghan king would come to his aid and capture both Delhi and the emperor. The Maratha commander, whose name was Dattaji Sindia, began to look round for allies and found one in Suraj Mal who, from his base at Bharatpur, was becoming something of a power in the land. Dattaji also sent envoys to Imad in Delhi, urging the wazir to join him in an attack on the potentially dangerous Rohilla, Najib Khan. He even volunteered 200,000 rupees for travelling expenses if Imad would set out at once. On 16 November 1759, after taking leave of the emperor, Imad left Delhi for the Maratha camp.

While Imad-ul-mulk was making for the Maratha camp, news reached him that Ahmad Shah Abdali was moving across the Punjab in the direction of the imperial capital. Imad sensed his own danger. If Ahmad Shah should capture the emperor again, it seemed highly probable that Imad would once more be dismissed from office, and perhaps killed this time. Two choices seemed to be open to him. He could either have the emperor brought to him at the Maratha camp, or could simply have him killed and replaced by someone more amenable to his demands, who would be less likely to enter into conspiracies. The latter seemed the more satisfactory alternative, and Imad sent the appropriate orders off through his chief adviser. As it would have been risky to murder the emperor in a public place, and almost impossible in his private apartments, he had to be lured to some suitable spot. The emperor, fortunately for Imad, affected a great interest in religion and holy men, so he was informed that a saintly dervish had arrived from Lahore to take up residence in one of the old Delhi forts. The saint, it was said, could work miracles. The emperor's curiosity was easily aroused. With a small party of retainers and courtiers he went to the fort and was shown into a chamber built in the bastions. Only one companion was admitted with the emperor.

The emperor Alamgir was stabbed to death. His escort, which included one of his sons, was quickly disarmed and sent back to the palace. The body having been thrown on to the river bank nearby, a false story was quickly circulated that the emperor had met his death by falling from the ruined walls of the fort. At midnight he was buried in the great tomb of Humayun, second emperor of the dynasty, by the light of a few torches, and without ceremony. Others died too. Imad at last took his revenge on his uncle, Intazim-ud-daula, whom he had formerly imprisoned but hesitated to kill. The former wazir was strangled and his body was thrown into the river, weighted with stones. The rumour was then spread that he had fled the city.

In the morning another prince was brought from the private quarters to be crowned under the title of Shah Jahan II.

The news of his father's death reached Shah Alam at the village of Ghotauli in Bihar, where he had gone after the end of the rainy season. It was 21 December when he heard, and three days later he crowned himself emperor. For the next few days there were celebrations, but the new emperor quickly appointed Shuja-uh-daula as his wazir and sent an agent to the Afghan invader, Ahmad Shah Abdali, asking for his support.

That Shah Alam was now emperor attracted more men to his standard. Some were trained and seasoned soldiers, but most were raw levies thrown together by dubious adventurers. Only in one way did the emperor have superiority. His Rohilla cavalry, mounted on fast-moving wiry ponies, was a superbly mobile fighting force. It was, however, no match for well-armed infantry supported by well-aimed artillery, and Shah Alam had to face an adversary lacking in cavalry of its own but based on infantry trained in the European manner, well furnished with arms and ammunition, and supported by guns operated by Europeans. Even his handful of Frenchmen under Jean Law was of little use in the face of such odds.

Nevertheless, it was essential for Shah Alam to go forward. With Delhi in dispute and a usurper on the throne, he could not remain inactive. His advisers were divided. Should he return, hoping that Ahmad Shah's deputy Najib Khan would aid him against the wazir, Imad, and his Maratha allies? Would the Afghan invader defeat the wazir and, if so, would he again depart from India leaving a legacy of chaos and danger for the new emperor? On the whole, it seemed better for Shah Alam to stay away from the capital until the situation began to resolve itself. This meant, however, that he had to put himself in the hands of the only power which seemed dependable—his new wazir, Shuja-ud-daula—who also seemed very unlikely to trust the legitimate emperor out of his sight.

The new wazir was, in fact, little better than the old. He was certainly no less ambitious than Imad-ul-mulk, and no less erratic. His main interests were hunting and violent exercise, but Jean Law considered that he had 'qualities of heart' not shared by Imad. Under pressure from Shuja-ud-daula, Shah Alam determined to attack Patna again so as to restore Bihar to the imperial dominions.

Clive left for England at the end of January 1760. Before he sailed, he heard that Shah Alam had again crossed the border of Bihar; he therefore instructed the English commander, Major Caillaud, to move on Patna to reinforce the governor's position. Caillaud's force of native and European infantry, with six guns served by Europeans, was accompanied by about fifteen thousand men, with twenty-five guns, led by the son of the puppet nawab of Bengal. The governor, however, when Shah Alam appeared outside

Patna, chose not to wait for the English force but to go out and attack the emperor, even though he had been warned of the possible treachery of some of his own men. Three of the governor's commanders did indeed desert to the emperor, and the governor was forced to retreat into the fort.

Rumours of the approach of Caillaud's force were becoming more insistent, and Shah Alam made no attempt to besiege the fort. Instead, he began to retire. Caillaud caught up with the imperial forces on 22 February 1760 and, in a short but bloody encounter, put them to flight. He was unable to pursue them as he had no cavalry and the horsemen in the force of the nawab's son would not take orders from the English commander. But Caillaud was still determined to follow Shah Alam.

The emperor now conceived the plan of leaving his heavy baggage behind and making a cavalry raid on Murshidabad, the capital of the nawab of Bengal. But this move having begun, it was hamstrung by hesitation, and the initiative was finally lost when a vanguard came in contact with Caillaud.

Caillaud mounted what was intended to be an attack on the main body of the imperial army, but when he reached its camp he found it a ruin of burnt tents and baggage. The emperor had doubled back to Patna yet again. Once more he was to be disappointed. After a forced march, a detachment of British troops entered the city and, with colours flying and drums and fifes playing, joined the defenders in the fort. Two days later, the emperor raised the siege and, after lurking for a couple of months in the south of the province, retired in August across the border to Oudh.

The rainy season came again, preventing military activity as the rivers swelled and burst their banks and the countryside became an impassable swamp. The emperor had been rejoined by Jean Law, who had not been present at the last attempt on Patna. Despite a shortage of ammunition and supplies, Shah Alam was still prepared to try again. With the French troops, few though they were in number, he thought that there might be a chance, especially as it was known the English were having trouble in Bengal and might be slow to respond to another provocation.

There was also the possibility that some agreement might be reached between the emperor and the British, who had just deposed one nawab and replaced him with a successor who would certainly need the seal of imperial approval. The British in Bengal did, in fact, begin to toy with the idea of putting the emperor back on his throne in Delhi by force of British arms, and Caillaud was instructed to take soundings of the situation.

Before anything could come of these, there was a change in the command of the British forces. Caillaud was relieved, and replaced by Major Carnac—who moved against Shah Alam and caught up with his force at the village of Suan, near Bihar city, on 15 January 1761. There, despite a gallant attempt by Law and his men to hold off the British, the emperor was routed and Law himself taken prisoner. Shah Alam managed to escape on a wounded elephant, closely pursued by Carnac. Indeed, the British were so close behind the emperor that Carnac reported: 'We sometimes find the fires of his camp still burning'. At last, on 6 February, tired of being hounded through the countryside, the emperor surrendered. Carnac received him with considerable ceremony and together they moved on to Patna, where the city prepared itself to welcome the man who had three times tried to take it by force.

At Patna, a hall in the British quarter was decorated with rich cloths and a couple of tables were covered with cloth of gold and cushions to do duty as a throne. The emperor appeared, borne on a litter, and escorted by a guard of honour consisting of European soldiers. The new nawab of Bengal, Mir Kasim, after receiving promises of safe conduct, came to pay his respects, bringing the customary presents and receiving imperial confirmation of his appointment. The emperor began to think that, in the British, he might at last have found allies who would carry him back to Delhi in triumph. There certainly seemed to be grounds for hope. Great events had been taking place around the imperial capital, and on the very day before the emperor's own defeat at Suan a vast Maratha army had been utterly crushed by the Afghan invader, Ahmad Shah Abdali, at 'the battle of the black mango tree'.

6
The black mango tree

WHEN THE news that Imad had murdered Alamgir II
reached Ahmad Shah, he had decided to press on towards
Delhi immediately. In his way stood the Maratha commander, Dattaji Sindia, and Imad's own contingent. In the first
skirmishes, Dattaji was forced to retire. Ahmad Shah,
joined by Najib Khan, moved up the river Jumna towards
the imperial capital, while Dattaji and Imad fell back before
them. At Delhi, Imad made preparations to defend the city
and Dattaji set up camp about ten miles to the north.

The defenders' situation deteriorated daily. Ahmad Shah
was being joined by large numbers of troops, and Dattaji's
men, demoralized by their defeats, were clearly outnumbered and not to be relied on. Reinforcements had been
promised by another Maratha leader, but it seemed certain
that they could not arrive in less than a fortnight. The whole
countryside, scenting Dattaji's plight, turned against him as
if the people knew that a day of reckoning was coming for the
Marathas who had so often plundered and abused them.

Dattaji sent off his heavy baggage, the spoils he had
accumulated, and the families of his officers and himself—
including his pregnant wife—to a safer place. Without them,
he would have more room for manoeuvre. It was winter and
the sharply honed winds blew bitterly from the distant
Himalayas. The river was at its lowest level and there was
no need to cross by the usual fords. Dattaji sent out detachments to watch the crossings, but it was impossible to watch
them all, and Najib Khan crossed secretly at one point;
there, on an island covered with dense shrubs and reeds, he
attacked a Maratha force with such vigour that Dattaji was
forced to go to its aid. As he went, dark and thickset, leading

his men on horseback, sharpshooters concealed in a thicket opened fire and brought him down with a bullet through the eye. At the same moment, Najib led a charge and put the Marathas to flight. The body of their chief was left behind. After the action, the victors cut off its head and sent it as a present to Ahmad Shah.

Dattaji's remaining force lost heart at their leader's death and failed even to go to the support of some of their comrades who tried to renew the action against Najib. The Maratha army of about twenty thousand men turned and fled towards Delhi.

When Imad-ul-mulk heard of Dattaji's death and the rout of his men, he hurriedly left the city and made for Bharatpur and the protection of Suraj Mal. The Marathas, though pursued by Najib, managed to regroup and—having little or no baggage and being unencumbered by noncombatants—to escape. They finally joined up with the reinforcements which were coming up from the south, and the combined force hovered to the south-west of Delhi, waiting for an opportunity to attack Ahmad Shah.

Even though Delhi now held no defenders, the Afghan king did not enter the city. He did, however, arrange to send officials to take charge of what was left of the imperial government. At his camp outside the city, Ahmad Shah received envoys and despatched letters to the rajas of Rajputana and to Suraj Mal, calling on them to pay tribute immediately, in cash and in person. The rulers were faced with a real dilemma. All were afraid of the military strength of the Afghans, but they also feared and hated the Marathas. On past form, Ahmad Shah seemed likely to return home when his demands had been satisfied. This would leave the Marathas in possession of the field, and they had no intention of leaving northern India. The rulers' envoys temporized, in the hope that some kind of decisive action would take place between the Afghans and the Marathas, removing at least one of them from the scene.

This procrastination did not suit Ahmad Shah. He decided to visit the rulers' domains and exert some degree of pressure. The first victim was Suraj Mal, who was not only nearest but had also offended by sheltering the murderer of Alamgir. On the journey, the Afghans completely defeated a Maratha detachment although they failed to catch up with the main body. The Maratha horsemen, now fined down for rapid movement and quick getaways, were easily able to outdistance the heavier horses of their opponents. One of the Maratha commanders, however, heard that Najib Khan was sending a treasure convoy to Ahmad Shah and halted for a few days to investigate. He was routed, with many casualties, by a strong cavalry detachment sent by Ahmad Shah.

On the whole, the Maratha tactics were not proving conspicuously successful, but they were taking up so much of the Afghans' time that the hot weather had begun and the Afghans were still by no means ready to depart for home. The Afghan troops found it particularly trying to have to fight in the height of the Indian hot weather which, in the Delhi plain and surrounding countryside, reaches temperatures of 110°F—a roasting heat which is intensified by severe dust storms. On the advice of Najib Khan, Ahmad Shah gave up his march to Bharatpur and settled at Aligarh, some seventy miles south of Delhi, until the heat and the subsequent rains should be over and the weather suitable for campaigning again.

A large Maratha force was reported to be assembling in their homeland of the Deccan, in preparation for a march northwards. There was little doubt that a great moment of decision was approaching. The Marathas' preparations for war included a search for allies. Even these supposedly fearless people still looked on Ahmad Shah with a certain superstitious belief in his invulnerability. But their agents' attempts to persuade Shuja-ud-daula to come over to their side failed. Because of the rains, too, they were unable to move troops into the area between Shuja-ud-daula's territory in Oudh and Ahmad Shah's position, tactics which would at worst have neutralized Shuja, and might at best have made him decide to join the Marathas after all.

The Maratha armies were under the command of
Sadashiv Bhau, a relative of the Peshwa. Though he was a
competent general, he had had no experience of northern
India and did not know the country. He was, however,
determined to crush Ahmad Shah, and when the Afghan
offered negotiations in June 1760 he kept the envoys
hanging about and then dismissed them. When the rains
came, the river Jumna was so swollen by flood water that the
Maratha forces could not cross. Neither could the Afghans.
Sadashiv decided to bypass Ahmad Shah's encampment and,
by a swift sortie along his own side of the flooded river, to
capture Delhi, which he knew was only lightly held by the
Afghans. In the palace there, ignored because there were more
important matters in hand, was the shadowy emperor Shah
Jahan II, whom Imad had left behind when he fled the city.

Sadashiv's force had now been joined by Imad. The
Marathas arrived outside the imperial capital on 22 July
1760 and broke into the city on the afternoon of the same
day. Ahmad Shah's governor had been able to gather only
a scratch force of men, and most of them deserted after the
attack began, leaving him with only a few score professional
soldiers of the Afghan army. There were not enough of them
even to patrol the battlements of the palace, and a Maratha
party was able to scale the walls while the garrison's attention
was diverted by an assault on another part. Instead of
opening the gates to their comrades outside, however, the
party which had broken in began looting. They were
discovered by a small group of defenders who shot some
down and forced the others to flee.

The Maratha commander began to besiege the palace.
Trenches were dug and guns mounted. Three guns on the
river bank opened up on the state apartments, some of which
were badly damaged, but the bombardment had very little
effect on the walls, which were massively constructed of red
sandstone. The defenders, however, had little food and no
hope of relief, and the governor offered to negotiate. He and
his men were allowed to vacate the palace, with their belongings, and to march off to join Ahmad Shah.

Shuja-ud-daula now entered the arena, not with troops but with suggestions for conciliation between the Marathas and Ahmad Shah. Shuja was prepared to mediate, on the understanding that the Marathas recognized Shah Alam as emperor and himself as imperial wazir. Not unnaturally, this antagonized Imad-ul-mulk and his protector, Suraj Mal, both of whom withdrew with their men from Sadashiv's camp and would not be persuaded to return. Sadashiv now had no allies in the campaign against Ahmad Shah and compounded the unfortunate situation by offending one of his own veteran commanders, Malahar Rao Holkar. On the other hand, the capture of Delhi had restored Maratha prestige and set Ahmad Shah's allies wondering whether they had made what might prove to be a fatal mistake.

Sadashiv himself would probably have preferred to negotiate with Ahmad Shah for an amicable division of the country between the Marathas and Afghans. There was room for both, and such a division would have been profitable. But Sadashiv's master, the Peshwa, would have none of it.

The Maratha commander, who, before the capture of Delhi, had shown considerable intelligence in his appreciation of the dangers of fighting Ahmad Shah, afterwards was so elated that he went to the extreme of believing that the Afghan forces were by no means as invulnerable as had been alleged. The opinion was endorsed by the reports of spies who discovered dissensions among Ahmad Shah's supporters. It was also said that ten thousand horses, camels and mules had died in the Afghan camp, and that many of the Rohillas had left for their homes 'beyond the Ganges'.

If the suspicion occurred that some of these reports were exaggerated or had been tampered with before they reached Sadashiv, there was no question but that he was fully aware of what was happening to his own forces around Delhi, cut off as they were from the fertile lands dominated by Ahmad Shah. Shortage of grass and dry fodder killed off most of the bullocks which pulled the guns and commissariat carts. At the beginning of September, Sadashiv was writing to the Peshwa that there was starvation in his camp and that he was unable to raise revenue out of the countryside. The troubles around Delhi, he lamented, had 'dispersed the bankers of this region—therefore no loan can be raised'.

Delhi, that milch cow for invaders, was almost dry. There was believed to be treasure still hidden in the palace but, oddly enough, the Marathas seemed unwilling to torture members of the imperial family or to break into the harem where the treasure seemed most likely to be concealed. Before he left, Imad-ul-mulk had ripped off part of the heavy silver ceiling of the Hall of Private Audience and taken it with him. Now Sadashiv, in his overwhelming need, took the rest. Melting it down, he struck 900,000 rupees which maintained the army and the imperial family for a month. But there was no more to take. The Peshwa had instructed the Rajput rulers to pay tribute to Sadashiv, but they were determined to part with nothing unless forced. They had already been squeezed by Ahmad Shah. If the Marathas came, they would be paid, but until then none of the princes intended to volunteer.

At this stage, with the cold weather approaching and the traditional season for war, Sadashiv decided to act against a strategic town, Kunjpura, which lay on the river Jumna eighty miles north of Delhi and controlled an important crossing. The town was the base of one of Najib Khan's partisans, and there were large stores of grain ready to supply the Afghan army as well as a hoard of treasure. The river being still in flood and uncrossable would, Sadashiv reasoned, prevent Ahmad Shah from going to the town's aid.

On his way to Kunjpura, Sadashiv sent two agents back to Delhi with instructions to depose Shah Jahan II, proclaim Shah Alam as emperor, and strike coins in his name. He also offered Shuja-ud-daula the appointment of wazir. In this way Sadashiv hoped to strike a wedge between Shuja and the Afghan king.

A few days later, the Marathas took Kunjpura by storm, with considerable plunder. It was now the end of October and the rivers were falling. The next news that came to

THE BLACK MANGO TREE

Sadashiv as he made his way slowly back to Delhi was that Ahmad Shah had crossed the Jumna, cutting the Marathas off from the capital.

This crossing had revived the spirits of Ahmad Shah's troops, who had been heavily depressed by their inability to go to the aid of their comrades in Kunjpura. At the crossing point, the swollen river had been so high and fast-running that it had been impossible to find a ford. Horsemen sent in to test the waters had been swept away and drowned. Ahmad Shah fasted and prayed for two days, and on the third a ford was found. This was greeted as a miracle and the army made its way across in some euphoria. As they advanced along the other bank of the river, they took Maratha concentrations by surprise and, driving them before them, approached the town of Panipat on the first day of November. There they met up with the main body of the Maratha force which occupied the town.

At this place some of the most decisive battles in the history of India had been fought. Among them was the one in which Babur had founded the Mughal empire in 1526. But there was nothing impressive in the scene—an empty plain and a town famous for its tombs of Muslim saints, now battered by the depredations of Sadashiv's men. Ahmad Shah made his preparations for battle with great care. This was an encounter that had to be won, in his own way and at his own time. He settled down to take the measure of his enemy and refused to be drawn into premature fighting. His troops were ordered not to respond to minor skirmishing. If the Marathas cut off a few horses or raided the supplies they were not to be pursued. Patience and preparation were the watchwords.

Ahmad Shah's peculiar passivity was taken by the Maratha commanders to mean terror and timidity, failings never before displayed by the Afghan king. The Afghans were also known to be short of supplies. Sadashiv was openly contemptuous. He wrote to the Peshwa: 'Ahmad Shah is called the "king of kings" . . . but having come to within four miles of us he has sat for eight days and dare not make a demonstration of his valour'. The general impression in the Maratha camp was that the Afghan would be glad to avoid a fight and would rather make his way home. If he chose to remain where he was then he could be starved into submission. All Sadashiv had to do was wait and see that supplies were prevented from reaching the Afghan camp. He therefore began to entrench his own position and set up his guns. Ahmad Shah did the same.

Two entrenched camps now faced each other across a treeless plain, both waiting. There were occasional skirmishes, some of them hard-fought and bloody, but none in any way decisive. Yet it was the Marathas who were getting the worst of it. Their casualties were higher than those of the Afghans. The first encounter took place on 7 December and, during it, one of the Maratha generals was killed. Unfortunately for Sadashiv, this was his most trusted and cleverest adviser. The other generals were men of worth but not of genius or even of outstanding competence. In a sense, the battle was already lost.

From that time onwards, the Afghans were on the offensive. No longer did they permit Maratha skirmishers to get away unharmed. By running patrols of cavalry around the Maratha encampment, they began to stop supplies from getting through. The road to Delhi was blocked by Afghan troops. The town of Kunjpura was recaptured. Sadashiv had to pay in cash for food from the north-west, and his last hope disappeared when a party conveying a large quantity of stores and ammunition was intercepted by the Afghans, who killed its commander and diverted the supplies to the Afghan camp.

The Maratha position was now so tattered by the failure of supplies that some action had to be taken. Even supplies for cash had been stopped. One evening, when some twenty thousand Maratha camp followers crept out to gather grass and wood they were attacked by five thousand Afghan horsemen, who killed almost all of them and piled their bodies into mountains which were clearly visible from the Maratha lines. According to a contemporary, at this even

Sadashiv 'began to yield to fear and despair'. At last he made
the attempt to induce Shuja-ud-daula to intercede with
Ahmad Shah on his behalf, sending him a piece of paper on
which he had made an imprint of his palm in saffron. This
was to be proof of the honesty of the proposals. But, though
there was some hesitation in the Afghan camp, the Rohilla
Najib Khan persuaded the Afghan leaders that they were
now engaged in a holy war against infidels—a view strangely
out of place in the shifting alliances of an India in which the
religion of the participants seemed to play very little part.
Yet it had some relevance. The Marathas were Hindus with
a record of resistance to Muslim power. To fanatical
Muslims, they seemed perhaps to epitomize the enemies of
God. Whatever the truth, Najib was persuasive, and the
Maratha envoys, baffled by this sudden injection of religion
into questions of profit and power, were sent back to their
master.

Inside the Maratha entrenchment, the blockade had first
brought hardship, then want, then despair and desperation.
On 13 January 1761, after the army had been two days
without rations, the commanders surrounded Sadashiv's
tent and shouted : 'Let us not die in misery but go out and
attack the enemy. Then whatever fate has decided will
happen'. After a great deal of argument, stretching far into
the night, it was decided that the army should move out
before daybreak and make a frontal attack on the Afghans.

In the morning, the Maratha army prepared for death.
The Hindus who made up the majority of Sadashiv's force
made their religious ablutions and said their prayers. Some
undid their turbans and smeared their faces with powdered
turmeric as a sign that they did not expect to come back
alive from the field of battle. On the Maratha side, despite
Najib Khan's attempt to give the conflict the special and
inspiring flavour of a holy war, there were also about eight
thousand Muslim troops. These were commanded by a
man who had been trained by a French general, and the
contingent was organized on French infantry lines and
armed with light muskets. Altogether, Sadashiv was able

to muster about 45,000 men, roughly three-quarters of whom were mounted. In reserve were 15,000 Pindaris, men from professional robber tribes who, since they preferred plunder to fighting, were more of a menace than a support.

Ahmad Shah had a great number of fighting men in the field—around 60,000, of whom two-thirds were mounted. In reserve lay another 80,000 men, mostly raw levies and untried troops. The Afghan cavalry was better mounted than the Maratha, their horses being of the superb breeds of Khorassan and Trans-Oxiana on which so many of the earlier Muslim invaders had ridden through the passes of the north-west to conquer India. The Maratha horses were greatly inferior, their poor breeding intensified by bad fodder and short rations.

An hour before dawn on 14 January, the Maratha army marched out of its camp. Each division was centred round its commander, and the banners moved in a long procession before fanning out to form a line of battle. The army moved in a vast cloud of dust; when it stopped, there was a wait of two hours before the dust could settle and the enemy became visible.

Ahmad Shah was also in line, his army spread out along a front of seven miles and extending two miles deep. The Afghans had assembled in a hurry, as the Maratha decision to fight had been so unexpected that the first the Afghans knew of it was the sound of iron-shod wheels and the cloud of dust.

Sadashiv had tried to avoid marching out to what he believed would be certain defeat by sending an envoy to Shuja-ud-daula. 'The flood has risen over my head', he wrote. 'If anything can be done, do it or else tell me plainly and at once that it cannot, for in a moment there will be no time for talk'. But Ahmad Shah was not prepared to talk, and Sadashiv was on the move, however reluctantly, with his army.

Ahmad Shah knew that he had the advantage. His men were well fed and better horsed. Fresh reinforcements had come to him from the harsh hills of his homeland, young men, vigorous and anxious for battle. The Maratha artillery was heavy, but his own was highly mobile—two thousand camels carrying swivel guns. Even his hand guns were superior, the long-barrelled Afghan flintlocks, firing heavier bullets and with a longer range than the light French *fusils* of the Maratha infantry. The Afghans were even better dressed than the Marathas. The Afghan officers wore armour, whose weight was easily carried by their horses, but the Maratha generals rarely wore either breast-plate or cuirass, preferring light clothes more suitable to the climate and the carrying power of their small ponies. The rank and file of the Afghan force wore padded leather and quilted jackets that could turn a sword thrust, while the Maratha soldier had often nothing more than a piece of cloth round his waist. The Afghans derisively called them 'bare-backs'.

The battle began at 10 a.m. with an inaccurate cannonade from the Maratha artillery. Then the Maratha infantry attacked and a bloody engagement continued for about three hours, in which European training was matched against Rohilla tenacity. When the fighting became 'breast to breast', the Rohillas' weight of numbers told and the Maratha infantry fled from the field leaving behind more than three-quarters of their number in dead and wounded.

Sadashiv himself now attacked the centre of the Afghan line. First the cannon roared and then there was silence. The Marathas, clustered around the great yellow banner of their commander, sent up a tremendous shout that could be heard in the Afghan lines. 'Hara! Hara! Mahadev!' they cried, in adoration of the great god Siva. A flash of sunlight was reflected from the upraised spears and the waving swords. Then a great phalanx of thousands of horsemen turned and rode towards the Afghan lines. The swivel guns of the Afghans cut through the horses and then the two armies were in hand-to-hand combat, in a dust cloud which 'hid the earth and the sky and from which blood dropped like rain'. Through the din of battle came the Maratha war cry and the Afghan reply: 'Deen! Deen!' [The faith! The faith!]

Such was the fury of the Maratha charge that it almost broke through; some Afghans turned and ran. 'Where are you running to?' shouted their commander. 'Our homeland is far away and you may never reach it!' The line reformed and held, fluidly, in group combat, and the Marathas were unable to follow up their initial advantage because of their lack of heavy cavalry.

It was now after 1.30 p.m. and it was a curious fact that the Hindu troops, about noon, whatever they were doing, were inclined to break off an action in order to prepare food. This was a complex, caste-controlled occupation. The Afghans—meat-eaters with few or no food prejudices and tabus—ate in the saddle and continued the fight. Some Marathas began to desert.

Sadashiv and his immediate supporters still held on, constantly counter-attacking, constantly separating and coming together again as they were attacked and dispersed. Many Marathas were killed by the Afghan muskets, constantly reloaded from inexhaustible supplies. Again and again the yellow banner of the Marathas was raised and the Maratha cavalry rode down in a wave on the Afghans, only to be slashed apart by the fire of muskets and swivel guns. Soon after two o'clock the news was brought to Sadashiv that his nephew had been killed. This, reinforced by the sight of the youth's body brought up to him on the back of an elephant, seemed to make up his mind that all was over. A desperate charge with death as the outcome seemed a fitting conclusion—the triumph of 'honour' over military expertise.

Sadashiv found death only with difficulty. He was wounded by a spear thrust, and a musket ball was lodged in his thigh. He lost his horse from a shot which threw him from the saddle. But he was still alive and only slightly hurt when the battle passed over him. His costly brocade coat smeared with blood, he limped along with the aid of a short spear, his great necklace of jewels shining in the sun. It was their gleam which attracted four Afghan horsemen searching the field for plunder. They called on him to surrender and save his life, but he launched out at them with his spear. Sadashiv was killed and his head cut off and carried away.

Elsewhere on the field of battle the Marathas were in retreat. Some had hardly fired a shot or waved a sword. On one wing, Najib Khan had moved slowly forward against a block of Maratha cavalry, his pioneers erecting earthworks as they went, to give shelter if the cavalry chose to attack. Face to face at last, Najib's rocket-men sent hundreds of missiles into the packed ranks of Maratha horse so that they turned and ran.

By three in the afternoon, the Maratha army was virtually leaderless, its principal officers dead and the rank and file scattered about a wide plain piled with dead and wounded. The Afghan army advanced all along the line, sweeping the remnants before it, into and through the Maratha camp, along a road already crowded with refugees, their carts and belongings. The pursuit continued for about twenty miles until the sun began to set and Ahmad Shah recalled his forces to spend the night bivouacked together in case the rout of the Marathas was not as complete as it seemed.

Next morning, the sharp winter sun shining through the cold clear air revealed a vast necropolis. The dead were strewn in mounds across the battlefield and inside the Maratha camp. Many fugitives died in the jungle they had hoped would shelter them. Some died of the cold; others were killed by wild animals. The town of Panipat was taken and the men who had sought refuge there were brought out and executed. As an appropriate act of revenge for the deaths of their comrades, the Afghan soldiers were allowed one day of indiscriminate massacre. From this murder of infidels, it was believed they would gain merit in the sight of Allah. Prisoners taken after this first day were not harmed.

Among the captives were a large number of women, the Marathas having taken advantage of the selection offered by the markets of Delhi and Lahore. The Hindu women captives were sold off to Hindu soldiers—for Muslim holy war or no holy war, there were many Hindu soldiers on the Afghan side. In the auction, the women rated about half the price of a horse!

The Maratha defeat at Panipat was complete and shattering. As well as Sadashiv, the Peshwa's own son and heir was killed in the fighting, as were many lesser chiefs and many thousands of ordinary soldiers. As the cypher report to the Peshwa said: 'Two pearls have been dissolved, twenty-seven gold [coins] have been lost, and of the silver and copper the total cannot be cast up'. The battle was to rule the Marathas out of the power struggle in northern India for ten years while they recouped their strength. For them, Panipat was always 'the battle of the black mango tree', where the fruit had withered and fallen from the branch.

7

A forest of wild beasts

NEWS OF the Maratha defeat at Panipat reached Shah Alam and the British after the emperor had surrendered to Major Carnac. Later came an envoy from Ahmad Shah informing the emperor that he intended to return home and suggesting that the emperor should make his way to Delhi. Ahmad Shah said that he had re-appointed Imad-ul-mulk as wazir and created Najib Khan commander-in-chief.

The emperor now required Mir Kasim, nawab of Bengal, to issue a proclamation of accession on his behalf. This the nawab was not prepared to do. He was already in conflict with the British, who were squeezing Bengal with almost as much thoroughness as Ahmad Shah or the Marathas had squeezed Delhi, and there were rumours that the emperor had offered to appoint the British principal collectors of revenue for Bengal. Such an appointment would have left the business of government to the nawab, while giving the British the financial control. The offer had in fact been made, but the British had as yet neither accepted nor declined it. While the British were trying to persuade the nawab to issue the proclamation—which he steadfastly refused to do until the emperor had left Patna—Shah Alam was endeavouring to decide whether to go to Delhi or not.

Shah Alam had no desire to place himself once again within range of Imad, who had murdered the emperor's father and could not be trusted not to make a similar attempt on the son. As a court historian put it, a river of blood lay between Shah Alam and Imad. Najib Khan was well aware of the problem. While Imad was hanging about waiting for an escort back to Delhi from his refuge with Suraj Mal, Najib persuaded the queen mother and Shah Alam's heir, who were in the city, that Imad must be kept out ; otherwise, with the emperor far away in Bihar, he might once again proclaim Shah Jahan II or some other prince as emperor in his stead. The result was that Najib made a ceremonial entry into Delhi in the company of Shah Alam's heir. This event was widely publicized, and when news of it reached Suraj Mal he decided to refuse Imad his support. Though, by avoiding involvement in the struggle between the Afghans and the Marathas, Suraj Mal was by now probably the most powerful prince in northern India, he was not prepared to restore Imad to power in Delhi without support. That support was not forthcoming. No one was prepared to trust Imad. Suraj Mal occupied himself instead in capturing Agra, where he took the fort by bribery after less than a month's blockade. This meant that the country south of Delhi was now in the hands of a man of the same race as the majority of the inhabitants, and that there was an identification between the ruler and the ruled.

In Delhi itself, Najib was for the moment supreme. As well as commander-in-chief, he had been made governor of the Delhi district and, even more important, regent of the imperial government. Shah Alam confirmed these appointments.

The emperor himself had now decided to return to Delhi. His wazir, Shuja-ud-daula, offered him an escort when the British refused one—sensibly enough, as they had neither the troops nor the resources for such an expedition. In any case, they had enough problems in Bengal. But they did provide Shah Alam with a party of troops to see him as far as the Karamnassa river, at the Bihar border, where he was met by Shuja-ud-daula. It was now June and the rainy season was about to begin. The emperor settled to await the return of the cold weather and the travelling and campaigning season.

In November 1761, Shah Alam and Shuja-ud-daula set off for Delhi, intending to conduct a few useful campaigns on the way. Shah Alam hoped to recover the imperial terri- tories in Bundelkhand, an area south of Delhi, lying between the Jumna and Chambal rivers, which had once been under the control of the Marathas. After Panipat, the local land-owners had risen against the weakened Maratha garrisons and shut them up in their forts. When Shah Alam entered the area in January 1762 he met with little opposition, which was easily overcome, and soon received the submissions of the chiefs. But all this took time, and Shah Alam had to withdraw to quarters for the next rainy season. He set up his camp at a place near Cawnpore.

It was early in 1763 before the emperor, escorted by Shuja, could march to the town of Sikandrabad and call on the local chiefs to accompany him to Delhi. One of these, the nawab of Farrukhabad, refused, and Shuja decided to mount an attack on him. Before he could carry this into effect, however, there arrived two important Afghan leaders, as well as Najib Khan, the imperial commander-in-chief in person. Unfortunately, Shuja-ud-daula's plan antagonized the Afghans—for the offending nawab was one of their countrymen. There was also an outbreak of fighting between Najib's and Shuja's troops who belonged to different Muslim sects. The situation was so uneasy that no agreement could be reached among the various parties which would allow the emperor to be installed at Delhi with any semblance of unity. Shah Alam himself was hardly a free agent, and was ultimately forced to retire with his wazir and master, Shuja-ud-daula.

Najib's position was now somewhat delicate. He was the agent of Ahmad Shah, who had only just left the Punjab where he had spent his time after Panipat. Ahmad Shah had not only confirmed Shuja as wazir, but had sent letters to the princes of India announcing that he recognized Shah Alam as legitimate emperor. Najib could not therefore afford to show antagonism to the emperor while the emperor had the approval of Ahmad Shah—who might possibly return at any time. Najib was also ill, probably of cancer, which slowed up his activity. Furthermore, he was threatened by Suraj Mal, whose army of Jats menaced Delhi. The forces of Suraj and Najib met in battle, however, and Suraj Mal was shot dead early in the engagement. After this, though superior in numbers, his troops fled from the field. Najib's men were so surprised by this unexpected victory that they did not follow the fleeing enemy, and the Jats were able to escape. But there were serious dissensions among them which gave Najib almost a year's respite before Suraj Mal's successor was in a position to try and avenge his father's death.

Meanwhile, Shah Alam, under pressure from Shuja, once again considered invading Bihar. Superficially, the situation seemed favourable. In Bengal, the British had forced the nawab, Mir Kasim, to proclaim Shah Alam. But Mir Kasim had simply been waiting to build up his strength for the showdown he intended to have with them. During the latter part of 1763, he finally acted against the British. In October, after capturing Patna, he had a number of Englishmen murdered—but when a British force approached the city, Mir Kasim fled into Shuja's territory of Oudh. The British were not strong enough to pursue him there. They stopped at the border and settled themselves at the town of Buxar, about halfway between Patna and Benares.

In February 1764, Mir Kasim went to visit the emperor. After contributing a large sum of money to the finances of both the emperor and his wazir, he suggested that an invasion of Bihar might be the prelude to the reconquest of Bengal. It was an idea which appealed to the emperor and his wazir, and in April 1764 a large force crossed the frontier of Bihar and made for Patna. The British commander at Buxar, afraid of being cut off from his base at Patna, retired in the direction of the city and, on 3 May, met up with the imperial forces. There was a sharp series of actions, lasting most of the day, in which the imperial forces came out badly and were forced to retreat. The British were too weak to follow up their victory.

The British commander was now removed from his post, because of jealousies and fear among his superiors at Calcutta, and replaced by Major Hector Munro, who was ordered to get his troops into a fit state to start a campaign against Shah Alam and his allies. When he took over, Munro was faced with a number of mutinies, some of which may have been incited by *agents provocateurs*. He acted with severity, however, and a number of rapid trials and swift executions soon restored military discipline. By October 1764, Munro was ready to move. With 900 Europeans, 5,000 native infantry, and 900 native cavalry he set off to find the imperial army, and came up with it at Buxar, securely entrenched with the river Ganges on its left and Buxar town and fort in its rear. Inside the defences were an estimated 40,000 men, including European gunners and a cavalry contingent which incorporated the famous Rohilla horsemen who had contributed so much to Ahmad Shah's victories.

Munro's attempt to attack the camp by night failed for lack of satisfactory intelligence about the enemy dispositions. The following morning, 25 October, the imperial forces decided to take the initiative, secure in their numerical superiority, and the battle began. Neither Shah Alam nor Shuja took part in the struggle which raged bloodily from 8 a.m. until after sunset. The various Indian leaders, not trusting one another, refused to co-ordinate their actions, and there was none of them with any claim to genius. All fought well, but—except for the European mercenaries—without discipline. It was here that the European training of the British troops began to have its effect. Well-laid artillery fire tore into the Rohilla cavalry, and disciplined musket fire broke up the advancing infantry. Slowly, fighting all the way, the imperial forces began to retire. Finally, a flight was precipitated when Shuja crossed the river to leave the field, destroying the bridge of boats behind him and leaving many men cut off.

The first to approach Munro for terms was the emperor, who protested through his envoy that he had been kept a prisoner by his own wazir and had not wished to attack the British. He asked for Munro's protection. The British commander, whose own force had suffered considerably, was not prepared to take the responsibility of receiving the

emperor into his camp and informed him that he could not
offer the emperor sanctuary from his wazir without the prior
authority of his superiors in Calcutta. Shah Alam remained
close to the British force as it moved towards Benares in
pursuit of Shuja.

Shuja himself sent envoys asking for terms. Those he was
offered included a demand to surrender the former nawab,
Mir Kasim, and a European known as Sumru who had been
personally responsible for the murder of the English at
Patna. Shuja refused, probably because these two men were
still in a position to threaten his safety rather than for reasons
of honour towards allies. He fled to his capital of Lucknow,
and then into the Rohilla country to the west. Mir Kasim
disappeared into the jungle. Sumru moved off in the direction of Delhi, in the hope of finding new employment for his
varied talents. Mir Kasim was not heard of again, but
Sumru still had a role to play in the violent history of
Hindustan.

Word finally came from Calcutta that the emperor, cling-
ing in fear to the fringes of the British camp, should be
given protection. At Allahabad he was lodged in the fort,
which Munro took over in his name from an agent of Shuja
in February 1765. Even from the emperor's point of view,
this was all very satisfactory. He was free of Shuja, and the
British seemed to be willing to pay him due respect, even to
the extent of supplying him with money for his small court
and personal needs. The British were already dividing up
Shuja's territory. They could, they thought, give the whole
of Oudh to the emperor in exchange for a grant of the city
and environs of Benares. When they raised the matter with
him, he found the idea very appealing, and was also prepared to reimburse the British for their efforts out of the
revenues of Oudh. But before these agreements could be
put into practice, Shuja-ud-daula reappeared, this time with
allies of proved value—the Marathas.

Shuja was just as much a prisoner of the Marathas as the
emperor had been of Shuja.

The British and the Marathas met at the town of Kora,

twenty-five miles from Cawnpore. Munro had resigned his command of the British force, and Carnac had been re-appointed. The Marathas, first put to flight by Carnac's heavy artillery fire, returned and were again driven off. During this engagement, Shuja-ud-daula, with an escort of four hundred men, broke away and made for the British lines where he was received with brittle courtesy. The Marathas withdrew from the field.

Shuja asked again for terms, but when Carnac sent to Calcutta for instructions he was told that no agreement should be made until Carnac was joined by the new English governor, who had just landed at Calcutta from England— Robert Clive, Mughal noble and now an Irish peer.

Clive reached Benares on 1 August and negotiations were opened with Shuja on the following day. A week later Clive, accompanied by the wazir, was at Allahabad discussing terms with the emperor. Shah Alam was by no means as penitent in face of the British as his wazir had been. He did not even accept that he had been defeated. Clive, as an officer of the Mughal empire, owed allegiance to it and to its head. Shah Alam pointed out that Bengal owed the imperial treasury considerable arrears of revenue!

Clive promised that he would be paid a monthly sum in future, amounting to over two-and-a-half million rupees in the year. He would also receive the territories of Allahabad and Kora (detached from Oudh), and a British force would be stationed at Allahabad to protect him. Shah Alam promptly accepted these offers and, in return, appointed yet another British nominee as nawab of Bengal and assigned to the British the right to collect the revenue.

On 12 August the emperor seated himself in Clive's tent on a throne made from an armchair, covered with brocade and mounted on a dining-table. He then formally handed to Clive the written allocation of the revenue. The British were now, *de jure*, part of the Mughal empire. And with such ease. As a contemporary Indian historian put it, the grant of the revenue collection which 'left neither pretence or subterfuge, and which at any other time would have

required the sending of wise ambassadors and able negotia-
tors, as well as a deal of parley and conference with the
[East India] Company and the king of England, and much
negotiation and contention with the ministers, was done and
finished in a less time than would have been taken up for the
sale of a jackass, or of a beast of burden, or of a head of
cattle'.

Four days later a treaty was signed with Shuja which
included his paying a large sum to cover the expenses of the
recent campaign against him. The emperor, who had
deprived Shuja of his office of wazir after the battle of Buxar,
now under pressure from the British reinstated him.

Everyone seemed to be satisfied. The British had a
legitimate position in the political structure of India. Shuja,
though somewhat lighter in pocket, had a defensive alliance
with the new and powerful force of the British. The emperor
had money even if, with it, came dependence.

Shah Alam settled down in some comfort in Allahabad
although he still wished to return to Delhi, the hub of the
empire. Until he was seated on his throne in the palace of
his ancestors, his authority would seem to have a slightly
tarnished air. The British promised to march back there with
him 'after the rains'—a promise that came to be repeated
every year. The British agent at his court constantly
reminded Shah Alam of the sadnesses and privations of his
past; far better, he implied, to remain in the comparative
comfort of Allahabad, however provincial it might be, than
to risk death, imprisonment, or at least humiliation at Delhi.
While the British paid their tribute regularly, such advice
carried weight. But it seemed to the emperor that, if the
British pension failed, everything would be lost.

Under pressure from Shah Alam, Clive had once written
to say that he personally did not have the authority to
commit British troops to taking the emperor to Delhi. Shah
Alam then decided to send an envoy to England to present
a petition to the king. The envoy left early in 1766, in
company with an English officer, and carrying gifts valued
at 100,000 rupees. When he was actually on the ship, the

envoy was informed that his letters were still ashore, having been confiscated by Clive. Clive had told the officer that he himself would present the letters and the gifts on his own return to England the following year. The letters were never presented, and the gifts were handed over with no accompanying message from the emperor. It seems likely, in fact, that Clive pretended they came from himself.

But, whatever was or was not happening in England, events in Hindustan were not standing still. In the heartland of the empire, 'all law and religion were trodden underfoot . . . and every individual as if amidst a forest of wild beasts could rely upon nothing but the strength of his own arm'. Yet the situation was not quite as anarchic as the contemporary chronicler thought.

The unexpected death of the Jat leader, Suraj Mal, and Najib Khan's failure to follow it up, had left Suraj Mal's successor time to consolidate his questioned heritage. He was assisted by an incursion across the river Jumna by the Sikhs, who were rising in the Punjab against Ahmad Shah's deputy at Lahore. Najib was compelled to buy them off.

The throne of the Jat territories had been seized from Suraj Mal's legal heir by one Jawahir Singh. Anxious to take revenge on Najib Khan, he made preparations to attack the imperial capital. He had the very considerable army of Suraj Mal, and had also contracted to hire a Maratha force of about 20,000 men as well as a force of Sikh mercenaries amounting to about 15,000 in number.

Jawahir's campaign opened in November 1764. His was a formidable army, further strengthened by some 30,000 cavalry and foot, and with a hundred pieces of artillery. Najib Khan could muster nothing like such numbers. As soon as he had heard of Jawahir's preparations, Najib had sent off a messenger to his nominal overlord, Ahmad Shah, who was then at Kandahar in Afghanistan; had appealed for help to his Rohilla brethren across the Ganges; and had sent envoys to Jawahir suggesting that there was nothing for them to fight about. Was it not destiny that Suraj Mal had died on the field of battle? Would he be brought back to life if his successor avenged himself on Najib? Najib had taken no Jat territory—what, then, was to be gained?

From Jawahir's point of view, it was honour, or the visible proof of honour, that was at stake. His father had to be avenged so that Jawahir's prestige with his own people should not be diminished, nor the prestige of his people in the eyes of the other powers of northern India. In the forest there were plenty of jackals waiting to bring down the failing tiger.

So Jawahir moved on Delhi while Najib set himself to organizing the city's defence. A number of skirmishes took place, but Jawahir's Maratha allies seemed reluctant to fight and he began to wonder whether they could be trusted. Nevertheless, he began to press forward on the defences and Najib's position was closely threatened. A certain non-chalance in the Jat attack enabled Najib's Rohilla marksmen to create deadly havoc; the Jats were only saved from annihilation by a fanatical attack carried out by a contingent of reinforcements. Jawahir was, however, able to cross the river and site guns to bombard the city. The countryside around the city was now in the hands of the Jats and their allies, and the bombardment of the city was taking its toll of men and buildings.

The Sikh mercenaries were brave fighters but had no guns, and when they approached the city walls Najib's men, expert with rockets, were easily able to drive them back. Shortly after a murderous but indecisive battle outside the walls at the end of January 1765, Jawahir was joined by a force of Hindu religious mendicants, fanatical fighters for their faith, who were quite prepared to die if they could take infidels with them. They too fought a desperate battle with Najib's men, but military expertise triumphed over fanaticism, and they were defeated.

In the meantime, Imad-ul-mulk had reappeared. Although he had joined Jawahir, both he and the Maratha leader had been in secret correspondence with Najib. When Jawahir heard of this, he realized that he could not count on their aid in capturing Delhi; on the other hand, he could not capture the city without it. Some of the former Jat commanders of Suraj Mal were also conspiring against Jawahir.

In February, Najib opened up negotiations. Envoys passed between the two sides and Najib himself came out of the city to visit Jawahir and his Maratha ally. Famine had begun to gnaw at the defences, so grain was sent into the city as a sign of good faith. An index of Najib's sense of victory appeared in his willingness to be reconciled with Imad-ul-mulk. At the end of February, as the Muslim holy month of Ramadan began, the citizens of Delhi saw the two men ride side by side on an elephant down the main street of the city. But Imad did not stay for long. Jawahir and his fickle allies, the Marathas and the Sikhs, soon departed too, for the news came that Ahmad Shah Abdali was in the Punjab yet again.

The Afghan king did not, however, descend on Delhi. When he heard that Najib was no longer in danger he angrily returned to Kandahar. Ahmad Shah's own kingdom was unsettled, and his army was turbulent with dislike for his Indian campaigns. The Punjab, too, remained in a flurry of violence as the Sikhs threatened the Afghan hold. In one sense, all this suited Najib Khan very well. He was supposed to be Ahmad Shah's agent, and responsible for collecting tribute. But this he had been unable to do. Now, however, after his success against the Jats, he began to reimpose his rule in the areas surrounding the imperial capital.

Though Najib succeeded to some extent in restarting the flow of revenue, he was constantly harried by Sikh attacks. These were sudden and swift. The Sikhs would descend on a place, plunder it, and take off rapidly again. Najib had to be constantly on the move against these raiders. Sometimes there would be bitter engagements. At other times, he would merely pursue the Sikhs around the countryside. He was never defeated himself, but neither was he able to crush the Sikhs.

At the beginning of 1767, Ahmad Shah appeared in India for the last time, for a campaign against the Sikhs who were divided amongst themselves. The Afghan king sent a message to Najib, among others, ordering him to visit him and bring with him the seven years of tribute money which had not been paid. Najib joined the Afghan camp at Ismailabad, near Ambala, in March. By then he was extremely ill. Ahmad Shah received him with great kindness, partly because there was a certain friendship between them and partly because, despite his condition, Najib had come himself instead of sending envoys as the Jat and Rohilla chiefs had done.

The campaign which Ahmad Shah now began against the Sikhs was not very successful. He himself was tiring of life in the saddle, and constant battles and the intrigues of his own court were beginning to affect his health. His army, too, was beginning to murmur against him once more. Finally, having made arrangements for the governing of the Punjab and having accepted Najib's offer to send on a part of the tribute money as soon as possible, he left for home. On his way, he was harassed by Sikh bands right up to the frontier.

Najib returned to Delhi, followed, like his master, by omnipresent bands of Sikhs who continued to threaten him even there. Conscious that he was dying, he wrote to the emperor Shah Alam: 'Until this very hour I have shown only the firmest loyalty to the princes in Delhi and to the queen mother. But now I am no longer able to give protection. Let your majesty advance to your capital and there defend your own honour'. To the queen mother, he wrote offering to have her and the heir apparent escorted to join the emperor at Allahabad. In his suffering, he talked of making the pilgrimage to Mecca or of retiring to some holy place to spend what remained of his life in meditation.

But the adventure was not quite over. The emperor did not come. Najib, now in Najibabad—the town he had built and named after himself—brought together his generals and, in their presence, declared his son Zabita Khan to

76

be his successor. His private advice to Zabita was that he should quickly crush those commanders who supported his step-brother's claims and who would be most likely to dispute the succession after Najib's death. Zabita acted quickly against them, and also took the opportunity of making peace with the Sikhs by buying them off.

The situation in Delhi remained unchanged. The imperial family remained in occupation of the palace, and Zabita Khan's men manned the defences. There was a lull.

In October, carried in a litter, Najib paid a visit to the emperor's heir apparent and was received with high honour. Zabita Khan was introduced to the prince and the queen mother, and his succession was confirmed. But these preparations for a future in which he would play no part did not reassure Najib. The Marathas, the wounds of Panipat healed, were flexing their muscles. Letters had gone out to the rulers of northern India demanding the payment of overdue tribute. Who was there to oppose the Marathas? Ahmad Shah Abdali was dying and could not be called on again. The Peshwa had managed to soothe the jealousies of the Maratha chiefs; he had even made peace with the rulers of the Deccan and Mysore, who might have threatened the Maratha homeland. Najib was sure that the Marathas had not forgotten that he had been one of the causes of their disaster in 1761. In one last attempt to save his family, he decided to try and reach some agreement with them.

It appears that the exact state of Najib's health was not known to the Maratha leaders. Perhaps it was not fully known to anyone but Najib himself, conscious of the cancer in his stomach. In any case, his overtures were received with relief by some of the Maratha leaders, for Najib Khan was still a name to be feared in northern India. At least one of the chiefs had been feeding Najib with information for many years and was still his friend. But to others such as Mahadaji Sindia he was 'the foremost of our enemies'. Powerful enemies, however, had to be deflected with diplomacy. The Marathas sent pledges of friendship and suggested that, as they proposed to invade the Jat dominions

77

from the west of the river Jumna, Najib might also choose to move against them.

Najib agreed, and his forces began to attack the Jat forts. Jawahir Singh had been murdered in July 1768 and power was now held by Nawal Singh, the man from whom Jawahir had originally seized the throne. Nawal was foolish enough to emerge from his fortress at Dig and was defeated by Najib, who had regained something of his old virility in one of the characteristic revivals shown by those dying from cancer. It was not a decisive victory, however, as Nawal Singh escaped the battlefield and retired into another of his forts.

The time had now come for a meeting between Najib and the Marathas. Mahadaji Sindia was among those present. Najib tried to explain away the deaths of Sindia's relatives at his hands by speaking of the ways of providence —'whatever God wills, happens'. To which Sindia replied: 'The will of God has been accomplished. Let us see what he wills *in the future*'. It was a sinister reply, and Najib was warned by his Maratha friend that treachery was in the air. As Najib moved away to a safer spot, his baggage-train was attacked. But the attackers were driven off and the rainy season prevented further hostilities.

Though the rains called a halt to military activity, they increased the diplomatic offensive. Envoys laden with threatening letters moved around the country. From Najib appeals for aid went out to the Rohilla chiefs. Conferences between the nominal allies were shadowed with distrust. Najib was blunt. If there was ill will towards him, he said, contacts should be broken off. With difficulty he was persuaded that no one wished to break off relations.

Even in mortal sickness, Najib was no dupe of the Marathas, however. Opening talks with the Jats, he brought them and the Marathas together. From his one partisan among the Maratha chiefs he asked support for his son and successor, Zabita Khan. On the last day of October 1770, he died. His last act was to prohibit his troops from molesting Hindu pilgrims at a religious fair near his camp.

Najib Khan had maintained himself against all opposition for nine years. He had survived less by force of arms—though he was a brilliant general—than by diplomacy. He was not strong enough to crush his rivals, but by juggling alliances kept them from combining against him. Now that the juggler was dead, the balls began to roll about. It seemed probable that someone would be hurt and the most likely victim was the emperor Shah Alam far away in Allahabad. The Sikhs looked as if they might take Delhi and put someone else on the throne; there were plenty of imperial princes for them to choose from. Or the Marathas might do the same.

In Allahabad, the news of Najib's death was received with apprehension. That lull of comfortable living sub-sidized by the British tribute was in danger. The standstill party, supported by the British, argued that even a moth-eaten court was better than none at all. In fact, save in contrast with the distant imperial past, the court was *not* particularly moth-eaten. The British tribute was paid regularly and without deductions. But although the British were not anxious for the emperor to forego their patronage, they had themselves no personal intention of handing him to the throne. They were, in fact, much occupied in south India. They made the attempt to convince the emperor that he was better off where he was, but were not unduly worried if he chose to disregard their advice. They could hardly stop him from pursuing his own path, although they might cut off payments. It was a risk Shah Alam had to take. If he did not go then, it seemed certain that he would never go at all.

At the end of 1770, Shah Alam sent an envoy to negotiate with the Maratha chiefs for an alliance which would restore him to the capital. After these talks, the envoy went on to Delhi and, in February, officially took possession of the city in the name of Shah Alam. Two days later, the Marathas began to bombard Delhi. There was no one to defend it, and the city capitulated.

The Marathas entered Delhi, took possession of the fort,

and posted guards at the city gates. When Shah Alam's envoy protested, the Marathas made it clear that they had not entirely trusted him and had occupied the capital as a safeguard. Under pressure, the envoy negotiated a treaty with the Maratha chiefs. By its terms, the Marathas agreed to escort the emperor to Delhi. In return they were to receive the sum of four million rupees and the revenue assignments of a number of areas. One million rupees was to be paid immediately and the rest was to come from the assignments. The details were drawn up in writing, and the heir apparent affixed his seal to the document on the emperor's behalf.

The emperor ratified the treaty as soon as he received it. The time of final decision had now come. Overruling those who preferred to stay in the modest comforts of Allahabad and ignoring the advice of the British, he set out for Delhi on 13 April 1771. He was accompanied by a large force, some of them European mercenaries and some consisting of troops supplied by his wazir, Shuja-ud-daula, who—in place of his person—provided the equipment for the emperor's travelling camp. He sweetened his own refusal to go to Delhi with a donation of 1·2 million rupees in cash. Though the British refused the emperor's request to supply troops to accompany him, they did order a large detachment under Sir Robert Barker to escort him as far as the frontier of the province of Allahabad.

On 13 April the emperor and his escort left Allahabad. Shuja-ud-daula marched with him for part of the way, but left early in June. At Bithur, at the end of the same month, General Barker told the emperor that he could go with him no further but that he would leave him a gift of four guns as well as the strongest assurances of British friendship and a promise of their readiness to assist him should he ever have to call on them again. The emperor thanked the British commander for all the kindnesses he had received at British hands.

It was a formal and empty farewell. The emperor knew that the British did not want to let him out of their grasp, and that they would certainly find some way of showing their disapproval—probably by taking over the provinces he was now leaving. But Sir Robert Barker had been instructed not to antagonize the emperor—just in case.

Shah Alam, accompanied by his own men—a small force, though trained on European lines—and a body of horse and foot left to him by Shuja, continued his progress until he met up with the Maratha chief Mahadaji Sindia. At Nabiganj, nineteen miles south-west of Farrukhabad, he halted. As ever, the rainy season brought the world to a standstill.

But on New Year's day 1772 Shah Alam came in sight of the imperial capital. Two days later he was joined by the heir apparent and the queen mother, who came out of the city with other members of the imperial family to meet him.

All that remained was for the exile to take possession of his inheritance. This he did on 6 January, entering with his cortège through one of the great gateways. By accident or design, this was the day which saw the end of a Muslim period of fasting, a day when all was rejoicing and gaiety.

PART TWO

Imperial Pride and Star-clad Power

Learn to sustain the loss of sight and throne;
Learn that imperial pride, and star-clad power,
Are but the fleeting pageants of an hour.

1

A shattered heritage

IN THE MOSQUES, public squares and private houses there was rejoicing at the end of thirty days of fasting. It was a rejoicing that was, in some minds, enhanced by hopes of return to the old days, when an emperor in the palace meant profit for the craftsmen, artisans and merchants of Delhi. For twelve years the imperial city had been the prey of adventurers, its population driven out to the countryside to escape oppression or simply to find bread.

From a distance, the proud domes and stately buildings of the city had shone with their old splendour in the eyes of the returning exile. But as his escort marched through the unkempt streets, whose paving stones were broken, whose sidewalks were lined with crumbling shops, Shah Alam saw little but decay and desolation. Outwardly, the great palace of the Red Fort was barely altered by the winds of war. The mark of a cannonball showed here and there, but it hardly touched the majesty of the façade. But inside the gates, the wreck of the years was undisguised. Trees, with the terrible aggressiveness of Nature, had broken through the building blocks. There were piles of rubble in the great courts. The palaces had been stripped not only of their treasures but of their most basic furnishings. Animals had filled the dead fountains with their excrement. The aqueduct that had fed the conduits—called, so dramatically, the Canal of Paradise—was stopped up with leaves and debris.

Worse still, the great store rooms were empty. The secret cellars of the treasury echoed only to the susurration of rats. The palace was a shell, still gorgeous with marble—a paradise lost.

The treasury was empty and if it were to be filled it would

be necessary to go out and conquer provinces that in time past had supplied the imperial revenues. On the whole, as Shah Alam looked round his shattered heritage, the rejoicings must have seemed somewhat premature.

If the view inside the palace was discouraging, the prospect from the battlements was almost unnerving. In his own right, the emperor controlled only his household troops, and they were not necessarily trustworthy. Around the walls of the city lay the Marathas, ostensibly allies but perfectly likely to turn on the emperor if they did not receive the money they expected. The provinces beyond were in the hands of powerful men with full treasuries and well-paid armies, who were unlikely to give up either without a fight. The two powers nearest the city were Zabita Khan, Najib's heir, and the Jat ruler, Nawal Singh.

The Jats of Bharatpur still looked like a formidable military power, even after their partial defeat by Najib Khan just before he died. But the ruler himself was by no means secure. After the death of Jawahir Singh in 1768, his immediate successor had spent a great deal of time and money on ostentatious display. On his accession, he had made a pilgrimage to one of the great holy places, and part of the religious celebrations had been adorned by a corps of four thousand dancing girls collected together at very considerable expense. The ruler had also acquired a private alchemist, who was commissioned to procure the Philosopher's Stone and to transmute metals into gold. The alchemist was a brahman monk and, like most tricksters, had a commanding presence and a shrewd insight into the psychology of dupes. But like many such men, he did not know at what point to give up and disappear with the profits. Instead, in April 1769, he stabbed the ruler as he was watching one of the transmutation experiments. The alchemist, however, did not have time to get away and was cut down by the guards.

The heir to the throne was an infant, and the regency was taken over by the leading Jat general. But Nawal Singh (who wanted the throne for himself) and his brother Ranjit spread rumours that the regent, who was not a member of the ruling family, was proposing to seize the state himself. The regent either did not hear these rumours or chose to ignore them, for he sent away his main supporter—a French mercenary, René Madec, whose force was trained on European lines and presented a definite obstacle to the success of any conspiracy—to put down some rebels in one of the provinces, leaving himself virtually unprotected in his mansion at Dig.

The two brothers had the regent's house surrounded and persuaded him to give in on the promise that his life would be spared if he went into exile. Once the regent had gone, however, the two brothers quarrelled over the succession. Nawal Singh's agents won Madec over to their master's side, and Ranjit retired into his fort at Kumbher. Nawal immediately attacked, but Ranjit had taken the precaution of hiring some Sikh mercenaries. It was rumoured that as many as 70,000 were on the way. Against such numbers, even the best of European military expertise seemed likely to be overwhelmed. Madec decided to raise the siege and move away from Kumbher. His aim was to catch the Sikhs on the march, attacking them when they least expected it. In this he succeeded, but the battle was long and bitter. Early in February 1770, Madec finally routed the Sikhs.

Wars of succession always offer an invitation to outsiders, and Nawal Singh was doubly unfortunate. Those great interveners, the Marathas, were on the march again, anxious to recover the prestige they had lost at Panipat. And Najib Khan, though dying, emerged in the field once more. From the subsequent battle, Nawal Singh escaped with his life, aided by the European mercenary, Walter Reinhardt—known as Sumru—who had massacred the English at Patna, served with the emperor, and finally taken himself and his men off after the battle of Buxar. The price of Nawal's escape was the destruction of an army and the deaths of some of his best generals. But it was by no means the end of him.

Decisive victory escaped the Marathas, as it so often did,

because of jealousies and quarrels in their own ranks. The overall command of the Maratha forces had been given by the Peshwa to a successful general named Ramchandra Genesh, but he had been instructed to act only with the approval of his principal adviser, Visaji Krishna—also a military man of great experience—and of two generals, Mahadaji Sindia and Tukoji Holkar. The latter was a young man who had inherited his father's counsellors, and they encouraged him to sustain his father's hatred of the family of Sindia. With this almost traditional hostility separating the two principal generals, whose armies consisted of men bound closely to their leader by ties of blood or sympathy, and with jealousy dividing the nominal chief from his deputy it was only to be expected that the Marathas would form two warring camps—Ramchandra and Sindia, Visaji with Holkar. The conflict between the two sides was so apparent that it was reported by the newswriters (the intelligence agents of the time) to the British, to the emperor, then still at Allahabad, and to the Peshwa himself.

The Peshwa's response was, in the middle of 1771, to recall Ramchandra. This removed perhaps the least important participant in the Maratha dissensions. Before his departure, the antagonism between Sindia and Holkar had intensified. Sindia had wanted to come to terms with the Jat ruler and accept a modest indemnity; afterwards, he proposed, the Marathas should move against those who had usurped their possessions following the defeat at Panipat. Above all, Sindia believed that they must turn on Najib, in whom he recognized the chief obstacle to Maratha pretensions in northern India.

Even though Sindia and Ramchandra were bound together against Visaji and Holkar, however, Ramchandra did not agree. In his view, the Jat Nawal Singh had been for all practical purposes crushed, despite his escape from the field of battle. Ramchandra thought that Nawal should be left for the Maratha tax-collector to squeeze, and that the main bulk of the Maratha forces should ally themselves with Najib, attack the Jat dominions, and divide the spoils.

Holkar agreed with this plan. Hindu agents of Najib had bribed Holkar's advisers to persuade their young leader that he should follow his father's policy of always backing Najib. The Peshwa also supported Ramchandra's view. All of them hoped that Najib would either help them against the Rohilla chiefs who had taken over Maratha territory, or else persuade the chiefs to surrender it voluntarily. When it came to the point, Najib did neither. The chiefs themselves, approached by Maratha envoys, bluntly told them that they were plain soldiers and knew nothing but fighting—and they would certainly fight if anyone attempted to take the territories from them by force.

To complicate a situation already bursting with tensions of one kind and another, Imad-ul-mulk arrived without warning in Sindia's camp and was received with the respect usually accorded to persons of consequence. The presence of the emperor Alamgir's murderer in the Maratha camp set the newswriters busily to work. Did this mean that the Marathas might be considering giving him their support? If so, it had to be assumed that Imad intended to replace Shah Alam with a ruler of his own, that he would return to Delhi as wazir, and that through him the Marathas would rule the empire. The news caused a great deal of anxiety, in Lucknow and Calcutta as well as at Allahabad. But there was no reason for it. The Marathas had given no thought to the matter; what they were concerned with was retrieving their own territories and punishing the men who had taken them.

Quarrels continued—over the size of the Jat indemnity, over whom to attack next. Najib persuaded the Marathas to leave his Rohilla countrymen alone and try for the Jat dominions nearer Delhi. He had already advised the Rohilla chiefs to stretch out negotiations for as long as possible, until the rainy season came to their aid by preventing military movement. The Marathas were consistently out-witted by Najib, and they had been unable to collect the indemnity—or even any substantial first instalment—from the Jat ruler. Their armies were beginning to feel the pinch.

'Your troops have nothing to eat', the Peshwa was informed. 'Until now we have carried on with loans but none is now obtainable and no tribute has been realized by us'. In fact, no one was prepared to pay up voluntarily until the Jats had first been forced to do so. It was Najib who, believing himself on the point of death, opened up negotiations with the Jats and settled the indemnity.

Najib's death at last seemed to remove the barrier to Maratha success. It was his influence and the memory of his past triumphs which had hamstrung Maratha policy. Now they swiftly turned to offensive action and met with success after success. Their sweeping movements reached as far as the frontiers of Oudh, and Shuja-ud-daula sent a force commanded by his son to oppose them. Shuja wrote to the British urging them to send troops from Patna to his aid. The Marathas, however, moved north on the road to Delhi. Imad, who was still an uninvited guest with Sindia's force, arranged a treaty with some of the chiefs by which they agreed a sum in settlement of the Maratha claims for past revenue. But Holkar refused to accept the treaty, demanded that Imad be sent packing and the chiefs immediately crushed. Imad disappeared from Sindia's camp in disgust and into obscurity, to be mentioned occasionally in spies' reports as having been heard of in Bombay or on a pilgrimage to Mecca. He is said to have died in British territory in 1800.

Imad's departure at least brought some relief to Shah Alam, though none to the dissenters among the Maratha leaders. On the contrary, for Ramchandra's and Holkar's policy had by now been utterly discredited. The triumph of the Sindia-Visaji faction led directly to the success of Shah Alam's envoy in persuading Sindia to support the emperor's return to Delhi. Though all the quarrels among the Maratha leaders had in the end helped Shah Alam's cause, they had left him to face the threat of the Jats—who had begun to recover—and of Zabita Khan.

When Najib died, Shah Alam had sent Zabita not only his condolences but a robe of honour, which invested

Zabita with his father's title of commander-in-chief. The emperor had also asked Zabita to go to Allahabad with his troops in order to escort him back to Delhi. Furthermore, he had called on Zabita to pay the usual fee for the succession and to settle the accounts for the revenue of those imperial estates around Delhi which Najib had administered. Whatever the emperor's opinion of Zabita—and he seemed to have had no ill feeling towards him—there was little else he could have done. His mother and heir were in Delhi, at the mercy of a garrison of Zabita's troops. It would have been foolish in the extreme to have antagonized their master.

But Zabita Khan had no intention of recognizing the emperor's authority. The imperial envoys, having been kept hanging about, were at last dismissed with a refusal either to pay up or go to Allahabad. Zabita did accept the robe of office as commander-in-chief.

Zabita's arrogance was soon to be somewhat deflated by the speed of events. The emperor made his arrangement with Sindia, the Marathas expelled Zabita's men from Delhi, and the emperor himself arrived to occupy the palace. It was, if ever, a time for caution, but Zabita Khan again refused to pay his respects to the emperor. For several reasons, the emperor decided he must act at once. The prestige of the emperor himself demanded it, and so did the state of the imperial army. His own troops had received nothing for eight months except the barest subsistence. The soldiers, seeing no likelihood of extracting their back pay from an empty treasury, were now demanding that they be let loose on Zabita's territory so that they could ease their own distress. It seemed that action against Zabita was the only way to satisfy everybody, including the Marathas. Without revenue, the emperor would not be able to pay them either.

2

Splendour of the state

THE EMPEROR'S position was a lonely one. The advisers
who had spent their exile with him were not men of action
or even of much imagination. As diplomats they were
excellent, and there would always be a place for them, but at
this hour the empire needed men of action. More, it needed
a man of genius. Fortunately for Shah Alam, there was
one—Najaf Khan, later to be given the title of Zulficar-ud-
daula ('splendour of the state') as well as many others. To
him, Shah Alam was to owe a period of ten years during
which the empire appeared to rise again from the dead
surrounded by a growing halo of prestige. Yet during most
of the time Najaf was to be menaced by ambitious enemies,
and by the weakness of the man he served.

Najaf Khan was a Persian, whose mother belonged to the
royal house of the Safavids. As a result, he had been imprisoned by the usurper, Nadir Shah, but had been
released in 1746 at the request of the Mughal ambassador.
Thereafter he went to seek service in India and found it at
Allahabad with Muhammad Kuli Khan, who was his sister's
stepson and a cousin of Shuja-ud-daula. When the fort of
Allahabad was captured by Shuja during Muhammad Kuli's
absence in Bihar with Shah Alam, Najaf decided to find
employment elsewhere. This was a wise decision, as
Muhammad Kuli was murdered by Shuja in 1761. Najaf
Khan made for Bengal where he was enlisted to raise a force
for the nawab, Mir Kasim. When Mir Kasim fled from
Bengal, Najaf followed and later found employment with
the princes of Bundelkhand—who spent most of their time
fighting one another.

Najaf was building a reputation for himself, and Shuja

invited him to join him and fight the English. Meanwhile, the English tried to bribe him into coming over to them. Najaf sensibly committed himself to neither until the battle of Buxar proved to him that European-trained and disciplined troops could defeat many times their number when they were opposed to traditional Indian armies. Najaf also realized that the British were a rising power with whom it would be best to be friendly. After Buxar, Najaf left Bundelkhand, plundering the countryside in the customary fashion, and joined the British at Allahabad in January 1765.

At Allahabad Najaf was able to advise the British on the defence dispositions of the fort, and they captured it without much difficulty. This, and later support given to the British force by Najaf's cavalry—a branch of the army which the British lacked—earned him not only respect but tangible gratitude as well. When Clive concluded the treaty of Allahabad, it included a provision which gave Najaf an allowance of 200,000 rupees a year. Further, on representations by Clive, Najaf was taken into the imperial service as a general. He was also appointed governor of Kora, which was one of the two areas made over to Shah Alam by treaty.

Najaf Khan's sudden elevation to a position of authority and power was not welcomed by the emperor's principal adviser who, until then, had considered himself the leading British partisan at court, and he managed to have Najaf dismissed on the false charge of not having collected the revenue. Though the British intervened on Najaf's part, he was not re-employed for over a year, a period which he spent neglected by the court and in comparative poverty. But the decision to march on Delhi brought a change of attitude. The times demanded his experience and military ability. Round the emperor there was no one who matched up to him. Relations were quickly restored, and he was given a sum of money with which to raise a contingent; it proved to be small but well-disciplined.

In Delhi, it was to Najaf Khan that the emperor turned for advice and Najaf's advice was to attack Zabita as soon as possible. The decision taken, Najaf marched out with his enlarged contingent of imperial troops, accompanied by the Maratha army. The emperor himself left Delhi only eleven days after he had entered it and, with another force, followed behind the main army.

Zabita's spies had informed him of what was going on and he made his own arrangements to meet the challenge. His treasure, and the families of his chiefs, he placed in a fort at his capital of Najibabad. He and a small force took up position some distance away, while the mass of his army was strung out along the river Ganges for about forty miles. The strategy was his father's. Unfortunately for Zabita, the tactics were his own.

The imperial forces, including the Marathas, arrived at the river and began to dig in on the bank opposite Zabita Khan's Rohillas. The Maratha generals had decided exactly where they would make the attack, and they proceeded to deceive the enemy by removing their baggage train from the point at which they intended to cross. Zabita Khan's men were duly deceived and concentrated their watchfulness at other, more likely, crossing points, leaving the true one badly guarded.

Three hours before sunrise on 23 February, the Marathas crossed the Ganges without being seen or even heard and surprised the defenders in their trenches. But the surprise was neither complete nor sufficiently demoralizing. The Rohillas rallied and began to press the attackers back into the river. Najaf Khan, who was by this time halfway across and had halted on a spit of sand, began to bombard the Rohillas with his camel-mounted swivel guns. The fire brought down most of the leaders, who were in the front ranks. At this stage, the majority fled, but their commander, though badly wounded, made an attempt to reach Najaf who was mounted on an elephant. Rushing forward shouting a battle cry, and covered with blood, he broke through the lines around Najaf. Shouting back down at him, 'Come, I am ready for you!' Najaf simultaneously thrust a long spear into the Rohilla's body.

The rout of Zabita's men was complete. The heads of commanders were cut off and despatched to the emperor, who had made his camp some ten miles from the river. It was Shah Alam's first victory—an omen, he thought, for the future. When Najaf went to his camp, he was received with the words : 'My honour has been saved by you'.

The victory, exaggerated by rumour, shattered Zabita's men. They deserted their posts along the river bank and Zabita's own position, though essentially strong, was threatened. Zabita appealed to his brother-in-law for help, but his brother-in-law refused, leaving the same night and later taking off, with his family and treasure, into the jungle. This desertion further demoralized Zabita Khan, and he fled on an elephant escorted by only forty men. After his departure it became a question of every man for himself, and soon the town was deserted, wide open to looters who plundered the place so effectively that when the Marathas arrived they found it barren and in flames.

This minor disappointment hardly worried the Marathas, who rarely wasted energy on mourning lost opportunities. In rapid pursuit of Zabita's fleeing army they soon arrived outside the fortress of Najibabad, where they were joined by Najaf Khan and the emperor. The fort itself was strong, admirably constructed by Najib Khan as his base. There were plenty of guns and ammunition, but there was not enough food for the large number of people who had been sent into the fort for safety. These included the wives and families of all the chief Rohilla leaders, now skulking in the jungle. After a fortnight, the commander offered to surrender on a guarantee that the lives of the garrison and the honour of the women would be spared. The offer was accepted and on 16 March 1772 the occupants marched out.

At the main gate waited the Marathas. First came the lesser figures among the people who had occupied the fort. They were stripped by the guards, searched, and sent off naked. When they saw this, the wealthier occupants threw their bags of money and jewellery into the moat, hoping to haul them out later.

The Marathas allowed the women and children of the Rohilla chiefs to go to the imperial camp. But there they were plundered and the men of the imperial army 'dragged away the women by the hand towards their own tents'. Fortunately, before they got them there, Najaf Khan arrived and rescued them. A few days later they were sent away under escort.

The Marathas took their revenge on the memory of Najib Khan by defacing his tomb. But that was merely an enjoyable pastime. The real business was to make as much profit as possible. The whole area of the fort was dug up in a search for buried treasure; those unfortunates who had thrown their possessions into the moat stood by and watched the Marathas drain it. So active were the Marathas in their search for loot that they managed to hold on to most of it for themselves, despite an agreement to divide the spoils with the emperor. Soon there was an open quarrel. Through the agency of Sindia, a compromise was reached but it was one which favoured the Marathas. They kept the cash and jewels, which the penurious emperor desperately needed, but scrupulously divided up the horses and guns, which the emperor could well have done without. The Marathas, however, had not chosen to help the emperor for the sake of the empire; their own ambitions and desire for profit were more important to them.

In this simple and occasionally equivocal attitude to Shah Alam, the Marathas were not alone. The emperor's own wazir, Shuja-ud-daula, nawab of Oudh, was hardly a paragon of loyal virtue. Sindia had, on a number of occasions, tried to induce him to join the emperor. As a sign of friendship, the two men had even exchanged turbans—a gesture more normally carried out face to face than at a distance. Shuja's turban, however, travelled to Sindia's camp without its owner's head supporting it, and attempts at negotiation always broke down. To add to the general confusion, Zabita Khan now took refuge with Shuja, a fugitive from the emperor fleeing for shelter to the emperor's chief minister.

Shuja now emerged as a mediator, for an important Rohilla chief had joined him. The Rohillas' position, with their families in captivity and their few men being slowly killed by the jungle, was too weak for anything but total capitulation. Shuja therefore negotiated a settlement and stood surety for its payment. Zabita Khan was allowed to return to his estates, and his family was released to join him. But all was by no means well. Sindia objected vehemently to the agreement, so much so that his relations with his chief Visaji Krishna became so strained that he would no longer visit him.

Once again dissension in the Maratha ranks deprived them of the profit of their campaigns. Private fortunes, of course, remained untouched—but the Peshwa's suffered. Where, he asked, was the indemnity? Where was his share of the loot? His agent at the Maratha camp reported at the end of May 1772 that everything was in chaos. 'Our leaders are not of one mind, but everyone acts independently. God only knows what the result of it will be . . . Nobody is paying . . . the promised contribution'.

There was not even any agreement as to what should be done next. Holkar and Visaji pressed the emperor, who now wanted to return to Delhi, to march westward and take Allahabad. The British had not been paying the revenue they had promised, and the two Marathas thought they should be forced to. Sindia inevitably disagreed. So did Najaf Khan, who had a healthy respect for the British. Indeed, there was nearly an armed clash between the opposing sides, and the emperor called on Najaf's men to protect him. At this the atmosphere cooled off, and the various forces began to move back on the imperial capital. As they went, the armies swept up what had been left behind during the campaign. Najaf's men were no more lenient than the others. 'Hardness of heart dominated all'.

The emperor's second entry into Delhi had all the appearance of a triumph, though this was an illusion not shared by the emperor himself. Shah Alam was not a fool. He had learned the way of his world in its harshest terms and was fully aware of his own fundamental weakness. But there was no reason to abandon the outward show. In July the court held a series of celebrations centred on the coronation of the emperor in the hall of his ancestors. The Peacock Throne no longer graced the ceremony, but the marble walls were clean and bright. The fountains played once again and there was perfume in the air. The nobles of the empire were richly attired in fine clothes heavy with embroidery and jewels. The imperial cortege, as it made its way to the great mosque with the drums and the fifes playing and the elephants elegant but majestic in their tread, was surrounded with soldiers. Pikes gleamed, gay pennants fluttered from the lances and armour glittered in the watery sun—for even the rains had played their part by holding off. It was all a charade. The rainy season, as always, had declared a hiatus. What was to happen afterwards when the bright winter ushered in the season of wars?

The respite had brought no better relations between the emperor and the Maratha leaders. The campaign against Zabita Khan had brought very little profit to the imperial treasury, and the Marathas were pressing continually for the payments promised on Shah Alam's restoration to Delhi. The Peshwa regularly bombarded his agents with demands for money. Something had to be done. The emperor had refused to attack the English for the sake of the Allahabad and Kora revenues, but where else was the money to come from? There was only one possible source—Zabita Khan. Though his fort had been sacked, his own treasure had not been found. The most satisfactory method for laying hands on it would have been for the emperor to pardon Zabita and appoint him to his father's old office. The Marathas would then have claimed a fee of a million rupees from Zabita, in return for their part in the deal. But there were a number of objections to this. Firstly, the idea was unacceptable to Sindia. Secondly, the emperor too was against it.

After the campaign against Zabita, Najaf Khan had gained not only credit but the ear of the emperor. His advice was fundamental and very appealing. The emperor, he said, must have reliable forces of his own. Only thus could he be independent, and until such a situation was achieved he would always be at the mercy of his 'allies'. The emperor commanded Najaf to raise an army and assigned to him several districts round Delhi whose revenues could be used for the purpose. As soon as the news began to circulate that the emperor was raising a new imperial army there was no shortage of volunteers. Veterans who had been disbanded and young men looking for a future flocked to Delhi, and during the rainy season a force of about 7,000 men was mustered, as well as a contingent of cavalry. It was this that led to tensions in the court, and the minister, Hisam-ud-din, frightened of Najaf's growing power and influence, suggested to the Marathas that they should persuade the emperor to placate Zabita Khan, who would then act as a counterweight to Najaf.

The emperor refused to pardon Zabita, but the Maratha leaders Visaji and Holkar decided that he must be forced to do so. They began to muster their troops for action. Yet there was a possibility that they might not have to act after all. At the end of the rainy season, Najaf Khan and his new army marched out of Delhi to invade the Jat territories to the south of the city. The two Maratha chiefs came to an agreement with the Jat raja that, in return for cash, they would not join in the attack. This allowed the raja to devote his whole attention to the imperial forces.

The vanguard of the Jat army was led by René Madec, the French mercenary. Najaf's men were still raw and inexperienced and at Madec's approach they fell back, giving up the few mud forts they had already captured. It seemed to the Marathas that the imperial army might fall into total disorder before Madec's well-trained and well-armed men. If Najaf were to be defeated, the emperor would be at the mercy of Visaji and Holkar and would have to agree to their terms. But the Maratha leaders were not aware that the emperor's agents were already at work on Madec. The Frenchman was promised that, if he went over to Shah Alam, he would be granted a substantial personal allowance as well as freedom to increase the strength of his own force, which he would naturally take with him. As an added inducement, the envoy took Madec a patent of nobility.

The negotiations were something of a mockery, though it seems unlikely that the emperor was aware of this. Madec had himself, by secret routes, instigated the imperial attempt at his own seduction. Though he was a mercenary, he was also a loyal Frenchman. The French presence in India had been severely curtailed by the recent British successes. The French had been routed in the south and completely expelled from Bengal. Now they hoped that, by infiltrating positions of influence at the courts of the Indian princes, they might be able to seize political control. There could have been no more potent place to realize such an ambition than at the court of the emperor himself. Madec had received instructions to go over to Shah Alam.

Madec had once been a sailor and had had little formal education. He had become a capable, but by no means inspired soldier. Nevertheless, he had ambitions and, more important still, dreams of making a fortune and of taking it home with him, where it would buy him rank in the frankly hierarchical society of pre-revolutionary France. His expertise saw him through a running fight with the Jats, whom he deserted without warning, and carried him almost intact to Delhi, where he arrived on 15 November 1772. His dreams were nourished by the honours with which he was received there.

At the gates of the city, Madec was welcomed by the emperor's envoy and transferred to a state elephant, whose howdah was hung with fine cloth and whose tusks were gilded. In his memoirs, he afterwards recorded: 'I can say without ostentation that that entry ... had the air of a triumph and that I entered ... more like a monarch than a private person'. The Mughal court had learned, over the years, how to flatter. But this was not all. At the palace, Madec was received by the emperor in the Hall of Private Audience—reserved only for visitors of great consequence—

and invested with a robe of honour made of cloth of gold, and with a jewelled girdle. The turban which was placed on his head by the emperor's own hand had an aigrette of precious stones. Madec was impressed. 'Considering the grandeur in which I found myself ... I could scarcely believe that it was not a dream'.

Madec had arrived in Delhi just ahead of the Marathas. Visaji, on behalf of his master the Peshwa, again demanded payment of the subsidy promised in 1771 in return for Maratha protection on Shah Alam's journey to Delhi. The emperor's reply was simple and to the point. During the recent campaign the Marathas had seized all the spoils; what had the emperor gained 'except hardship and debt'? To the reiterated demand for Zabita Khan's installation as an officer of state, the emperor, Madec reported, countered with: 'I am the sovereign and the ... Rohillas are rebels who have usurped territories rightfully mine'.

On 21 November, the Maratha forces were reported to be only eight miles from Delhi. Inside the palace, the factions were at work. The emperor vacillated. Madec prepared for action. Early in December the Marathas were at the gates. The emperor's attitude hardened and he rejected once again their demands for Zabita's installation. Najaf Khan, ready for the assault that was now certain to come, sallied out as far as the old Delhi fort. The two armies faced each other, indulged in an occasional skirmish, but finally retired to their respective camps without any major engagement. Najaf began to dig trenches in the sandy banks of the river Jumna below the fort, but was unable to hold them against constant enfilading by the Maratha cavalry. It seemed that neither side was really ready for a major encounter, but the skirmishes intensified in both frequency and animosity and on Friday 17 December 1772 a decisive encounter took place.

On the emperor's side there were European-trained and European-led soldiers and artillery, a small but powerful force commanded by Madec and officered by mercenaries of various nationalities. In the morning, the imperial forces drew up near the old fort, their flank resting on the river.

In front were fields of corn which formed some kind of protective line by reason of their thorny dividing hedges, which promised difficult going for the Maratha horses. Madec regarded it as a good position, and it was. But there was an enemy other than the Marathas—inexperience, which even a general of genius would have been unable to transmute.

The imperial cavalry wavered for a moment before charging, and was charged itself instead. Two powder chests on the imperial side were hit by a Maratha shell and exploded, killing four hundred men. Out of nervousness, the musketmen fired while the enemy was still beyond range and could not reload quickly enough to fire again before they were overwhelmed. Madec was hard pressed and forced to form his men into squares. In doing so, he had to give up not only ground but some of his guns. He managed to hold his own, however, though the imperial artillery was badly served and most of its shot was wasted. The Maratha cavalry broke through the line of guns and Najaf Khan himself was forced to take refuge inside Madec's square.

From the walls of the city all that could be seen was a sea of Maratha horsemen, swirling round a point hidden by dust clouds. This was Madec's position, firmly held, the guns firing rhythmically. He was holding his own but no one else was. The Marathas swept up to the gates of the city, through Madec's camp and baggage train, pursuing the imperial cavalry and driving all before them. On the city walls, the minister Hisam commanded the artillery and made no attempt to aid Najaf and Madec. Afterwards he was accused of firing blank charges so as to give the impression that he was assisting the imperial forces. His men, instead of going to their comrades' defence, were seen pillaging Madec's camp—in consort with the Marathas. Soon after, Hisam and his troops vacated the walls and left the city with its ramparts undefended. The Marathas actually broke through, but they were so busy plundering that a force of defenders which hurried to the spot was able to drive them out again.

After sunset, Madec and Najaf decided to break the

square and make for the city. The Marathas had drawn off
in more profitable directions and they were able to get most
of their men into the city, but even this could not disguise
the extent of the disaster. The Marathas were in complete
control of the environs of Delhi, and though Najaf and
Madec were anxious to continue the fight the failure of
Hisam and the virtual collapse of the emperor himself made
it impossible.

As soon as news of the Maratha success spread, the
vultures arrived in preparation for the feast. The Jat raja
made his appearance. Walter Reinhardt and his men,
always averse to the reality of fighting but happy to collect
the loot, arrived and ostentatiously set up their guns. It
might have been possible for the imperial defences to hold
out, but not for long. Najaf's new force had collapsed under
the strain, and what remained was so demoralized that it
would have run if it could. The emperor decided to give in,
completely.

The terms were shattering. Zabita Khan was to be
appointed commander-in-chief, Madec was to be dismissed
and Najaf Khan's troops disbanded. The Jats were to have
back all the territory Najaf had seized. And there was, of
course, to be a substantial subsidy for the Marathas. All
this was agreed, but secretly. The Marathas had no desire
to reduce the emperor's credibility; though they had
attacked him and forced him into an agreement which
deprived him of any hope of personal power, they did not
intend that this should be apparent to the rest of India.
Deference to the Mughal name, the fount of legitimacy, was
here taken to absurd lengths. Yet another imperial charade
was arranged.

On 26 December, after having had the palace carefully
searched and their own guards posted at strategic points,
Visaji and Holkar entered the audience hall with Zabita,
their wrists bound together with silken cloths as if they were
in fact captives. All presented gold coins in token of submission, and the ties were then removed from their wrists.
The emperor gave them robes of honour and other gifts,

and Zabita Khan was formally appointed commander-in-chief. A few days later, Madec was dismissed and the order was given to disband Najaf's force.

The façade hid an abundance of intrigue. Hisam had returned to Delhi and his place by the emperor's side, hinting that it had been a mistake to overrule him when he had first counselled caution. Fearing that Najaf would have him assassinated if the Marathas left, he offered Visaji a sum in cash if they would insist on Najaf's banishment from court. The Maratha chiefs, realizing that they were very unlikely to extract from the emperor the subsidy he had promised them, went even further and demanded that Najaf be handed over to them. Najaf's spies and wellwishers having informed him of this move, he began to fortify his mansion, which lay close to one of the city gates, claiming—with every show of defiance—that he had a perfect right to do this 'as a private person'. It looked for a while as if there would be an armed encounter.

The Marathas were invited to eject Najaf, and the imperial artillery was set up on the walls commanding Najaf's house. But in a climate of constantly shifting alliances, anything was possible. The Marathas feared Najaf, while he knew that if it came to a battle he would be crushed. Envoys passed between the two sides, and an agreement was reached. Najaf was to move out of Delhi with his remaining troops and, for a payment of 3,000 rupees per day, join the Marathas in their intended campaign in Rohilkhand and Oudh. When profit beckoned, there was no place for sentiment. Najaf and the Marathas were accompanied by Zabita Khan.

The main object of the campaign was to capture the provinces of Allahabad and Kora. The emperor had previously refused to make the attempt, partly because his own experience told him that he was likely to come up against the British, and partly because Najaf Khan had confirmed that, if this happened, the chances were that the emperor would lose. It is possible that Najaf now hoped the Marathas would so far involve themselves that the British would be forced to attack them and, with luck, defeat them. Visaji and Holkar, however, had no intention of fighting if it could be avoided. The Marathas were not at full strength as Sindia had left them before the taking of Delhi and another force had been detached for action in the south. Visaji also knew that both Najaf and Zabita were in communication with Shuja-ud-daula, and that even Madec—whose bid for a position of power at the Mughal court now seemed to have failed—had applied to Shuja for employment. But Visaji was armed with imperial authority to take over the two provinces, and he appears to have thought that this, plus a general dread of the Marathas, would assure a peaceful take-over.

He was wrong. Shuja had appealed for aid to the British in Calcutta, and they regarded it as in their interest to supply it. When Shuja moved off towards the banks of the Ganges at the end of January 1773, he was accompanied by a British force consisting of both European and Indian soldiers. When, a few days later, he continued up the river to face the oncoming Marathas, he was joined by more troops under the British commander-in-chief, Sir Robert Barker.

While these manoeuvres were taking place, the Maratha forces had moved quickly into Rohilkhand. When Visaji heard of the concentration of Shuja's troops with those of the British he was convinced that the campaign ought to be called off, but Holkar would not have it. Taking Najaf Khan with him, he crossed the Ganges and made for Ramghat. Visaji remained behind with half the army and all his baggage. When Holkar began to besiege the fort, however, the British troops approached and he withdrew, plundering as he went, to rejoin Visaji. After an encounter with another British force, Visaji had moved away to avoid an open fight which he felt he would lose. As he was carrying with him the accumulated loot of about three years' campaigning, it was a sensible decision.

There was another and equally pressing reason for the Maratha withdrawal from a campaign which now seemed overweighted with dangers. News had arrived that the Peshwa was dead, and it was in the interests of all the

Maratha chiefs to collect at the Maratha capital of Poona. Because of this, Visaji opened up negotiations with Shuja and the British. Shuja promised to collect an indemnity from the Rohillas on the Marathas' behalf, presumably because he anticipated collecting at the same time the subsidy the Rohillas had promised him for helping in the present campaign. It was the best the Marathas could hope for, and time was pressing. Najaf Khan was courteously dismissed with presents and a grant of land. Zabita Khan was sent off without gifts but with a reminder that the Marathas would return. Najaf Khan, whose sense of diplomacy was almost as pronounced as his military ability, took the precaution of paying a farewell visit to General Barker before he left.

On the whole, everything had worked out reasonably well for Najaf. His instinct to take on the Marathas before Delhi had been right, even though his army had failed him. But the failure had been compounded by the minister, Hisam, who had not wanted to fight at all. Najaf had warned the emperor constantly against the Marathas and had been proved right every time. Even now, they were very unlikely to divide any of their spoils with Shah Alam.

Najaf Khan had managed to survive not only the enmity of Hisam and the pro-Maratha faction at court but that of the Marathas themselves. He had even ended up being rewarded by them. All this appealed to the emperor, whose spies had also told him that Najaf was on excellent terms with the British. It seemed possible that his influence in that quarter might persuade the British to begin paying the revenues again. Furthermore, Najaf was the only soldier of quality still attached to the emperor. When he returned to Delhi in May 1773, he was welcomed with the highest honours.

3

The irresistible will

RELATIONS between the emperor and the British could not have been colder. The British had undoubtedly supported the emperor's nominal wazir in face of a Maratha invasion, but it was unfortunate that the invaders had been backed by imperial authority. Nothing better illustrated the general chaos of the situation in northern India at the time than the campaign which had just ended—where the chief minister of the empire, supported by the emperor's revenue-collectors in Bengal, fought an army consisting of the commander of the imperial troops, allied with agents who had been instructed by the emperor to attach the revenues of two of his provinces, which were in reality under the control of the emperor's chief minister!

The British were, of course, defaulters, but the emperor had no intention of trying to force them to pay up. Occasionally, they replied to his demands by saying that, when things were better, they might be willing to resume payments. But they never did, and for perfectly straightforward reasons. The new governor of Bengal, Warren Hastings, saw no good reason to divert money from Bengal, which was suffering the effects of a terrible famine, in order to 'supply the pageantry of a mock king'. Hastings was astonished that the British should even think of paying the emperor such 'dangerous homage' while he was 'the tool of the only enemies we have in India [i.e. the Marathas] and who want but such aids to prosecute their designs even to our own ruin'.

The emperor had done his best to convince the British that they should support him and that, with their aid, he might manage to achieve some independence of action. His attempts to bypass the British in Bengal and approach the king of England had not been successful. His letter of 1766 had disappeared into the limbo of Clive's pocket. Another letter in 1769, though it had been forwarded to England, had brought no reply. In 1772, after his return to Delhi and when the subsidy had suddenly and almost totally ceased, the emperor tried again. This time he appointed an Englishman as his personal envoy to King George III. His choice was unfortunate. Major John Morrison, who had joined the Bengal army in 1768, had decided that there was no longer much profit to be made there. In 1771 he left in the hope of finding employment with some Indian prince where the gleanings might be richer. Those offered by Shah Alam, now determined to return to Delhi, seemed promising, and Morrison was able to persuade the emperor that he was a man of much experience and military expertise. The news of Morrison's appointment did not please the British in Calcutta, and Hastings thought of demanding that the emperor dismiss him. But it seemed probable that Shah Alam would refuse such a demand. He had departed for Delhi without British help, and their failure to provide it still rankled. As Hastings put it in a letter to General Barker, 'nothing exposes weakness so much as demands that cannot be enforced'. Morrison therefore continued in the emperor's employ, though in what capacity was at first somewhat obscure.

The next the British heard of Morrison was that he had been given the rank of general in the imperial forces and appointed ambassador to the Court of St James's. This bombshell arrived in the form of a letter from Morrison to Warren Hastings, telling the governor of his appointment, asking whether he 'would receive him in his public character, and demanding a passage in one of the [East India] Company's ships to England'. Hastings replied that he would neither receive Morrison nor give him a passage. The imperial envoy returned Hastings' reply unopened, complaining that it had not been addressed to him by his ambassadorial rank. The governor, in turn, chose to be insulted. Who was Shah Alam to be sending ambassadors to the British, who had done so much for him and received nothing but ingratitude in return? It was, Hastings thought, all a plot to try to deprive the Company of its position in Bengal.

In view of the state of relations between the British government and the Company's directors in England, this was not entirely irrational. The Company had powerful political and commercial enemies who would have been quite prepared to accept a grant of the revenue collection in Bengal from the emperor, and to use it as an excuse for depriving the Company of its Indian possessions by abrogating the charter from the king of England on which the Company's authority depended. Hastings insisted that it was absolutely essential that the contents of the letter Morrison carried, as well as the background to his mission, should be known in England before the envoy himself reached there. It was easy enough to find out the contents of the emperor's letter, which was addressed to 'Our Brother dear to us as Life'. It offered King George III the territories now occupied by the Company. Hastings did his best to slow Morrison down by preventing him from embarking on a foreign ship. He succeeded in stopping him from travelling on a Danish vessel, but was unable to repeat this manoeuvre in the case of a Dutch ship—even though, as he complained, the Dutch customarily had a rule that foreigners were not allowed to travel to Europe in Dutch ships.

What happened when Morrison reached London is not known, but the emperor received neither acknowledgement of, nor reply to his letter, despite his expressed hope that the 'doors of correspondence be kept open, for the arrangement of the concerns of this World is dependent upon Friendship'.

In 1773 Hastings took the decision not only to stop the subsidy altogether—which was by then an almost academic exercise—but to return the provinces of Allahabad and Kora to Shuja-ud-daula in exchange for a payment of five million rupees. His argument, a very good one at the time, was that the Company was desperately short of money. Later, he was condemned for being short of morals, too. But Britain was an *Indian* power, however reprehensible the fact to such people as Edmund Burke and later critics of the situation. If it had not acted as such, it would not have survived.

Hastings' arrangement with Shuja included a promise to defend his territory if it came under attack by the Marathas or the Rohillas. Oudh was important to the British presence in Bihar and Bengal. It was their own buffer against the Marathas and anyone else inclined to attack them, and Shuja knew this. 'My country', he once wrote, 'is in reality the door of Bengal'. He recognized that he could be reasonably sure—as sure, that is to say, as it was possible to be in the case of any alliance in India—that he could call on British aid in protecting his own frontier, though he also knew he would have to pay for it. As a result, he made an offer in advance.

When the Rohilla leader, Hafiz Khan, had found himself menaced by the Marathas, he had promised Shuja a substantial payment in return for his aid. But the payment had never been made, which gave Shuja a satisfactory excuse for attacking, and if possible annexing, Rohilkhand. Shuja suggested that, if the Rohillas continued to refuse payment of the sum involved, the British might help him to teach them a lesson. For this, he was prepared to pay four million rupees in cash. The offer was immediately accepted, but before the campaign could be mounted, on however valid a pretext, a number of potential dangers had to be neutralized. Among these was Zabita Khan, still alive and well, and himself a Rohilla, who might suddenly decide to aid his countrymen. There was also the emperor, or, more accurately, Najaf Khan; what kind of role might Delhi choose to play?

Najaf was, in fact, preoccupied with other matters. On his return to Delhi he had assured his position by inducing the emperor to appoint a nominee of his own to succeed Hisam, whose policy had now been totally discredited. Into this post of deputy wazir—which was, in the absence of Shuja, effectively that of chief minister—stepped Abdul

Ahad Khan. He had been a member of the trusted entourage of the dead Najib Khan and, after the father's
death had stayed with the son, Zabita. Captured after the
fall of Najibabad fort, he had been pardoned by the emperor
and had gone with the court to Delhi. There he had remained, though without employment. Abdul Ahad was a
Kashmiri, with a smooth tongue and a veneer of culture. At a
court which was not conspicuous for scholarship or charm,
he soon captivated the emperor, who had scholarly tastes
and was himself a poet of some quality. With no official
position at court and no hope of winning one through
military talent, Abdul Ahad naturally gravitated towards
Najaf Khan, a powerful figure who was nevertheless almost
as isolated as he was himself.

Abdul Ahad's appointment, which owed much to Najaf's
enhanced position after the retirement of the Marathas,
meant that, for the time being at least, Najaf did not have to
worry about the intrigues of those who hoped to diminish
him in the emperor's eyes. This left him free to raise a new
army. Professional soldiers were again attracted to Delhi by
the news, and this time more attention was paid to training
new recruits. Najaf's lieutenants were also men of quality
and experience. There were Najaf Kuli Khan and Afrasiyab
Khan, two men so close to Najaf that they were often
referred to as his adopted sons. There was, too, Tahmasp
Khan who, under the pseudonym of Miskin, wrote memoirs
which are an invaluable source of information about the
times. René Madec also returned with his men, and there
were to be other European mercenaries in Najaf's forces.
The imperial army grew quickly, and at its core was a body
of men who had fought in almost all the battles of the recent
past; these consisted of three thousand Rohillas, most of
whom joined in order to escape destitution. Najaf soon had
twenty thousand well-trained and experienced men. Unfortunately, they had to be paid and the treasury was, as
always, empty.

An unpaid army was a threat to the state. Abdul Ahad
managed to find 200,000 rupees which he gave to Najaf

so that the force might be moved out of Delhi to make an attack on the Jats. During all the comings and goings of the last months, the Jats had been left alone and were still in possession of their riches. Nawal Singh, the Jat raja, was due to be taught a lesson, and the profit could be divided between the emperor and Najaf Khan. There seemed an excellent chance of success. In the past, the Maratha presence had always prevented any decisive settlement with the Jats, for the Marathas were ever ready to reach an accommodation which would be to their own advantage— never that of the empire. This time, however, the Marathas were occupied in their own territory, trying to influence the Peshwa's succession. It seemed that the imperial forces might be able to carry out at least one campaign without their interference.

Najaf's force was very well armed. It had a large supply of artillery, rockets, and hand-arms. The infantry was European-trained. Najaf himself was a general of some genius. The opposition consisted of an army which had never taken to European ideas and was still, in every sense of the word, a rabble, distinguished only by the bravery of the individual soldier and the stupidity of most of his commanders. The wars of succession for the Jat kingdom had killed off most of the best military talent in the state. Factions at court destroyed the government's ability to make decisions. The only European mercenary still in the Jat service was Walter Reinhardt, and he was only waiting for a suitably phrased invitation from the emperor before changing sides. In any case, Reinhardt always—on principle—avoided actual fighting if it was at all possible.

The Jats had one good general left, and he took the offensive by advancing into imperial territory south-east of Delhi. There he was met by Najaf and forced to retreat. Turning and making a stand, the Jats attacked Najaf's line on 16 September 1773, when they were literally torn to pieces by disciplined artillery and musket fire, their commander being bayoneted in the charge. It was a rout in which 3,000 Jats were killed and the remainder fled. A force personally commanded by Najaf Khan was at this time moving south, deeper and deeper into Jat territory, meeting little opposition and brushing it aside. There were defections from the Jat army, and at no point was any real defence mounted. The soldiers, reported Miskin, marched through the autumn fields, feeding themselves on the standing millet and plundering villages as they went. The Rohillas who had joined Najaf were transformed, their 'leanness turned into fatness from eating the provisions they looted and their very appearance, for they were now clothed in plundered apparel, changed from that of wild beasts into human beings'.

The Jats soon realized that victory was on Najaf's side. Panic struck them. When they saw a natural dust-cloud they assumed it to be caused by Najaf's men on the move, and Jat encampments were immediately and hurriedly evacuated. But skirmishes and Jat retreats were of no use to Najaf. What he needed was a decisive engagement, and it came at the end of October. The battle itself has a place in military history for it was the first to be fought in northern India, outside Bengal, between infantry and artillery trained by Europeans. Walter Reinhardt was for once forced to fight, and was severely cut up in the process. The battle was brisk and bloody, and came to an end when the Jat raja, Nawal Singh, fled from the field. Reinhardt, a capable officer when he had no alternative, formed his men into a square and began to retreat in good order. Najaf's force had already disintegrated into individual looters, but Najaf and a few personal retainers made a vigorous effort to stop him. They failed, though Najaf managed to get his artillerymen back to their guns in time to open fire on Reinhardt's rearguard, killing its French commander.

No pursuit was attempted. The spoils of victory were at hand. Najaf's strategy was not to waste time attacking and capturing Nawal Singh's forts one by one, but to move past them towards the former imperial city of Agra, a much more important prize in terms both of plunder and prestige. When he arrived outside Agra early in December, Najaf was approached by envoys who offered to give up the city without a fight provided his men would neither plunder the private houses nor rape the women. The terms were accepted and kept, though the Agra fort remained in the hands of its garrison which refused to accept Najaf's terms.

While Najaf's army was moving from success to success, Nawal Singh was trying desperately to drum up aid from any quarter. His envoys went to Shuja-ud-daula, reminding him of past friendship between their two families. Nawal offered the Agra fort as a bribe in return for help against Najaf, and Shuja had already begun to move in the direction of the city before he heard that Najaf had captured it. With the news came a request from Najaf himself for a loan of siege artillery which could be used to reduce the fort. Shuja was now in something of a quandary, but he did not allow himself to remain in it for long. Najaf was obviously winning, and Shuja did not intend to be on the losing side. His plans embraced wider issues than the safety of Nawal Singh and his dominions, which seemed, in any case, to be lost already. So Shuja sent Najaf a large force commanded by one of his officers, a Swiss named Major Polier, who was an expert engineer. With Polier's assistance, the fort was induced to surrender in the middle of February 1774.

Shuja now decided that the time had come for his own attack on the Rohillas. He had previously hoped that Najaf would remain neutral, but now felt that, if only in self-defence, he would have to ask for his active assistance. Shuja therefore sent an envoy to the emperor asking for imperial troops to join the expedition and offering to divide the spoils. On the emperor's instructions, Najaf Khan met Shuja at the town of Etawa at the end of February to settle the details. Shuja gave him an extravagant welcome, for he wanted Najaf to persuade the emperor to take part in the coming campaign in person. This appealed to Najaf, as it meant there would always be somebody to keep an eye on the wazir, and he returned to Delhi to report to Shah Alam. The idea appealed to Shah Alam, too. Though he was unwell, preparations were made for the march; but eleven days after the emperor left Delhi, on 5 April, he had to return because of the illness of his favourite son. Najaf Khan was sent on to join Shuja, but by the time he arrived at Shuja's camp, the wazir had fought his war—and won it.

It would have been more exact to say that the British had fought Shuja's war, although he had taken the profits. A brigade under Colonel Champion had been sent to assist him and, as it turned out, it was this brigade that did all the fighting. On 17 April, the British force crossed into Rohilkhand, ignoring a letter from the Rohilla leader, Hafiz Khan, suggesting an accommodation. Six days later, the two forces met in battle and the Rohillas were neatly and expeditiously cut down by disciplined artillery and musket fire. Hafiz himself was killed in the encounter.

This victory was followed by systematic and ruthless plundering on the part of Shuja's men who, according to Colonel Champion, had taken no part in the battle. Champion resented the whole affair, and complained bitterly over the brutality involved. His statements were later used against Hastings, but they reflected primarily the anger of a disappointed man. Shuja, insisting that the British had been no more than mercenaries who had already been adequately paid, maintained that they had no rights in the matter of loot. The British officers, demanding prize money, came very near to mutiny when it was refused. But the British as a power, if not as individuals, made a profit. They had moved the frontiers of the buffer state of Oudh further westwards, and had enlarged the *cordon sanitaire* between themselves and a doubtful future. Only the Rohillas really suffered, and even they regarded their defeat as the workings of an unfriendly destiny. 'The will of God is resistless', wrote Hafiz' widow. Certainly, the easy way in which the Rohillas had been swept aside seemed to confirm this estimate. But, as a later conqueror was to say, 'God is always on the side of the big battalions'.

Najaf Khan viewed the matter rather differently. What he wanted, on his master's behalf—and, indirectly, on Shuja's was half the spoils, as agreed. But Shuja maintained that the share-out had been predicated on solid aid from the emperor in person. Though the terms of the agreement had included no such proviso, the British supported Shuja, murmuring about the need to *honour* treaties (as if they themselves regarded all treaties as sacrosanct) while they publicly claimed that the settlement was no business of theirs. Najaf was hardly in a position to contest the issue, for the reduced force which had accompanied him would have been no match for Shuja's army. So he returned empty-handed to Delhi.

4
Plots and counterplots

WHILE Najaf Khan had been almost constantly away from the capital during his campaign against the Jats and his abortive visit to Shuja-ud-daula, his enemies at court had been trying to discredit him in the eyes of the emperor. This was not a particularly difficult task. The emperor was still a cipher in his own palace. His direct control over even the most minor matters was virtually non-existent. He was little more than a presence. Najaf Khan was now the only real power in the state. He led the state forces, and though many of the men were now supplied by other powers in return for grants of land, the most efficient element was Najaf's own contingent of disciplined soldiers and artillerymen. In order to pay them, Najaf had taken over the revenues of what were, formally, crown lands supplying the privy purse. None of this money now reached the emperor, and much of the plunder from the Jat campaign had been held back by Najaf in order to provide for his troops in the future.

This situation, perfectly reasonable when assessed on the simple necessity of paying the state forces and thus assuring their loyalty, was distorted by the arguments of Abdul Ahad Khan. The minister suggested to the emperor that Najaf was trying to build himself up into the sole power in the state, so that he might control its affairs as he thought fit. The emperor, Abdul Ahad implied, might easily find himself brushed aside, and there was no one on whom he could now call for help. The British were obviously hostile. Shuja was not interested. The Marathas were immersed in their own complicated problems. Furthermore, Najaf did not belong to the same religious sect as the emperor. It was possible that he might decide to support his co-religionist,

Shuja-ud-daula, who had already—without consulting the emperor—offered Najaf the post of deputy wazir, i.e. the post held by Abdul Ahad.

Many of the arguments which Abdul Ahad fed to the emperor were contradictory, but Shah Alam had been left dangling by apparent contradictions before. His own position *was* delicate. Without forces of his own and with an empty treasury, he was beginning to lose faith in his own future, which had seemed so bright only a year before. The court of Delhi was an immense whispering gallery, full of unidentified and often unidentifiable murmurings of plots and counter-plots. The emperor could give unreserved trust to no one around him, not even to members of his own family, and he tended more and more to withdraw into the comparative security of the harem, where the demands upon him were of a different kind—and more easily satisfied. But Abdul Ahad was closer to the emperor than most of his court, and he was capable not only of playing on the emperor's fears but of supplying an answer to them. What Abdul Ahad suggested to the emperor was a solution hallowed by tradition. It was that a strong man should always be balanced by one equally strong. Zabita Khan was Abdul Ahad's candidate for the position of counterbalance to Najaf Khan.

The suggestion of such a candidate showed Abdul Ahad's ignorance of the realities. Since his defeat by the Marathas, Zabita had ceased to be a military power of any consequence. He had neither the men nor, more important, the prestige to challenge Najaf. Nevertheless, in Najaf's absence, Zabita was summoned to court and spent some time there before returning to his own estates, which were being threatened by raiding Sikhs. Zabita did, however, put in an appearance at Delhi on the same day as Najaf arrived after his abortive visit to Shuja-ud-daula.

The conflict between Najaf and Abdul Ahad now came into the open. The emperor personally demanded from Najaf his share of the conquests, as well as the keys of the Agra fort. Najaf was accused of using the wazir's seal, given to him by Shuja, for making treaties without the authority of the emperor. Another charge was that, though the emperor's own agents had bought Walter Reinhardt and his force after the Jat collapse, Najaf Khan had taken them on to his strength. All these charges were, of course, well founded. After discussions and mediation by some officers of the imperial cavalry, Najaf agreed to share the territories he had conquered with the emperor and to hand over the keys of the fort at Agra. But this was not the solution Abdul Ahad had been hoping for. His aim was to destroy Najaf.

Abdul Ahad planned to provoke Najaf into taking some action which would seriously prejudice his position with the emperor and, more important, with others who now supported him. Early in October 1774, on Abdul Ahad's orders, Najaf was refused entry to the palace and insulted by the guards. In reply, Najaf stayed away from court for two months. The emperor, becoming frightened, personally intervened in an attempt to bring the two men together. In the meantime, Abdul Ahad had been searching for allies. He had sent letters in the emperor's name to both the Sikhs and the Marathas, inviting them to come to Delhi and assist in the reconquest of former imperial territories. The Marathas were preoccupied, however; when they decided to come, they would need no invitation. The Sikhs recognized the implication that they would have to fight Najaf; they preferred to continue raiding rebels and loyalists indiscriminately, on their own behalf.

Najaf's spies kept him well informed of the minister's intrigues, and he merely laughed at them. But he had his own problems. One was an attack of fever early in 1775 which kept him in his bed for some time. The other was the ever-recurring need for money to pay his own and the imperial troops. The most immediate source remained those Jat governors who had not been defeated in the last campaign and who were still holding out in their various territories. Nawal Singh himself was still safely ensconced in his fortress at Dig, because he had not been pursued after his defeat. In all the campaigns of this time there was an element of 'living to fight another day', because they were rarely more than punitive expeditions with the limited aim of destroying an army and collecting plunder. Almost inevitably, a defeated ruler would find an ally somewhere for an attempt at a come-back. Nawal Singh found his in the raja of Jaipur and the body of 3,000 Maratha horse which had been left behind as a revenue-collecting force in the area south of Jat territory.

The Jaipur raja, who had been annoyed by the capture of one of his forts, assembled an army to recapture it. Najaf immediately hurried from Delhi to reinforce his own local general against the imminent attack, but was greatly out-numbered and had to retreat. As always in Indian wars, negotiations were promptly opened up, this time by Walter Reinhardt, and a settlement was reached with the Jaipur raja which entailed Najaf's returning the fort in exchange for a promised subsidy. This settlement unfortunately an-tagonized one of Najaf's generals, who had been promised the fort for himself, and in disgust he went over with his men to the Jats. With the rainy season approaching, Najaf urgently needed a victory, and he was supplied with an excellent opportunity by the Jat raja. Nawal Singh was ill, in fact dying, and he wished to make a pilgrimage to an important Hindu shrine at the sacred city of Govardhan, not far from his fortress at Dig. Choosing a holy day in June, he arranged for his army to guard the route while he went with a heavily-armed escort to the shrine. Najaf's spies at the Jat court sent him the news and, moving rapidly, he advanced towards Dig. He divided his force into two, one section led by René Madec and the other by himself, and they descen-ded on the unprepared Jats, defeating them in a series of engagements. Nawal Singh again escaped, but not for long. He died early in August 1775.

The Jat campaign now entered a new phase. The general who had left Najaf's service in protest against the return of the fort to the Jaipur raja attacked Madec's force during a rainstorm and succeeded in putting it to flight after inflicting serious casualties. It took Madec several months to reconstruct his shattered contingent. After this escapade, the victor retired to the fortress of Dig and, while the defenders were distracted by the death of Nawal Singh, entered the fort, took a child from the royal harem, proclaimed it raja, and himself regent. But a midnight dash by Nawal Singh's brother, Ranjit, defeated the enterprising usurper—who did, however, escape. He made for Delhi and there, such was the luck of the game, found employment with Abdul Ahad. He was sent off to attack some of Najaf's territories, but Najaf sent a force against him and he was shot dead in the encounter.

Najaf's problem remained what it had always been, the town of Dig. This was a substantial system of fortifications protected by high ramparts and, on one side, a swamp. The main fort was the raja's palace, which stood on a rocky ridge. Except by means of treachery, of which there seemed little likelihood, the only way to take the town was by siege. This Najaf's men were not good at. One of his French mercenaries, the Comte de Modave, when asked his opinion of the army's breaching operations, replied frankly that 'if apes attacked each other they would undoubtedly construct such siege-works'. It was now December 1775 and Najaf was anxious to get back to Delhi. Attempts to escalade had failed; indeed, one such attempt which had been bungled by Madec almost led to Najaf's death. He had only been saved by the rapid fire of Reinhardt's guns, which had driven off the Jats who had sallied out to attack the attackers.

The siege dragged on. Najaf's troops had not been paid and were short of food, yet he did not dare to raise the siege or his enemies at court would have been certain to use it against him. Time was on his side, if only he could hold his army together. The Jats were divided among themselves. Najaf's men were able to blockade the town and very few supplies were getting in. The garrison, of about 60,000, and the population swollen by refugees, soon ran short of food, and shortage quickly deteriorated into famine. Disease spread, as the bodies of the dead could not be burned. Parties of soldiers began to slip out of the city at night and make their way into the countryside by routes deliberately left unguarded by the besiegers. Ranjit Singh next permitted the poorer inhabitants to leave the city, on the principle that it was preferable for them to be a burden on the besiegers rather than the defenders. Najaf did not drive them back into the city ; instead, he set up a refugee area in which the refugees were protected by a special body of troops. When this treatment became known, they were joined by men of consequence and even by some members of the ruling family.

In the end, conditions in the city became so bad that Ranjit Singh and a few followers slipped out and managed to elude Najaf's patrols and escape. When news of their flight became known, the imperial soldiers entered the fort and began looting. Part of the city was set on fire. Hindu shrines were defaced. As usual, women were raped, and three widows of former rulers committed suicide. When Najaf entered the city, he tried to stop the plundering, but it took three days to bring the troops under control. By that time, most of the treasure had disappeared and, when Najaf came to calculate the profit, it turned out to be insufficient to pay the soldiers their arrears.

One small party still held out in the citadel, despite a heavy bombardment, but at last—after killing their women —the defenders made a sortie in which all were killed. It was the end of the Jat state, although this brought no great relief to Najaf Khan. One by one, the Jat raja's feudatories had to be attacked as well as those who had taken advantage of the troubles to usurp some of his dominions. This took time, and the campaign was still in progress when Najaf Khan was recalled to Delhi in January 1777.

While he had been away from the capital, his rivals had not been idle. Abdul Ahad was still engaged in his intrigues against Najaf, though all had failed because he had no military support. He had pinned some of his hopes on the worthless Zabita Khan, but, knowing his own weakness, the latter had refused to become involved in Abdul Ahad's plots. This turned the minister against him, and he persuaded the emperor to send an army against Zabita. There was, in fact, good reason for taking action as Zabita had not paid the revenue due to the emperor. Abdul Ahad wanted Zabita taught a lesson by men of his own choosing, while Najaf was still away. Command of the force was given to his younger brother who, though a man of some quality and personal bravery, was reluctant. When he left with his men in October 1775, he remarked : 'My brother is sending me to my death'. He was right.

The first part of the campaign consisted of a series of small and bloodless victories while negotiations were simultaneously being carried on with Zabita. But Abdul Ahad was determined on crushing Zabita and he forced his brother into an open fight when diplomacy might have given better results. Zabita had with him a body of Sikh mercenaries who, by enticing the imperial forces into a trap, were able to disperse them. Only their commander and about fifty men were left on the battlefield. The commander refused to submit, and was finally shot. His head was cut off and taken to Zabita, and the body was later sent to Delhi in a handsome coffin, accompanied by a letter from Zabita offering condolences and maintaining that there would have been no need to kill the minister's brother if he had had enough sense to surrender.

This attempt at reconciliation, improbably, bore fruit, though Zabita's son and representative at the imperial court, Ghulam Kadir, fled home to his father. Zabita was invited to Delhi with solemn assurances of safe conduct, though there seems to have been a plot to kill him while he was a guest at the minister's house. After being presented to the emperor, however, Zabita left for his own estates and there continued his defiance of imperial authority. There seemed no alternative but to recall Najaf, so that he might settle Zabita once and for all.

One last attempt was made to induce Zabita to submit, but he would neither give up the lands he had seized nor pay the sums owing to the emperor. His title of commander-in-chief was taken away from him and given to Najaf Khan, and in May Najaf, accompanied by the emperor, set up camp outside Zabita's only remaining fortress at Ghausgar. With peculiarly irrelevant politeness, Zabita Khan was allowed to leave the imperial camp after the breakdown of negotiations, and returned to the fort which was now all that remained of the dominions of the great general, Najib Khan.

Najib had built the fort, and its defences were well sited and strongly entrenched. The last remnants of Najib's once almost invincible army were now in the fort under the command of his brother. All the wives and children of the principal chiefs were there too. The countryside aided the defences of Ghausgar, for the land was pitted with deep hollows and swamps which made it difficult for Najaf to concentrate his men and yet allowed Zabita's Rohillas to carry out their favourite tactics of swift attacks and ambushes, especially at night, in terrain they knew intimately. The real weakness of the imperial forces, however, lay in the determination of Abdul Ahad—who accompanied the emperor—to frustrate every plan of Najaf's and see that he gained no credit from any victory. In pursuit of this design, the minister, who was old, sick, lacking in military experience, and apparently heartbroken at the death of his wife, appointed himself second-in-command.

Abdul Ahad was virtually in charge of the expedition, and in constant conflict with Najaf. This fact was very soon known to the enemy, who took every advantage of the friction between the two men. The bickering continued for so long that the rainy season began, turning already difficult terrain into an actively inimical element. The hollows filled with water and the swamps spread outwards. Dry river-beds suddenly burst into life under an unusually heavy fall of rain. The imperial forces were constantly repulsed by quite small bands of Rohillas. Even Najaf Khan's reputation suffered. Abdul Ahad made the most of it.

The rains had turned the emperor's camp into a marsh. The fashionable nobles who had accompanied the court now found out what it was like to campaign in the wrong season.

There was grumbling and discontent, much of which helped Abdul Ahad—who naturally blamed Najaf for the whole predicament. One night, the imperial camp was penetrated by a band of Sikhs who almost reached the emperor's tent before they were driven off by his personal bodyguard. The rest of the imperial forces were under constant guerrilla attacks which, though they did not inflict high casualties, kept the men on edge. In the circumstances, it seemed wise to begin negotiations, but though Zabita was willing to talk terms his relatives were not. His envoys were instructed to inform the emperor that it was to be war to the death.

The imperial army was harassed by ever-increasing difficulties. Supplies were short, and prestige, which was so fragile that it depended on visible success, began to crack. The population, basically friendly to Zabita, began to attack food convoys. In the imperial camp itself, the tensions that already existed were exacerbated by the secret withdrawal to more comfortable surroundings in Delhi of many courtiers and officers of state. Only Najaf remained active. In one well-timed manoeuvre, he saved a grain convoy from a Sikh attack while the deserted Sikh camp was burnt by another force. His envoys were permanently at work trying to seduce Zabita's allies—with some success, though the Sikhs refused to be bought.

As the rainy season drew to a close, Najaf sent for reinforcements from Agra. By the middle of September, he was ready for a major assault. This turned out to be unnecessary, for the two armies met on the battlefield where superior fire-power and discipline won the day over an almost hysterical bravery. Zabita Khan fled from the field with his Sikh allies, leaving Ghausgar undefended. His son, Ghulam Kadir, was taken prisoner and within a few days, on a guarantee of full protection for persons (though not, of course, for property) the fort surrendered. The wives and children of the Rohilla chiefs were sent to Agra under guard, the town was stripped of its treasures, and the emperor was able to return to Delhi.

It was not quite the end of Zabita Khan. After the collapse at Ghausgar, he and his Sikh allies fled to the Sikh settlements on the west bank of the Jumna, to the north of Delhi. There Zabita remained for some months, maintained by the generosity of the Sikhs. He was totally without resources. In order to ensure the continued support of the Sikhs, he turned Sikh himself, taking the name of Dharam Singh. It seemed the sensible thing to do, and when Najaf Khan found himself involved with some of the Rajput rulers in 1778, Zabita and his allies crossed back over the river into his old territories and finally arrived outside the fortress of Ghausgar. The imperial reflex was arrested by Abdul Ahad, ever ready to take the opportunity of discrediting Najaf Khan and his supporters. But when the imperial army did move under the command of two of Najaf's most trusted generals, Zabita and his Sikhs were defeated in a running fight which lasted until the Sikhs were forced to agree to terms. These included a promise not to shelter or aid the emperor's adversaries, nor to attack Najaf Khan's lands. Zabita Khan was promised a high post in the state and the release of his women and children from Agra fort as soon as, with proper humility, he approached the emperor for pardon.

This gambit on Najaf's part was designed to protect his own position against the intrigues of Abdul Ahad, as well as to sustain a buffer between his own lands and those of the Sikhs. In order to bind Zabita more closely to his side, Najaf had the treasure taken at Ghausgar, which had been kept untouched at Agra, restored to him. In return, Zabita gave one of his own daughters to Najaf in marriage. It was a very astute move, and a timely one, for the final struggle for power between Najaf and Abdul Ahad was about to take place.

5
Doomsday in Delhi

THE CAMPAIGN against Zabita Khan had been carried on by Najaf Khan's generals. The commander-in-chief himself had been occupied elsewhere, clearing up some of the after-effects of the imperial troops' poor performance before Zabita's fort at Ghausgar. Though the town had ultimately fallen and Zabita had fled, the action had seriously damaged the prestige of the imperial forces. One evidence of weakness was all that was necessary to release the rebellious instincts of every ruler or petty landowner in the empire. Ranjit Singh, the Jat raja whom Najaf had allowed to retain the fortress of Bharatpur and some of the lands around it, decided to try and win back his lost domains. There were plenty of ambitious men to support him. At hand was a vassal of the Jaipur raja, Pratap Singh, who was anxious to extend his own territories at the expense of his overlord. In April 1778 the throne of Jaipur passed to an imbecile; the resulting confusion left the state wide open for plunder of one kind or another. Pratap Singh felt himself ready to take advantage of the situation, and was willing to side, quite impartially, with whoever seemed most likely to bring him nearest to realizing his ambitions. His first choice was Ranjit Singh.

With Pratap Singh and a mercenary force of Marathas, the Jat ruler moved towards Agra, burning and looting as far as the city walls. But he could not take the city, which was too well defended by Najaf's agent. When news of the Jat offensive reached Najaf, he left Delhi in November 1778 and, pushing rapidly towards Agra, began a reign of terror. A mud fort at Sonkh was quickly stormed and then demolished. The Jat defenders, some 3,000 of them, were massacred and the women and children sent to the slave markets. This had the intended effect, and Jat defiance crumbled. Ranjit Singh and his stepmother were forced to surrender the great fort of Bharatpur. But there were no reprisals. Najaf was collecting friends, not enemies, and the Jat raja had his fort and lands restored to him.

Taking advantage of the Jat collapse, Ranjit Singh's erstwhile ally, Pratap Singh, had himself taken possession of two important Jat strongpoints by the simple expedient of buying their commanders. But Najaf, in turn, purchased the Maratha mercenaries and Pratap Singh was left facing Najaf's army alone. Sensibly, he offered to deal, but before he could be pressured into accepting Najaf's terms, Abdul Ahad intervened. Abdul Ahad, hoping to make a profit which would not have to be shared with Najaf, requested the presence of envoys from both Pratap Singh and the Jaipur raja. Pratap Singh, hoping he would be offered easier terms in Delhi, sent an envoy who was welcomed with a promise of full protection and the information that Najaf Khan was to be disowned. Abdul Ahad even persuaded Shah Alam, still hankering after the unobtainable, to march out in force and take over from Najaf. Naturally enough, when Pratap Singh heard all this, he refused to continue negotiations with Najaf.

Najaf responded to Abdul Ahad's enterprise by sending him a letter pleading with him not to imperil the interests of the state. All was going well, he said, without interference. Unfortunately, the minister took this approach as a sign of weakness, another indication of Abdul Ahad's inability to recognize the realities of power. He rejected an attempt by one of Najaf's generals to bring about a reconciliation. At this stage Najaf decided to take action. He ordered his two leading generals, Najaf Kuli Khan and Afrasiyab Khan, to march on the imperial capital, and thus frighten the emperor into dismissing his minister. When Adbul Ahad heard of this, he immediately sent away the envoys of Pratap Singh and the Jaipur raja and hurried the emperor back into his palace. He covered this retreat by announcing that the stars were not propitious for the emperor to leave the city, and that an unfavourable conjunction had convinced the astrologers that the emperor might be in danger if he took the field.

All this left Pratap Singh in a dangerously exposed situation. He therefore made terms with Najaf and handed over the down-payment on a large indemnity, borrowing it from the Jaipur raja and then refusing to pay it back. The raja's minister, as a result, asked Najaf for help in recovering the loan. An imperial force was sent to assist the Jaipur army. As an additional complication in the ever-changing alliances and partnerships of convenience and profit, Pratap Singh had now been rejoined by the Maratha mercenaries who had earlier deserted him at the offer of a payment by Najaf.

Pratap Singh still felt it would be wise to try and placate Najaf while he took time to decide on his next move. A meeting between the two was therefore arranged, but a rumour that Pratap would attempt to assassinate Najaf gave the meeting an additional air of tension which so ruffled the tempers of those present that Pratap finally, with a show of truculence, refused to pay any more of the agreed tribute. While Pratap was permitted to return to his camp, his Maratha mercenaries were secretly approached and induced—for the inevitable cash payment—to change sides and help in an attack on him. As dawn was breaking a few days later, Pratap Singh was surprised at his morning prayers and was only just able to cut his way through the attackers to safety.

Najaf's forces now entered Pratap's territory, plundering and burning as they went. Just as it seemed that he would have to submit, news arrived from Delhi that Abdul Ahad—with, no doubt, the support of the stars and recovered from his fear that Najaf would move against him—had persuaded the emperor to march into the Rajputana in order to exact a tribute which was urgently needed to pay the troops raised by the minister in Najaf's absence.

Shah Alam was reluctant to leave Delhi, but it was

forcefully put to him that, though Najaf was having considerable success in his campaigns, none of the profit was reaching the emperor's treasury. The new raja of Jaipur owed the emperor a succession fee, and if Shah Alam did not go and collect it himself Najaf Khan would. Again, the prospect of action was alluring and the emperor agreed, leaving Delhi late in 1778.

The imperial force met with no opposition. Local rulers were received and the amount of their tribute fixed. As the emperor's camp approached the Jaipur frontier, envoys came and arrangements were made for the Jaipur raja to be confirmed on his throne by the emperor in person. So far, Abdul Ahad Khan had had the field to himself, but at the end of January 1779 Najaf Khan arrived at the imperial camp with a large force. A few days later, the Jaipur raja put in his appearance and was received with some pomp, the emperor himself making the sacred mark on the raja's forehead and placing a robe of honour about his shoulders. The size of the succession fee was agreed and, to the minister's annoyance, Najaf undertook to collect it. There was now no point in the emperor's continued presence in the countryside and, accompanied by Najaf, he returned to Delhi.

Najaf did not, however, remain long in the capital, for Pratap Singh bounced up once more and the emperor ordered his commander-in-chief to bring him to heel.

With Najaf out of the way, Abdul Ahad resuscitated his intrigues. There seemed at first to be no one to turn to. Zabita had proved useless, and was in any case now a partisan of Najaf. The Jat raja had been crushed. There was no point in calling in the Marathas, who were still entangled in their own problems. An earlier approach to some of the Sikh leaders had come to nothing; they had been given robes of honour by the emperor and had responded by burning a mosque. But there was no one else. The Sikhs it had to be. There were plenty of them to choose among, for the Sikhs were cruelly divided and there were many who would be happy to provide help in exchange for imperial assistance against their own enemies—who were usually other Sikhs.

Some Sikh chiefs in Delhi promised the minister that, if he would move northwards, they would assist him in retaking the old imperial provinces, even that of Lahore ! Abdul Ahad not only believed them but persuaded the emperor to send a force headed by one of the imperial princes. The minister had hoped to make the emperor go himself, but Shah Alam had been unusually firm in his refusal. It was the height of summer, he said, and he had recently been ill with fever. What if he died on the way? Where would the minister be then?

The troops left Delhi in June 1779, accompanied by the prince, with Abdul Ahad in command. As he moved northwards, he expelled the tax collectors who had been appointed by Najaf and replaced them with his own men. He recruited Sikhs into his army and generally set out to win over their leaders. It was a policy heavy with its own failure. Ostensibly, the imperial aim was to restore the emperor's rule. But the minister had also agreed to go to the aid of the Sikh raja of Patiala against other Sikh rulers who were threatening his lands. These were the very leaders with whom Abdul Ahad was making terms as he moved forward. Naturally, this did not endear him to the raja of Patiala, who had hoped to overawe his enemies by his alliance with the imperial forces.

It was obvious that Abdul Ahad was completely out of his depth in a situation which became more and more complicated daily. He had no clear-cut plan of campaign and was continually changing his mind on the advice of those who happened to be nearest to him. Because he seemed to be achieving success, he began to believe that he was strong enough to impose whatever conditions he wished. When the Patiala raja sent an envoy with an offering of half a million rupees and a request that he march away again, the minister angrily replied : 'I have come here at your call and in every way that I can I shall extract from you everything I have spent'. He demanded that the raja himself should come to the camp.

The raja was prepared to do no such thing, as he felt that the imperial minister could not be trusted. Instead, he offered a larger sum. But Abdul Ahad was not to be deflected. He intended to teach the raja a lesson and, at the same time, make it clear to the emperor that Najaf Khan was not the only one who could win battles. The imperial forces entered Patiala territory and besieged the capital. Negotiations led to nothing, and in an encounter following their breakdown the raja was driven from the field to take refuge in his fort. But the imperial army was falling to pieces. The Sikh mercenaries were bought by the raja. Other contingents demanded their pay; without it, they said, they would fight no more. Mutinies broke out, some of them fomented by agents of Zabita Khan, and there were rumours that a large army of Sikhs was on the way to support the raja. The minister made the only possible decision. He decided to withdraw.

The retreat of the imperial forces from Patiala was constantly harassed, and the Sikh horsemen were kept off only by well-handled artillery. At Panipat, that battle-haunted field, the enemy pulled off and the army was able to rest before completing the journey back to Delhi. News of Abdul Ahad's failure had already reached the court. At first, it seemed likely that the imperial army would be totally destroyed and, with it, the only force under the emperor's direct control. Worse still, the imperial capital would once more be at the mercy of an attacker, for it seemed impossible that the Sikhs should not continue all the way to Delhi. The emperor sent a messenger to recall Najaf Khan.

This unwelcome news brought Abdul Ahad hurrying back to Delhi in an attempt to reach it before Najaf. His reception was at first cold but, by minimizing his failure and playing once again on Shah Alam's fears of Najaf, Abdul Ahad managed to force the emperor to send a message countermanding his instructions to Najaf. Najaf, however, ignored the new orders and made his encampment outside the city early in November 1779. It was a moment for dissimulation. Taking one of the imperial princes with him, Abdul Ahad paid a visit to Najaf's camp on the pretext of accompanying him back to his audience with the emperor.

Najaf had already taken control of the centre of the city, including the area surrounding the palace. The palace guards had been instructed not to oppose Najaf's men and, by slowly pressing through the gates of the palace, Afrasiyab Khan was soon in possession. All this took place while Abdul Ahad was still in Najaf's camp. Only when a signal was hoisted on the ramparts did Najaf agree to accompany the minister. He took his place on the same elephant as the imperial prince—though, with calculated modesty, behind him, in the seat usually reserved for servants. When Najaf was conducted into the hall of private audience, he found the emperor awaiting him. A gift was made, and a robe of honour given. There was an exchange of empty courtesies, and the minister then, as a mark of honour, conducted Najaf to the gate. Najaf had been urged to arrest the minister inside the audience hall, but had refused to do so in the presence of the emperor. Outside, it was a different matter. For a moment, it looked as if the minister might be assassinated, but one of his friends rushed between the two men and tried to calm Najaf's supporters. Unsure of what he should do, and unwilling to murder one of the emperor's ministers, Najaf had Abdul Ahad confined in one of the gatehouses while he himself went to the palace mosque to think.

The emperor, hearing that his minister had been detained, warned Najaf's emissary that he must not be harmed. A recital of the minister's sins left him unmoved, and angry only with Najaf. Abdul Ahad's supporters begged the emperor to call for armed help to drive Najaf's men from the palace, but he hesitated until he was told that large numbers of people had gathered outside the palace to support the minister. Then, putting on armour and taking up a crossbow, he had himself borne out of the harem in a small litter, surrounded by members of the imperial family and by harem servants, intending to drive Najaf's men out. Before he reached the outer apartments, however, he had been persuaded to draw back again for fear of humiliation.

It was a night of increasing anxiety. The emperor would not give up Abdul Ahad. Najaf, still in the mosque, insisted that he should. Inside the palace walls Najaf's men prepared for action. Outside, the minister's supporters began to mass. In the city itself tensions began to rise. It was like doomsday, a contemporary recorded. 'A terrible noise rose from every lane and house. None knew what was happening inside the fort which was occupied by Najaf's followers, while Abdul Ahad's retainers stood outside the walls, their hearts set on bloodshed'.

Najaf's plan was simple. His agents were active, persuading where they could and buying where they could not. Soon it became obvious that the minister's friends were deserting him. He gave in. In return he was offered a guarantee of his life and property, Najaf explaining to the emperor that his sole aim was to exclude Abdul Ahad from the imperial presence. On 15 November the minister was escorted to Najaf's camp outside the city walls.

There was nothing but satisfaction among Najaf's entourage. The most persistent enemy of the commander-in-chief—and, in most opinions, of the empire—had met his doomsday, his day of judgement. It was now time for Najaf to assert his control over the state. It was easily done. At the emperor's invitation, Najaf entered the hall of private audience the day after Abdul Ahad had been taken to his camp. There was a small display of pomp, and Najaf offered the emperor a gift of 200,000 rupees, some jewels, twenty suits of costly cloth, and five horses. In return, he was appointed regent of the empire. In a new distribution of offices, a number of imperial princes were given positions of nominal authority, though nothing was to be done without Najaf's approval nor authorized without his seal.

The new regent took up residence in the capital and a new sense of security grew in the city. His forces were active in the containment of rebels. There was a revival of trade. New houses were built—a sure sign of confidence. 'All the chiefs', recorded the memoir-writer Miskin joyfully, 'were happy, prosperous and exalted'. But for how long?

6
Ruining the world

THE REGENCY of the empire kept Najaf Khan in the capital. Never again was he to take the field in person. His very real talents as a general were to be submerged in his need to keep his hand on the affairs of the empire. At the time of his triumph, Najaf was forty-two years old and his lungs were slowly giving way to the effects of tuberculosis. He had made his position without relatives or friends in the nobility of the empire. He belonged, like Shuja-ud-daula, to a minority sect of Islam which antagonized many and brought him no friendship from the nawab-wazir of Oudh to balance it. He had earned his high office by military expertise, diplomatic skill, and an immense and driving ambition tempered by what was, in the terms of his own times, a gentleness which on many occasions prevented him from taking ruthless action against his enemies.

During his two years as regent, an almost unbelievable change came over Najaf's character. From being abstemious, he became a drunkard. A man of carefully calculated decision, he became a prevaricator. A man of his word, however subtly, he now made promises that he had no intention of keeping. There was no doubt that he was frequently ill and constantly in pain. He may have turned to drink and drugs to help him through the dark night of what he perhaps knew to be a terminal disease. For the same reason, he seems to have progressed from reasonable indulgence to a frenetic search for sexual excitement. The reports of spies are full of descriptions of days and nights spent with dancing girls and a few chosen cronies. In particular, there is mention of a woman introduced to Najaf by Latafat Ali Khan, who was experienced at arranging erotic entertainments. Some reports say that she was one of Latafat Ali's wives, and that he deliberately used her to divert Najaf from taking an active part in the affairs of state.

Latafat Ali had been a partisan of the fallen minister, Abdul Ahad, and had probably been responsible for saving his life at the gate of the hall of private audience. But, in his relations with the regent, there is no reason to think that he was acting on anyone's behalf but his own. Latafat Ali had once been in the service of the nawab-wazir of Oudh and personally controlled a body of some 5,000 men with artillery. Now, he seemed almost to rule the state, with the approval or at least the connivance of Najaf Khan. Latafat Ali's men collected their own customs dues and drove out of the city any who tried to interfere with their activities. They enjoyed the profits of an indiscriminate protection racket. Appeals to Najaf, from the highest and the lowest of their victims, received no response. The emperor himself could extract no satisfactory answers and was, in fact, consistently ignored. Najaf's failure to exercise direct supervision over his agents led to abuses which in turn produced continuing civil disorder in the areas surrounding the city. It was here that the revenues for the upkeep of the administration and the palace were supposed to be found. But what was collected went mostly into the pockets of the tax collectors themselves, and when their oppressions became too great to be borne the peasantry rose up in rebellion and attacked them. Villages and standing crops were burned by the collector's troops, which only ensured that the source of revenue was destroyed for many years to come. Empty fields produce neither food nor wealth.

The ministrations of the tax collectors were compounded by an unfortunate series of dry years. The failure of the rains produced intense droughts throughout upper India from 1780 onwards. There was starvation not only in the villages. The imperial troops, who could not be paid, could not be supplied with food either. There was even a severe

shortage inside the palace. Though Najaf had promised
to pay the emperor's monthly allowance promptly and in
full, he was soon in arrears. The situation in the palace,
with its thousands of inhabitants—the imperial family, the
immense harem, the hundreds of state prisoners—became
so bad that the emperor's women declared they would link
arms and throw themselves in the river Jumna, as they had
neither money nor credit left. To Najaf's emissaries, who
came bearing excuses, Shah Alam was abusive. To his own
people, he suggested that they go to Najaf Khan's house
and sit outside, fasting, until they shamed him into making
some payments to relieve the distress. 'The king of the
world', he wrote, 'is ruining the world, through Najaf
Khan'.

Najaf's own position, though there always seemed to be
money for his dancing girls and entertainment, was by no
means as comfortable as the spies reported. He was constantly being pestered by officers of the imperial forces,
demanding their pay, and replied only with promises which
were never redeemed. At last, some of his commanders had
had enough. 'We cannot go on accepting your promise to
pay us tomorrow, because that day never comes. Tell us
plainly there is no money and let us go from your service,
but do not treat us as if we were children'. Many of Najaf's
men did leave him in the hope, usually forlorn, of finding
employment elsewhere. This frightened the emperor, for
an uncontrolled and angry soldiery was a perpetual menace
to the state. 'They are dispersing', he complained, 'in
bitterness of mind'.

Najaf's forces were the essential prop of the state. Whatever the financial situation, it was essential that he should
keep the force together and in a reasonable frame of mind.
The imperial army in 1781 consisted of Najaf's own troops,
i.e. thirty battalions of infantry trained on European lines,
5,000 rocket men, 3,000 swivel guns mounted on as many
camels, and 400 pieces of wheeled artillery. With this force
as the core, there was a further 73,000 cavalry and infantry
supplied by dependent chiefs, and mercenaries for whose

support land had been allocated. These were allowed to fend for themselves, but Najaf's own men had to be paid in cash. The monthly bill amounted to over 300,000 rupees.

Najaf's recent campaigns had produced very little money or jewels. What had been acquired had soon disappeared in day-to-day expenses. For the rest, he had had to accept promises of tribute, and these could only be ensured by a threat of force. Najaf himself could not leave Delhi, nor could he send his best men, for the Sikhs—after their triumphs over Abdul Ahad—were lurking in the northern margins. Yet money had to be found. At first, Najaf gave bills on his banker, but after a while these ceased to be honoured. His reputation still attracted soldiers of fortune of all races ; he continued, in spite of everything, to cast new guns under the supervision of a French armourer; he never turned away a commander whose fame had reached his ears, even if he could offer no more than promises of payment. But his personality alone could not hold things together indefinitely.

The principal lieutenants of Najaf's army were out in various parts of the country trying to produce some kind of orderly administration in areas recently conquered. Pacification was a long and tedious affair, and it would have been impossible to withdraw all of these commanders to take part in some other action. But action was necessary against the Jaipur raja, who had, on receiving his succession from the hands of the emperor, agreed to pay a fee of two million rupees and had failed to do so. He had not even sent anything on account. When the imperial armies had returned to Delhi, and after Abdul Ahad's fatuous expedition against the Sikhs had diverted attention from Jaipur, its ruler had sensibly taken advantage of the fact. Najaf decided that the Jaipur raja must be taught an immediate lesson.

Fortunately, one of Najaf's lieutenants, Najaf Kuli Khan, was having considerable success in an area on the way to Jaipur. He had moved out of Delhi in November 1779 to regain territory seized by the Rajput raja of Kanud. The fort at Kanud was in a waterless plain, and Najaf Kuli decided that he could not take it by force. He therefore pretended that he was prepared to come to an accommodation and even returned to the raja's agent such villages as he had captured on his way to the fort. For some reason—probably the sound and well substantiated Indian practice of changing sides for money—the raja believed Najaf Kuli, and sent his son to visit the Mughal general. As soon as the young man had entered Najaf Kuli's camp, he and the nobles who attended him were assassinated. Najaf Kuli advanced on the fort, hoping to take it by surprise, but despite the fact that the defenders had lost most of their leaders in this coup they held out for nearly three months. During this time the besiegers had to have their water brought from the nearest wells by relays of camels. The fort was finally surrendered on 17 March 1780.

Immediately after the fall of the fort at Kanud, news reached the regent in Delhi that Mahbub Ali Khan, one of the most famous generals in the service of the nawab-wazir of Oudh, had left his master's employ in disgust and, travelling with his family and an escort of 600 soldiers, had halted at Agra.

Shuja-ud-daula had died in 1775, though his passing had made only a slight ripple in the turbulent sea of Delhi politics. It was said that he had been poisoned—an automatic reaction at the sudden death of any Indian prince—but if he was, it had been for reasons that had nothing to do with his nominal position as wazir of the empire. His son, Asaf-ud-daula, had problems of his own which precluded him from any involvement in the affairs of the empire. The British were driving him, and were really in control of the state. There seemed to be no future there for a distinguished military leader. As a result, Mahbub Ali had decided to make the pilgrimage to Mecca.

As soon as Najaf Khan heard of Mahbub Ali's arrival in Agra, he sent him an offer of service in the imperial forces. Mahbub, whose determination to visit the holy places of Islam was apparently not very deep, accepted and was instructed to raise a force on the promise of payment out of the tribute and loot he would win from Jaipur. Mahbub's repute was such that it had only to be announced that he was in business again for military adventurers of all kinds to be attracted to his banner.

The situation in Jaipur was ripe for an invasion. The court had been shaken by a number of palace revolutions which had left in charge of the administration—a tailor. He had contrived to catch and hold the favour of the young Jaipur raja, who was charitably said to be mad. Najaf Khan hoped through Mahbub Ali to conquer the state, and for a while it looked as if this were what was about to happen. Mahbub Ali's troops ravaged the countryside and by October 1780 were within sight of Jaipur city itself.

But the Jaipur raja was able to hold out in his fort, and Mahbub Ali soon found himself without resources, his men deserting for lack of food or plunder. Having lost faith in him, Najaf allowed the raja to open up negotiations directly with Delhi. A deal was arrived at, and when Mahbub demanded reinforcements from the regent he was told that he could not have them. Mahbub went himself to Delhi but was unable to extract anything from Najaf for the very good reason that the regent was without funds himself. Promises failed to induce Mahbub to remain in the imperial service and his desire to visit the holy places revived. He informed his men that he intended to leave Najaf's employ, and their response was to mutiny and seize his property. 'At last', the chronicler recorded, 'Mahbub set out for Mecca as a penniless fakir'.

Unfortunately, though not reduced to quite such desperate straits as Mahbub, Najaf Khan made very little profit out of the Jaipur affair. There was a small down-payment from the raja, which satisfied at least some of the demands being made on Najaf's bounty, but within a month the money had disappeared. Najaf was also ill. Conditions in Delhi were extremely unhealthy, and the spies' reports continually refer to an unusually heavy mortality, not only among ordinary people—where it was to be expected—but inside the palace and among the imperial family as well.

KING OF THE WORLD

There were epidemics of typhoid and cholera, all intensified by the growing shortage of food. Najaf, though advised to reduce his intake of alcohol, would not listen. In 1780 he was forced to take to his bed, apparently close to death. Although he recovered on this occasion, it appears that he now became convinced that death was not far off.

Such an awareness hardly solved his most immediate problems. The failure of the Jaipur mission, by which he had hoped to collect enough to keep at least his own men quiet and to relieve, even a little, the misery of the emperor, had been close to disastrous. The emperor himself had reached such a state that he hoped for death. His public outbursts, intended no doubt to put pressure on Najaf, were becoming more frequent. 'I am sick of this life', he exclaimed one day. 'I cannot bear the shame of it any longer'. On another occasion he confided to the Maratha ambassador that he had no second robe to wear. Najaf was unaffected, and would have been unsusceptible to such rhetoric even if he had had enough money to silence it. Yet after his illness he went to court and laid his head at the emperor's feet, weeping tears of shame. It was only a momentary weakness. Convalescence restored his immunity and began a feverish search for other sources of revenue.

There did not seem to be any. Najaf's armies were having a measure of success in various parts of the country but all they gained was eaten up in keeping them on the march. There was no permanent or regular income for the state, but there was constant demand for money to meet everyday expenses. In looking around him for prospects, the only one that seemed to Najaf Khan to offer appreciable profit was the British. But his respect for their military expertise was such that he could not anticipate attacking them unless he could find allies so powerful that victory, if not assured, would at least be likely. The only allies who might conceivably fit the description were the Marathas.

Unfortunately, while Najaf Khan had been preoccupied in Delhi with the events which had led to his assumption of full power, the Marathas had been suffering a series of defeats at the hands of the British. After their failure at Panipat in 1761, the Maratha chieftains had turned back into their own territories to attend to their own problems. The latter were compounded by the peculiar constitution of the Maratha 'state'. In fact, there was no such thing— though the British never understood this—but instead a confederacy of virtually independent chiefs bound together by sentiment and tradition and owing a kind of variable allegiance to the ruler known as the Peshwa. One of the problems the Marathas had to face while they were recovering from their shattering defeat by the Afghan, Ahmad Shah, was that of the succession to that office.

In 1774, the holder of the position was assassinated, probably by his uncle, Raghunath Rao, who seized power for himself. But a son was born posthumously to the former Peshwa and formally invested, at the age of six weeks, with the office. Raghunath, who was generally disliked by his own people, now tried to interest other Indian powers in his cause. One of the powers he approached was the British— not the British in Calcutta, but those nearer to him, in Bombay. As the British there had always coveted the island of Salsette and the port of Bassein, which were close to Bombay and would have given the British much-needed protection for their highly vulnerable settlement, they offered help to Raghunath. The fee was to be the cession of Salsette and Bassein. Raghunath, however, dared not give up portions of the Peshwa's territory; he would, by doing so, have alienated such few supporters as he had among the people. His refusal did not upset the British authorities in Bombay; they simply took Salsette by force. Raghunath, who had fled from the Peshwa's capital at Poona, was persuaded to ratify this unofficial act of war by signing the treaty of Surat in March 1775. In return, he received a promise of British military support.

When news of the treaty reached the senior British authorities in Calcutta, Warren Hastings condemned it as 'impolitic, dangerous, unauthorized and unjust'. The treaty, he informed Bombay, was cancelled. By the time his instructions reached the west, however, the war with the Marathas had already begun. The British had managed to achieve a victory, though it was so closely fought that it was almost a defeat, and when Hastings heard of it he changed his mind. However misguided and foolish the original tactics of the Bombay authorities had been, he felt it would be unwise to lose initiative by means of a hasty withdrawal. It would, he thought, be better instead to send military assistance to Bombay. Hastings's opinion was overruled by a hostile majority on his own council and, after much negotiation, a treaty was concluded in 1776 with the representatives and supporters of the infant Peshwa. Though convinced that another clash was inevitable, Hastings preferred to choose his own time for it. Delay in transmitting news and instructions between Calcutta and Bombay, however, was always productive of confusion. Once again, Bombay acted precipitously and ruined Hastings's plans.

In 1778 war broke out in Europe between Britain and France. There was a French envoy at Poona and it seemed not unlikely that he might induce the Marathas to mount an attack on the British. Hastings therefore decided to send a force, overland, across India to attack the Marathas. The distance was about 1,000 miles through uncharted, unknown, and certainly unfriendly country. The force set out in May 1778. When Bombay heard that the force had left Calcutta, it was decided to send troops from Bombay itself to attack Poona, where it was believed there were dissensions among the Maratha chiefs.

The Bombay force was defeated and compelled, in January 1779, to agree to terms which Hastings, when he heard of them, said were enough to make him 'sink with shame'. Fortunately, the incompetence of the Bombay army was not matched by Goddard and Popham, commanders of the overland force from Calcutta. When Goddard reached western India, after a formidable journey, he stormed the town of Ahmadabad, in February 1780, and soon overran Gujarat, establishing friendly relations with a number of local chiefs while he did so. He did, however, make the mistake of trying to move rapidly on Poona.

The Peshwa's administration was now in the hands of a man of great strength and subtlety, one Nana Farnavis, who was fully aware that the British were in serious difficulties in the south, where their settlement at Madras was being menaced by the ruler of Mysore. When Goddard sent the Marathas a peremptory demand for surrender, Nana Farnavis knew it to be a bluff. The young Peshwa was sent away to safety, and Nana Farnavis collected the Maratha armies to surround Goddard's force. Goddard escaped from the trap only with heavy casualties and the loss of a great deal of his baggage.

Goddard's fellow-commander, Popham, repaired the effect of this partial disaster by allying himself with a local chieftain and driving the Marathas before him 'with great slaughter'. Finally, in a night attack, he took the allegedly impregnable fortress of Gwalior, the stronghold of Mahadaji Sindia. It was a victory both real and symbolic. As Hastings put it: 'The name of Gwalior has been long famous in history. In this country [the] effect [of its fall] is not to be described'. Gwalior was taken in August 1780. In December of the same year a recovered Goddard captured Bassein. But all was not well. Sindia, appalled at the loss of his fortress, began to harry the British. A force commanded by Major Carnac was surrounded by an army led by Sindia in person. He broke out only with difficulty, constantly pursued by Sindia's men. But Carnac was by no means defeated. Without warning, he suddenly turned and, in a night attack on Sindia's camp, completely routed his army and captured an immense quantity of stores as well as Sindia's personal standard.

This totally unexpected reverse led Sindia to open up negotiations almost immediately. The result was the treaty of Salbai, concluded in May 1782, which settled matters not only between the British and Sindia but with the other Maratha leaders as well. Sindia acted as mediator.

While all this activity was in progress, the Peshwa's

minister had been urging the emperor and Najaf Khan to help him in the war against the British. The imperial response was favourable, but loaded with conditions. The emperor was fully prepared to send an army to help, if the Marathas would in turn send an army to defend Delhi against any possible attack by the British. It seemed a self-cancelling proposition, but negotiations continued, though the Maratha envoy at Delhi soon became convinced that Najaf Khan was merely procrastinating. 'He is really waiting to see which side proves to be the stronger', was the gist of his report.

The fall of Gwalior worried Najaf Khan. The Marathas had done their best to keep the news quiet, but without success. As news of the Maratha defeats reached Delhi, Najaf feared that the British might move against the imperial capital itself, but there was in fact little likelihood of this. The British were in great trouble in the south, and were just as anxious to end the war with the Marathas as their enemies were.

With so much in flux, Delhi could do little but await the outcome. The emperor's favourite son was married with a pomp which would not have seemed possible a year earlier. Then another prince died suddenly. Astrologers began to examine their charts with greater care and to foretell all varieties of disaster. Nature complied with an unusually violent duststorm in June 1781. Later, there was a severe earth tremor which brought a number of buildings crashing down and caused a number of graves to open. To add a final touch, a glowing meteor fell not far from the city.

On 6 April 1782, as a grand climax, died Najaf Khan, Zulficar-ud-daula, regent of the empire and its last defence against the deluge.

7

All Hindustan is lying bare

THE PERSONALITY of Najaf Khan, however flawed, had
been the rock on which the whole edifice of the empire's new
power rested. At his death, that power seemed greater than
at any time in the preceding thirty years, but it was all an
illusion sustained by the reputation and military capability
of one man. During his short term as regent, Najaf Khan
had shown no capacity for administration, or even for
appointing men of quality who might have remedied his
own deficiencies in that field. Instead of setting the revenues
of the state on a firm basis, he had parcelled out the lands
round Delhi among his lieutenants who had diverted them
for their own use. These men, controlling troops, almost
independent in their commands, could only be kept in
order by a man of strength. When Najaf died, none remained. He left no male heir, and it was his principal
lieutenants who were to fight among themselves for his
inheritance.

In the palace, Shah Alam was distracted by conflicting
advice. The best proposition was that he should himself
assume the supreme command of the armies and take the
field in person in order to reconquer those territories which
rightly belonged to him. But Shah Alam was no longer the
young man who had cut his way out of a Delhi mansion and
conducted his own campaigns with hired troops. He was
now fifty-eight years old—a considerable age in the India
of his time—and, though still vigorous in body, his mis-
fortunes had made him timid and fearful of losing what
little he possessed. He therefore looked around for a
successor to Najaf Khan.

The choice appeared clearly to lie among Najaf's four

principal lieutenants. There was Afrasiyab Khan who, as a Hindu boy, had been captured by Najaf, converted to Islam, and made his slave. It was a position which did not last for long, and Najaf soon came to treat him as his adopted son. He controlled the fort of Aligarh and territories worth an annual income of 2,500,000 rupees. His forces numbered over 25,000. Afrasiyab had no reputation as a soldier, but he did have the very unusual distinction of handling money affairs well. The dying Najaf had recommended him as his successor, and he had the support of the regent's sister.

Another of Najaf's favourites was a Persian who had, out of respect for his master, taken the name of Najaf Kuli Khan. He was a reckless commander—when he felt like fighting—but preferred smoking opium and the pleasures of a well-stocked harem. Of the remaining two, Muhammad Shafi was very young at the time of Najaf's death. As the son of the late regent's nephew, he at least had the claims of blood. But though he had an army of 20,000 men and was respected for his high spirits, he was easily fooled by men of greater cunning. Among these could be numbered the sinister figure of Muhammad Beg Hamadani, an Afghan mercenary who had married a daughter of Najaf Khan but was disliked and distrusted by Najaf's closest retainers.

After the three days of mourning for Najaf Khan were over, the emperor called these principal lieutenants to the palace. They were asked themselves to elect a new commander. Naturally, they could not agree, except on one point. They did not want Afrasiyab Khan, because he was a convert who had once been a slave. This did not prevent the emperor from taking the advice of Najaf's sister and appointing Afrasiyab commander-in-chief. The choice was facilitated by Afrasiyab's promise of a succession fee. The emperor, his pockets always empty, was easily swayed by offers of money. The problem for Afrasiyab was how to make good his offer.

His simplest solution seemed to be to go out and recover the territories that had been usurped by rebels of one kind or another during the last few months of Najaf's life. This entailed first paying the army and buying stores. The late regent had left most of the administration of his affairs in Afrasiyab's hands, but such money as there was was soon exhausted. An attempt to bully the minor chiefs into supplying their contingents to the army caused nothing but antagonism. Very soon, a conspiracy was formed to replace Afrasiyab with the youthful Muhammad Shafi.

The conspiracy included some very significant figures—among them Shah Alam himself, although his support was kept as secret as it could possibly be. There was also Najaf's sister, who had turned against Afrasiyab and whose opposition was, on the other hand, almost ostentatious. Aware of the threat to his position, Afrasiyab began to make arrangements to meet it. He first attempted to placate the emperor by removing his troops from the palace and handing over the control of the gates to the emperor's personal guard. Further, he withdrew from his official residence, taking with him the ex-minister, Abdul Ahad, whom Najaf had kept as a prisoner of state. Together, the two men repaired to Abdul Ahad's old mansion. Afrasiyab's intention was to restore Abdul Ahad, who had never lost Shah Alam's affection, to his old position. But such plans took time to work out. Abdul Ahad had no resources of any kind and was unwilling to be used as a pawn by Afrasiyab. The army, on which all depended, was becoming extremely restive, and before any of Afrasiyab's designs could come to fruition, Muhammad Shafi arrived and was invited by the emperor to visit him.

To the horrified but knowing eyes of the inhabitants of Delhi, it was becoming obvious that a clash was imminent. On one side, there was Afrasiyab Khan who now had the support of Najaf Kuli and that of Latafat Ali, who had profited so much from Najaf's illness. With them—a trump card, they hoped, as far as the emperor was concerned—was the still reluctant Abdul Ahad. The opposition included Muhammad Shafi, powerfully supported by the late regent's sister and by Muhammad Beg, who was busily concluding a small

KING OF THE WORLD

campaign against one of Afrasiyab's major supporters and threatening Afrasiyab's own fortress at Aligarh.

With no overt, firm authority in the city, law and order broke down. The army did not know who its leader was and, in anticipation of trouble was already forming itself into factions. The court was full of partisans of one side or the other, who shifted their allegiance according to the promises made. For two months there was an uneasy quiet, broken only by the constant passage of envoys in and out of the palace. Then the emperor decided for Muhammad Shafi, on the understanding that he would pay half a million rupees into the emperor's treasury in exchange for the privilege of being made commander-in-chief. When Afrasiyab heard this, he countered by begging the emperor to restore his old friend, Abdul Ahad, to office. Obviously, Afrasiyab hoped to settle a grateful friend at court, but what the emperor hoped to gain from the transaction it is difficult to decide. Apparently, he was so pleased to welcome his old favourite back after three years of enforced separation that he gave no thought at all to the consequences. Abdul Ahad was restored to all his former offices, and Muhammad Shafi's appointment as commander-in-chief was postponed.

Tensions in the city increased. Inside it were two large armies, as well as a miscellany of uncommitted troops. The likelihood of a clash was there every time they met. One day in August 1782, an argument between a captain of Afrasiyab's force and a German mercenary belonging to Shafi's following developed into a major confrontation. The two sides began to dig trenches, and artillery was brought into the streets. Only appeals from the emperor stopped a full-scale outbreak. In an attempt to forestall any further such incidents, the emperor ordered Afrasiyab to leave the city and go to the defence of Aligarh, which was still threatened by Muhammad Beg. Behind him Afrasiyab left his fellow conspirator, Najaf Kuli.

No sooner had Afrasiyab gone than Muhammad Shafi took action. Najaf Kuli had become careless. On the night of the feast of rejoicing which brought a month of fasting to an end, he spent his time drinking. His house had only a small guard, reinforced with a few guns. During that night, Shafi's men surrounded the house as well as that of Abdul Ahad and, though Najaf Kuli put up a defence, he was forced to surrender to superior firepower. Abdul Ahad offered no defence. Both men were put under arrest.

Five days later, on 15 September, Shafi was given the appointment of commander-in-chief. But the ballet of shifting alliances was not yet in its last act. Shafi tried to make friends with his former enemies and succeeded only in alienating some of his friends. Latafat Ali—engaged, as always, in intrigues—was now active on behalf of Shah Alam! His first success was to persuade Shafi's German mercenary, Pauli, to change sides; then some of his agents induced Shafi's troops, who had not been paid, to mutiny; Shafi, however, managed to placate them with a payment on account.

On 16 October, Latafat came out into the open and, with Pauli and his contingent, marched on Shafi's mansion. The emperor himself emerged from the palace to add his countenance to the expedition.

Shafi did not wait to be attacked, but fled in the direction of Agra, taking Abdul Ahad with him but leaving Najaf Kuli behind. The roundabout now returned Afrasiyab to imperial favour, but not for long. The fugitive Shafi met up with Muhammad Beg and together they began to march towards Delhi.

Again it seemed that Shah Alam's plans were in danger. Latafat and Pauli persuaded him to move out of the palace and into camp as a preliminary to taking the field against the two rebels. There, envoys came asking for the emperor to pardon them and restore their titles. The inevitable bargaining now took place, as well as a simultaneous attempt to detach Muhammad Beg from Shafi. The incentive was an offer to make Muhammad Beg commander-in-chief. The plot failed, however, as Muhammad Beg told Shafi about it. Together, they agreed to let the intrigue continue in the hope of being able to use it for their own advantage.

The opportunity came when Latafat Ali invited Muhammad Beg to meet him so that he could be presented to the emperor. Naive conspirators, Latafat and Pauli arrived at the meeting place with a very small escort which was soon overwhelmed and put to flight. Muhammad Beg immediately sent a detachment into the city to seize Latafat's property, but it was too late—Shafi's brother had already acted.

The last tableau was still to come. The emperor, in his camp, was without support and had no alternative but to accept the protestations of loyalty from Muhammad Beg and Shafi and appoint the latter commander-in-chief. The finale, which no one regarded as incongruous, came on the emperor's return to his palace when he was borne into the private apartments in a palanquin supported on the shoulders of Abdul Ahad, Afrasiyab Khan, Muhammad Beg and Muhammad Shafi. There was no charade, however, when it came to the treatment of Latafat Ali. Next day, on the orders of Muhammad Beg, Latafat was blinded. Pauli, who refused to submit quietly to having his eyes put out, was hacked to pieces instead.

Shafi now had the unenviable task of pacifying the imperial provinces and producing some revenue. Accompanied by one of the emperor's sons and Najaf Khan's sister, Shafi took possession of Agra and spent two months in the area. Here he received an envoy from the British. The death of Najaf Khan had led all the powers in India to reconsider the problem of Delhi. While Najaf lived, the British believed they had nothing to fear but in the changed situation they decided they must know at first hand what was going on. They therefore settled on sending an agent to Delhi to report on the state of affairs and advise the British on what their policies should be. The man appointed was Major James Browne.

Browne was experienced, had seen service in the recent Maratha wars, and had a sound knowledge of languages. He was also close to the governor-general, Warren Hastings. Unfortunately, he was neither a shrewd judge of men nor devious enough to follow the intricate windings of Delhi politics. Browne left Calcutta in August 1782 and reached Lucknow, the capital of the nawab-wazir of Oudh, in November. There he engaged as his native agent a man who had had long experience of the court of Delhi. From Lucknow Browne sent off a letter asking for Shah Alam's permission to proceed to the imperial capital. He received a reply inviting him to come directly to the palace.

Browne set off in December 1782, but received another letter on the way in which the emperor informed him that the recent troubles in the capital were now over. British assistance was no longer required, and Shah Alam recommended that Browne return to Calcutta. Attitudes towards the British at the court in Delhi were frequently at variance. The emperor himself occasionally felt that he would be better off if he had British help, but at other times he feared that, if they were once allowed into Delhi, he would never be able to get rid of them. Imperial agents of varying ranks and levels of authority had been sent to Calcutta to talk about aid, but none had at any time carried the emperor's real authority. They had also been supplemented by agents sent by members of the imperial court, by aspiring military commanders, and by ministers. Generally speaking, however, the court did not wish to be beholden to the British, who were by now becoming recognized as a major power in the land.

There were others who also feared British influence at the court in Delhi. The Peshwa frequently wrote to the emperor and to Mahadaji Sindia, warning that 'if the English once plant their feet there [Delhi] no power would be left independent in India'. Muhammad Shafi seems to have thought the same; it was he who persuaded the emperor to tell Browne to return to Calcutta.

But Browne had no intention of being ordered back. He sent his native agent to Delhi in the hope that he might persuade the emperor or his ministers to rescind the refusal to receive the British envoy at court. Though not entirely successful, the agent did manage to extract an imperial

letter instructing Browne to see the new commander-in-chief
Muhammad Shafi, at Agra. Browne made his camp on the
opposite side of the river from Agra. In his suite there was a
Savoyard soldier of fortune, Benoit de Boigne, who was
later to play a decisive role in the affairs of the empire, as
well as the artist and Royal Academician, William Hodges,
at that time making his way round India working on draw-
ings which he was later to publish with an account of his
travels. The effect on Hodges of his first sight of the once
great imperial city was one of sadness. 'It was impossible',
he wrote, 'to contemplate the ruins of this grand and
venerable city without feeling the deepest impressions of
melancholy. . . They extend, along the banks of the river,
not less than fourteen English miles. . . The great Musjid or
Mosque, built of red stone, is greatly gone to decay.
Adjacent to it is the Choke or Exchange, now a ruin ; even
the Fort itself, from its having frequently changed its
masters in the course of the last seventy years, is going
rapidly to desolation'.

The first meeting between Browne and Muhammad
Shafi was arranged for 27 February. Browne was escorted by
Afrasiyab Khan to a tent made of crimson velvet, lined with
gold-embroidered silk. It looked very fine from a distance,
but when the party entered they could see that the hangings
were torn and moth-eaten. Shafi, who was suffering from the
effects of an attack of fever, did not rise to meet the British
envoy but touched his turban in salute and waved his guest
to a European chair whose upholstery, once rich, was
ragged and threadbare. Though Browne reported that
Shafi was 'not very conversable' the meeting was cordial.
So, too, was a meeting with Najaf's sister, who was also in
camp. Later, Browne was received by the emperor's son,
Sulaiman.

Browne reported that Shafi's troops were mutinous for
want of pay ; they were so pressing, in fact, that the commander-in-chief took himself off into the Agra fort in
order to escape them. But not for long. In March, an urgent
call for help came from the emperor. The Sikhs, always

willing to take advantage of other people's troubles, had swept down as far as the outskirts of the capital, burning markets and killing a number of people. Another body of troops was, however, nearer the capital than Shafi's, and they were able to drive the Sikhs off while Shafi devoted his attention to other matters—particularly to the affairs of the Jat raja who, like everyone else, had taken the squabbles at Delhi as an excuse to default on his tribute. Though he and Muhammad Beg had reached an agreement, Shafi refused to honour it and set about ravaging the Jat country and investing the raja's forts. Shafi's rejection of Muhammad Beg's agreement marked another stage in the steady erosion of good relations between the two men.

Muhammad Beg's support for Shafi had been bought with promises which the latter was unable to fulfil. After the seizure of Latafat Ali and Pauli, Muhammad Beg had allowed his troops to plunder along the road to Delhi, dismissing Shafi's protest that it was not proper for imperial subjects to be oppressed by an imperial official. Muhammad Beg also increased the price to Shafi of his support. Now, he wanted not only more assignments of revenue but half of the late Najaf Khan's artillery and the entire imperial claim on Jaipur. Taking his rights for granted in the latter case, Muhammad Beg set off in the direction of Jaipur intending to collect the tribute himself. On the way, he showed leniency to the Jat raja, so that he might be sure—or as sure as it was ever possible to be—of a friend when the clash between himself and Shafi broke out into open war.

Shafi responded in the customary manner by attempting to suborn his enemy's principal commanders. As usual, they had not been paid for some time and, as Muhammad Beg's forces continued to grow in size, the likelihood of payment appeared to diminish daily. Shafi's concern was with how to crush Muhammad Beg, for crushed he must certainly be. Shafi could not do it unaided, but he did not want British help in the task, and he was already worried by signs that the British were moving troops near to the imperial dominions. He was not reassured by Browne's explanation that the troops were there only to prevent the Sikhs from attacking the nawab-wazir of Oudh. The only other possible ally seemed to be Mahadaji Sindia, who had emerged from the conflict with the British with his prestige only slightly tarnished and his forces virtually intact. Sindia, with a large army, was not far away, and Shafi decided to approach him.

During his negotiations with Sindia, Shafi was also playing a double game with the British. Browne tried to convince Hastings that a formal alliance should be concluded with Shafi, and that this would later be ratified by the emperor; indeed, the emperor had himself sent a letter to Browne, which was to be forwarded to Calcutta, asking for military aid against the Sikhs. It is difficult to tell from the correspondence and from the spies' reports whether any of this was taken seriously by any of the participants other than Browne. After Shafi and Sindia met in June, Browne became almost hysterical in his demands. Hastings, he said, should send a brigade of troops to Delhi to seize the city and the emperor, and to take control of affairs. Failing that, an alliance must be made with Shafi. This, he insisted, was the only way to avoid a Maratha take-over of the Mughal state. Sindia, though superficially amicable towards the British since the treaty of Salbai, was, wrote Browne, 'one of our most dangerous friends'.

The meeting between Shafi and Sindia had taken place in an atmosphere of considerable cordiality all round. Although Shafi and Muhammad Beg had reached an ostensible reconciliation, it was still very fragile, and Sindia insisted that Muhammad Beg should not attend the meeting. Shafi therefore went accompanied only by the prince and Najaf Khan's sister. After their first meeting at Sindia's camp, the Maratha leader paid the prince a visit. The British agent at Sindia's court was also introduced, and Major Browne—who had accompanied Shafi—was presented to Sindia. In the outcome, Sindia promised Shafi that he would go to Delhi after the rainy season.

Sindia's unwillingness to move there and then was partly a result of other preoccupations—he was attempting to retake the fortress of Gwalior—and partly of an instinctive feeling that it would be better not to become too deeply involved at that particular moment. In consequence, another plot began to crystallize.

Afrasiyab Khan had obtained from the emperor approval for opening up negotiations with the British. Arriving in Shafi's camp, he offered Browne a treaty assigning the revenues of lands around Delhi towards the cost of a British force. Browne, who was forever changing his mind over the question of whom to support, now favoured Afrasiyab. He did not trust Shafi after the meetings with Sindia. Afrasiyab appeared to be acting legitimately on behalf of the emperor. Browne had also heard rumours that Shafi had been in touch with a French envoy, who had secretly accompanied Sindia to the meetings. And finally, Shafi would not allow Browne to leave camp and go to Delhi to present himself to Shah Alam.

In the meantime, others had become involved in plots against Shafi. Abdul Ahad had sent letters direct to Calcutta appealing to Hastings—whom he referred to as 'the off-spring of this Royal House'—to join with Afrasiyab in deposing Shafi and restoring Shah Alam to a position of real power. While the British were discussing this proposal and Browne's repeated argument that 'the whole Mughal empire, with its unhappy master, look to you for redemption from the utmost distress and confusion', Afrasiyab was negotiating with Muhammad Beg, who had sniffed the wind of the meeting between Shafi and Sindia and had not liked the aroma. The two men decided that Shafi must be assassinated.

Shafi had still learned nothing about the ways of his world. He called Afrasiyab to advise him on what should be done about Muhammad Beg! Afrasiyab went through the motions of starting talks with Muhammad Beg, and gave the impression that he was acting as an impartial mediator. Though some of Shafi's closest lieutenants tried to convince him that there was a conspiracy in the making, Shafi believed in Afrasiyab. Reporting back to Shafi,

Afrasiyab said that Muhammad Beg was ready to wait upon
Prince Sulaiman, the emperor's envoy, to make his submission. Before that, however, Muhammad Beg asked for a
friendly meeting with Shafi so that he might receive personal guarantees of safety on his visit to the prince's camp.
Again his advisers warned Shafi not to be too credulous,
but he laughed away their misgivings. Had not Afrasiyab
said that all would be well? The interview was fixed for
23 September.

Four hours before sunset, Muhammad Beg advanced
from his camp to the meeting place, which was a few miles
from the great fortress of Dig—now occupied by the
commander-in-chief. Shafi had not, it seems, taken the
elementary precaution of consulting his astrologers about
the future. Perhaps he did not believe in the stars ; his turban
fell off as he was mounting his horse, and he refused even to
take that as a bad omen, though it was well known to be so.
Once again his attendants tried to persuade him not to risk
the meeting but, remounted on an elephant and surrounded
by only a small escort, he made his way out of the fort. As
he proceeded, his spies returned to report that, contrary to
the arrangement, Muhammad Beg had arrived at the meeting place with a very large force. But Shafi still did not
observe even the edge of the shadow.

As Shafi and his escort approached, Muhammad Beg
himself became visible, mounted on the back of an elephant
and surrounded by five or six other elephants carrying his
principal lieutenants and a number of armed men. As Shafi's
elephant drew up level with Muhammad Beg's, Shafi stood
up to embrace him. Shafi was small and delicately built,
Muhammad Beg a large and powerful figure. Grasping
Shafi's hands, Muhammad Beg failed to release them. As
Shafi struggled in his opponent's grip, Muhammad Beg's
nephew vaulted on to Shafi's elephant and stabbed the
helpless commander-in-chief in the stomach. One of Shafi's
attendants grappled with the assassin and both men fell to
the ground while another of Muhammad Beg's retainers
stabbed Shafi again, this time in the heart. Some of Shafi's

escort were killed, others fled back to Dig. Afrasiyab, who had arrived on the field after Shafi, took himself off the moment he saw the attack begin.

Treachery had triumphed, and once again the thin fabric of imperial authority had been torn. 'Muhammad Shafi is dead', reported the Peshwa's agent. 'All Hindustan is lying bare'.

8

Preventive of great evils

ON THE murder of Muhammad Shafi, Afrasiyab took over control of the dead commander-in-chief's troops by making a show of grief and promising vengeance on the assassins. At the same time his agents were busy persuading Muhammad Beg to depart for his own territory, with an immediate cash donation, confirmation of his right to the Jaipur tribute, and a promise that, as soon as the scandal died down, Afrasiyab would see to it that the emperor granted him a pardon. Afrasiyab seemed to be in a position to carry out this secret agreement; as soon as the news of Shafi's death reached the emperor in Delhi he appointed Afrasiyab to Shafi's old office and commanded him to return to court, with the prince. The emperor had felt that he had no alternative, though Najaf Kuli Khan tried to persuade him to give the appointment to Shafi's brother. This sensible suggestion was overruled by the fear of Shah Alam and Abdul Ahad that the British might persuade Afrasiyab to declare Prince Sulaiman emperor.

This idea does not seem to have occurred either to Browne or Afrasiyab. Browne was, in fact, enthusiastic about his protégé's change of fortune. He regarded Afrasiyab as timid and easily dominated, a man who would make a weak commander-in-chief. Nothing could have been more to the British advantage. Though Shafi's murder had been an evil deed, Browne wrote to Hastings, it would 'be productive of good consequences, and preventive of Great Evils'. Browne had an almost infinite capacity for self-delusion which was not, fortunately, shared by Hastings. There was, however, one small shadow over Browne's optimism.

Afrasiyab seemed very unwilling to let him go to Delhi on his own to see the emperor.

With Browne in tow, Afrasiyab spent the next months establishing his own rule in place of Shafi's at Agra and many other forts. He did not arrive in Delhi until the second week in December. Browne had managed to leave him, but any advantage he had hoped to gain was lost when he went down with a fever which kept him in bed for nearly two months.

Afrasiyab could not stay at court for long. Recent events had once more brought out the rebels and those who hoped to make profit out of chaos. The Sikhs were on the march again north of Delhi. Very soon they were joined by Muhammad Shafi's brother. But Afrasiyab defeated the Sikhs and reached an arrangement with Shafi's brother, then, having settled matters to his satisfaction, returned to Delhi where his colleague, Abdul Ahad, was slowly undermining his position. In this task, Ahad hoped for Major Browne's support.

A week after Afrasiyab's return, Browne was at last well enough to be received by the emperor. The day fixed was 5 February 1784. As Browne was still weak from his illness, the ceremonies were somewhat curtailed.

Shah Alam had revived the extremely complicated etiquette of the Mughal court. There was an obeisance which had to be carried out by placing the back of the right hand on the ground, slowly raising it until the body was erect, and then placing it upon the crown of the head. Three of these genuflections had to be made when a person was first introduced, a further three when the emperor made a presentation of a robe of honour or some other gift, and another three when the visitor left. As a gesture of goodwill on the part of the emperor, some of these obeisances were abandoned in Browne's case.

Browne was received, as were all ambassadors, in the Hall of Private Audience. After the obeisances, the envoy presented his gifts, and the emperor then gave him the obligatory robe of honour. The quality of such robes was very carefully graded according to the recipient's status. Browne described his own to Hastings as 'of the most honourable Degree'. It was, in fact, a dress of seven pieces, only one fewer than in that worn by the emperor himself. The officers of Browne's escort were also honoured, and Browne then presented a gift on behalf of Hastings, who had been given a title by the emperor. Shah Alam enquired courteously after the health of Hastings and Mrs Hastings.

After these ceremonies, the emperor retired from the audience hall into a suite of rooms in the private apartments, and Browne was invited to join him. Here the conversation was less formal. The emperor sat on a low throne and some of the protocol was relaxed. Afrasiyab and Abdul Ahad were present, and so was the emperor's son and heir, Jahandar Shah, who pleased Browne by maintaining that, though he himself had not been with his father in Allahabad and therefore had not had first-hand dealings with the British, he was convinced of their reputation as a 'nation famous for veracity'. Browne once again assured the emperor of the loyalty of the British to his throne and cause, and then left the presence.

This audience seems to have convinced Afrasiyab that there was some understanding between the emperor and Abdul Ahad on the one hand, and the British on the other. He was not sure what it was, but soon brought himself to believe that, if he were to leave Delhi without taking the emperor or one of his sons with him, Abdul Ahad would call in the British. There was no doubt that Abdul Ahad was in frequent touch with Hastings directly, as well as through Browne. The British envoy himself was hard at work trying to assemble an anti-Maratha faction among the leading officers of state, and Afrasiyab made it clear that he was fully prepared to co-operate in return for support of his own position. Letters allegedly from Sindia were shown to Browne, in which the Maratha leader asked for imperial backing against the British. Afrasiyab pointed out that, if the British would not give him their aid, he would have no alternative but to accede to Sindia's demands. When news reached Delhi that Hastings was on his way to Lucknow, Afrasiyab wrote to him suggesting a meeting.

Information that the British governor-general in person was arriving in the capital of Oudh was at first taken to mean that the British intended a march on Delhi. But Hastings, in his reply to Afrasiyab's letter, denied the intention and ignored Afrasiyab's request for an interview. Now that Afrasiyab had settled himself in the saddle, there was, Hastings wrote, no need for the British to come to his assistance. Instead of being reassured by this, Afrasiyab became convinced that something was going on behind his back. And something was, though it was not quite what might have been expected. In the middle of April, the heir apparent, Jahandar Shah, fled from the palace.

The night of 14 April 1784 was extremely dark. There was no moon, and a violent dust-storm made the blackness even more impenetrable. The prince and a few followers made their way to the ramparts of the palace on the river side, and let themselves down on a rope sixty feet to the ground. From there the party made its way along the river bank to a village where it was joined by a group of cavalry.

When it was discovered that the prince had gone, no one was sure where he had gone to. Browne thought he might have made for Sindia's camp, as he suspected that for all his fine words at the audience Jahandar Shah really disliked the British. Another rumour was that he had been involved in a conspiracy to overthrow Afrasiyab. There had indeed been such a conspiracy, and it had failed only a few days before the prince's flight. At the centre of this, as of almost every other intrigue, was Abdul Ahad. Supporting him was Shafi's brother, Zain, who firmly believed—as did many others— that Afrasiyab had been involved in the murder of his brother. Zain had sent five men who hid themselves in Afrasiyab's office, obviously intent on murdering him, but they had been caught by some of Afrasiyab's men before they could do him any harm. Ultimately, Abdul Ahad was arrested and sent as a prisoner to the fortress of Alighur.

Jahandar Shah had not gone to Sindia, but to Lucknow.

This put Hastings in something of a quandary. He had allowed Browne to convey the impression to Shah Alam and Abdul Ahad that he would be prepared to support the emperor by sending troops to Delhi, but whereas in 1783 a British force might have been able to take over control of the court and the Mughal state, the situation in 1784 was somewhat different. Hastings seems to have decided that it would be better policy to allow the troubled inheritance of Delhi to fall on Sindia's shoulders. In such an event, Sindia would find himself so preoccupied that he would have no interest in attacking British possessions. Furthermore, it seemed clear that if one of the Maratha leaders gained control of the empire, this would probably intensify the usual jealousies among the others and make it improbable that the Marathas would ally themselves for long enough to form a real menace to British pretensions in the south. Whatever Hastings's real views—and they are still unknown—the arrival of the Mughal heir apparent in Lucknow seemed to call for some kind of action.

Hastings first assured the emperor that Jahandar Shah had not come to Oudh at *his* invitation. Meanwhile, in Delhi, the emperor was assuring Browne that Jahandar Shah had not gone to Oudh at *his* instigation, nor even with his approval or consent. The most reasonable explanation of the heir apparent's flight from Delhi to take refuge with the British is that he was genuinely afraid of being thought to have been in the conspiracy to assassinate Afrasiyab. The emperor's second son, too, was jealous of Jahandar Shah, who may have suspected that he was planning to supersede him as heir to the imperial throne—for the Mughal emperors did not accept the right of primogeniture. If Jahandar Shah had fled to Sindia, he might have found himself in the uncomfortable position of being held as a hostage. So he sought refuge with the British, and it seems certain that he expected Hastings to give him help. Hastings, however, was no more willing to involve himself in a war of succession than he was to give concrete support to the man who already occupied the throne.

At the emperor's request, Browne left Delhi for Lucknow to discover the governor-general's intentions and to persuade him to send Jahandar Shah back to his father. He also carried a message from the emperor asking Hastings to renew payment of the tribute, so as to give the emperor 'some relief from his present emergent Distresses'. At Lucknow, Browne discovered that Jahandar Shah had been received by Hastings and the nawab-wazir with considerable pomp, all of which had been noted down by the spies for the information of their various masters at the courts of India. Hastings had seen the prince every day, and had asked the artist, Zoffany, then in Lucknow, to paint the prince's portrait. But he was not prepared to make any promises other than of protection and asylum if the prince chose to remain in Lucknow. On the whole, Hastings preferred that the prince should return to Delhi, for it seemed unlikely that he would cause anything but problems if he remained with the British. Browne was instructed to arrange for the emperor's forgiveness. To ensure the prince's safety, the British were prepared to provide him with an escort. They also requested from the emperor a guarantee of safety and security of office for Afrasiyab Khan.

When the terms were put to Afrasiyab Khan he accepted them without comment, but Shah Alam refused. Mahadaji Sindia now returned to the centre of the stage. His envoy in Lucknow suggested to Hastings that his master would be the best person to restore the prince to imperial favour and protect him once he was back in Delhi. Hastings accepted the proposition, but it did not appeal to Browne or to Afrasiyab, who had left Delhi with the emperor in June on the way to Agra, where he hoped to meet Sindia. Afrasiyab felt himself menaced by the recent reappearance of Muhammad Beg and was anxious for Sindia's aid in disposing of him. Muhammad Beg—who had received none of the promised money from Afrasiyab—now learned from his spies that he was to be attacked. His response was to invade imperial territory and plunder loyal chiefs. Afrasiyab appealed to Sindia to come as soon as possible.

The time, unfortunately, was during the rains and Sindia's progress was impeded by serious floods. His camp was flooded on more than one occasion and his astrologers, who had advised him not to move in the first place as the stars were unfavourable, urged him to go back before matters became even worse. As his wife was about to give birth to a child in the retaken fortress of Gwalior, Sindia decided to accept the advice of the stars and the inclination of his own heart. He did, however, send his deputy, with a large escort, forward to Agra to wait on the emperor. It was not until the last week in September that Sindia set out again, driving Muhammad Beg's men before him.

Afrasiyab himself moved out of Agra to join Sindia in an attack on Muhammad Beg. The latter appealed to Sindia to remain neutral while he destroyed 'that slave-child', Afrasiyab, offering as a bribe to hand over the fort at Agra. Sindia was not interested. Agra was merely a city, and he was playing for an empire. His way lay through friendship with Afrasiyab, who could never be a challenger. The two met on 23 October and again the following day. On Afrasiyab's visit to Sindia's camp a few days later, the terms of their alliance were agreed. Muhammad Beg's camp would be blockaded by Maratha troops and Muhammad Beg starved into submission.

The two leaders now moved on Muhammad Beg's position. Afrasiyab made his camp and then set out to reconnoitre the terrain with his principal captains, who included Shafi's brother, Zain. It was 2 November, and Afrasiyab fixed on the following day for the attack. Returning to his camp, he went to the tent of his principal adviser and spent an hour playing chess and talking about the victory that would certainly be his on the following day. At 11 a.m. he went to his own tent to take his midday meal, accompanied by his officers and Zain. Taking off his turban and coat, he called for his food. One of Zain's retainers went forward while Afrasiyab waited, and presented a petition. As Afrasiyab was reading it, the man stabbed him in the chest. Blood streaming from the wound, the commander staggered to his feet, took a few steps, and then collapsed. The murderer was cut down by Afrasiyab's servants, and Zain slipped away from the tent, unnoticed in the confusion.

Zain rode immediately to Sindia's camp. The Maratha leader was asleep when he arrived, and Zain gasped out to Sindia's retainers the story of Afrasiyab's murder, claiming that he had himself fled because he would certainly be suspected of having inspired it. Sindia refused to see him, and he was put under arrest until there was further information about what had happened. For some time there was very little. Afrasiyab's lieutenants put out the news that he was not dead at all, but merely wounded. At about three o'clock in the afternoon, Sindia and a few of his closest advisers rode over to Afrasiyab's camp to find out the truth for themselves. The general was dead, and Sindia immediately returned to his own camp.

There he examined his position. It was not altogether free from danger. With the imperial commander-in-chief dead, his troops might well decide to join forces with their co-religionist, Muhammad Beg, against the Hindu, Sindia. In the confusion, Muhammad Beg might even decide to mount an attack. As it happened, Muhammad Beg did not do so as he did not discover what had taken place at Afrasiyab's camp until it was too late to take advantage of it. Meanwhile Sindia had moved quickly against him. An appeal for a truce was pushed aside. Muhammad Beg would be allowed to leave if he surrendered his artillery and his transport animals. He refused. He was prepared, he said, to give up some of his guns, but not all. If Sindia wanted them he must take them by force.

While these manoeuvrings were going on, Muhammad Beg's agents had infiltrated into the imperial forces and were trying to persuade Afrasiyab's men to desert. There was even a plan to rescue Zain from Sindia's camp and make him the new commander-in-chief. But all came to nothing in the end. Sindia attacked Muhammad Beg's position, and he— weakened by the blockade of his camp, deserted by his own men when the attack started—was forced to surrender. He was treated with respect but stripped of his power, and his family were sent as hostages to one of Sindia's towns.

The news of Afrasiyab's death reached Agra on the following day. Now, the emperor had no one to turn to. Of the four heirs of Najaf Khan, two had since died by violence. The most competent of the four, Muhammad Beg, was a rebel. Najaf Kuli, who nominally commanded at Delhi, seldom moved out of his harem. Of all the great officers of state there only remained Abdul Ahad, now a captive in the fort of Alighur.

Ever distrustful of Sindia, the British envoy, Major Browne, tried to push the anti-Maratha faction at court into advising the emperor to salvage Abdul Ahad. Such a course inevitably appealed to the emperor, who had never lost his maudlin affection for the man who had caused the throne such endless trouble by his unsuccessful intrigues. An order was sent to the commander of the Alighur fort instructing him to despatch Abdul Ahad to the imperial camp. When Abdul Ahad reached Agra however, the commander there—without consulting Shah Alam—re-arrested him and confined him in the fort.

The emperor's response was the only possible one. He could not call for British help, however much Browne might have wished to provide it, and he therefore placed himself under Sindia's protection. Early in November, two imperial envoys arrived in Sindia's camp with letters from the emperor and robes of honour. Sindia sent them back with a message inviting Shah Alam to move to the deserted Mughal city of Fathpur Sikri, near Agra. Transport elephants and camels were sent for the imperial baggage, as well as an escort of 5,000 cavalry.

The meeting place was to be Afrasiyab's old camping ground, which the emperor reached on 12 November. Two days later was fixed as an auspicious time for the actual confrontation. The emperor's favourite son, Akbar Shah, welcomed Sindia, who then proceeded to the imperial presence. When he arrived there, he made a ceremonial presentation of 101 gold coins and placed his head, as an act of symbolic submission, between the emperor's feet. Shah Alam assisted the lame Sindia to rise, and invited him to seat himself. The meeting was entirely formal, an exchange of flowery courtesies hiding the harsh realities. But Sindia *did* listen to the emperor's request for protection. Next day, both the Maratha and the imperial forces lined the route as the emperor, mounted on an elephant and surrounded by his guards, made his way to Sindia's camp.

At a secret meeting three days later the emperor begged Sindia to take over the affairs of the empire. It seemed that, from every point of view, the coup could be a swift one. The imperial forces were without a commander and still without pay. Around Sindia's camp there were thirty thousand men in a state of confusion, angry about their present and worried about their future, for without their pay they found it difficult to acquire food. If discipline were to break completely, there would be chaos. There was also the danger of intrigue; everybody with an interest in the matter was conspiring to have his own nominee appointed to supreme authority. One group favoured the emperor's awarding the office of commander-in-chief to Afrasiyab's three-year-old son. This group planned to bribe the emperor with over a million rupees in cash, and the attempt was made to buy Sindia's ministers' support of the claim. To prevent the movement of agents, Sindia posted his own men around the emperor's camp. No one was allowed in or out without permission.

The central problem of the empire—or what remained of it—was money. The emperor demanded money for the maintenance of the palace and its inhabitants. The army demanded money so that it could eat. The state, lacking the economic foundations for its administration, was in complete disorder. If Sindia were to take on the empire, then the first thing he had to do was put it, at least temporarily, out of its financial misery. There was only one source which, despite the twists and turns of imperial financing, had always managed to remain virtually unsqueezed—the ever-defaulting raja of Jaipur. After much discussion, Sindia decided to move against this, the richest of the nominal vassals of the empire.

His armies made their way slowly towards Jaipur, stopping only at Pingora for an important ceremony. On 1 December 1784 the Peshwa, Sindia's nominal overlord, was appointed regent of the empire with Mahadaji Sindia as his deputy. Everyone knew, of course, that the real power lay with Sindia rather than with the young boy many miles away at Poona. But the appointment put an end to the dreams of all the conspirators, including Major Browne who, to the very last, clung to his belief that the British should have taken up the emperor's cause.

9
The nominal slave

THE APPOINTMENT of Mahadaji Sindia to the highest
office in the empire—even though he appeared only as the
deputy—had a certain irony. In the seventeenth century the
Marathas had been the symbol and the actuality of Hindu
opposition to the Muslim empire of the Mughals. Their
aim had been to replace the Mughals with an empire of their
own. That pretension had been destroyed at Panipat in 1761,
and the Maratha confederacy itself fell to pieces, its parts
ever in conflict. Now the most powerful of the Maratha
leaders had made himself the protector of the empire his
ancestors had once vowed to destroy. Like all those before
him, of course, he pretended not to have seized control of
the state but to be no more than the emperor's servant. But,
as an Englishman who was later to help crush the Marathas
once and for all remarked, he was 'the nominal slave but the
rigid master'.

At the time of his success, Sindia was nearly fifty years
old. His family had first made a small mark on history when
one of its members had been named guardian of the Peshwa's
slippers—which sounds menial enough but was at least a
court office, with the promise of being converted into a
position of influence. The first holder of this office did so
well that he achieved a place in his master's bodyguard, a
position of real trust in the fateful courts of India. He left
four sons, three legitimate, and Mahadaji who was not.
Providence and war removed the other three and almost
destroyed Mahadaji.

At Panipat, Mahadaji was pursued by an Afghan trooper
who persisted in following him even though Mahadaji had a
fine mare and the trooper a rather slow one. Whenever

Mahadaji stopped to rest, the trooper appeared on the horizon. Finally, Mahadaji's horse threw him, the trooper attacked him with a battle-axe, severely wounding him below the knee and leaving him lame for life, stripped him of his possessions and left him to die. But another fugitive, a Muslim water-carrier named Rana Khan, found Mahadaji and, placing him on his bullock, carried him to safety. Mahadaji rewarded him and treated him as his brother. The water-carrier rose to be a general in Sindia's army.

Sindia's injury prevented him from taking exercise and he had become very fat. His complexion was unusually dark for a Maratha. His tastes were simple but, unlike many of his contemporaries, he could both read and write. While he was perfectly capable of being cruel to those who injured him, he was an indulgent master. Most people who met him and recorded the experience found him amiable and intelligent. His almost active dislike of luxury included an impatience with ceremony, though he was fully conscious of the purpose and even the advantages of the intricate protocol of Indian courts. Sindia, too, was well aware that his new position, for all its high-sounding titles, was little more than ceremonial. The extent of the empire he controlled ended at the perimeter of his camp.

Sindia had hoped that, on the emperor's order, the governors of Delhi and Agra would hasten to make their submissions to the new regent, so he waited before embarking on the move against Jaipur. By the end of the year—still waiting—his debts exceeded eight million rupees and his running costs were ruinously high. His own army cost 700,000 rupees a month to maintain, and the imperial forces another 300,000. The maintenance of the emperor and his camp cost another 130,000 rupees a month. And there was nothing coming in. It was absolutely necessary before moving on Jaipur to impose his authority on the officers of the empire and to ensure that revenues now diverted to their use would go to him.

Rumour had it that Afrasiyab Khan had salted away in his fortress at Alighur treasure to the value of ten million rupees. His partisans still held that fort as well as a number of others. The fort at Dig was easily taken by the simple expedient of giving the garrison its arrears of pay, and Agra fell in the same manner. Aligurh was a different proposition. From Agra, the holders of the fort were ordered to give it up to the imperial representative. The defenders, commanded by Afrasiyab's brother, Jahangir Khan, gave the impression they were prepared to do so, but secretly devoted themselves to preparing their defences and searching for allies. Jahangir Khan had received messages from some of the Mughal officers in Sindia's train encouraging him to hold out, presumably in the hope of making things as difficult as possible for Sindia. What the officers hoped to gain from this is not clear. Intrigue and conspiracy were so much a part of life that many men found themselves at a loss without them. For Jahangir there was every excuse. He did not believe in Sindia's protestations of friendship.

Among the parties whom Jahangir appealed to for help were the British and the nawab-wazir of Oudh. There was a brigade of British troops stationed on the Oudh border, and Jahangir sent a message to its commander, Sir John Cumming, asking for assistance. To the nawab-wazir he pointed out that, if the Marathas took the fort of Alighur (which stood on the frontiers of Oudh), it would make a good assembly point for invasion. He offered half the treasure in the fort in return for aid. Cumming, without referring to Calcutta, moved his force to within a few miles of Aligurh and even allowed Jahangir to visit him. When news of this reached Sindia, he protested to the British agent at his court over what he interpreted as an unfriendly act. The protest, sent on to the governor-general, resulted in a reprimand for Cumming and the recall of his force.

Sindia continued to try and bring pressure on Jahangir to surrender the fort without a fight, but all his efforts failed. As soon as Cumming had withdrawn, Sindia sent a troop of cavalry to attack the fort. By the time they arrived, the hot weather was at its height, many of the wells around the fort had dried up, and there was a shortage of water.

That other enemy, cholera, broke out among the troops and there were soon signs of mutiny; Sindia was now also suffering from the customary lack of ready cash to pay them.

Knowing something of the commander's troubles, Jahangir decided to make an attack on the Maratha camp, which was near the town of Koel, a short distance from the fort. The attack was only just repulsed, but the defeat was enough to discourage the garrison in Koel, which fled to the fort. The Maratha commander now began to invest the fort itself by digging trenches around it. But the rainy season was just beginning and the besiegers soon found themselves cut off from Sindia as the river Jumna rose behind them. The siege dragged on. Every day of defiance reduced Sindia's prestige.

As soon as the rains were over, Sindia called the emperor from Delhi and together they made for Aligarh, in the hope that the presence of the emperor in Sindia's camp would convince Jahangir that he ought to surrender. Though shortage of supplies may have been a more persuasive factor than the presence of the emperor, Jahangir opened negotiations and agreed to vacate the fort. Inside, Sindia's men found only 40,000 rupees in cash and jewels. When asked what had happened to the great fortune Afrasiyab was known to have sent to Aligarh, Jahangir disclaimed all knowledge of it. Sindia heard, however, that Jahangir had been sending valuables out of the fort to safe keeping in Oudh, and had him arrested. Afrasiyab Khan's widows were taken to Sindia's camp and searched. A few jewels were found but it was obvious that the great bulk of Afrasiyab's fortune had been sent off out of Sindia's reach.

So far, though Sindia was managing to impose his authority, he was not gaining very much from it. He had had to detach a force to protect the imperial capital, yet again menaced by the Sikhs. As well as Jahangir, there were other rebels and recalcitrant landholders, and these occupied Sindia's forces for a great part of the year 1785. For most of the time the emperor remained at Delhi. Major Browne, who had been following him around while still trying to persuade his masters in Calcutta that they should support the emperor and place no trust in Sindia, found himself recalled. Hastings had gone home to England and the acting governor-general, John Macpherson, saw no purpose in keeping Browne at Delhi. Calcutta did not share Browne's intense and almost hysterical hatred of Sindia, and his attempts to create an anti-Maratha faction seemed likely to result in nothing but trouble.

Macpherson's letter to Browne contained a postscript. If Shah Alam offered him a title, it said, he was not to accept one which gave the impression that the governor-general was a servant of the emperor. The British dominions were sovereign and though, in theory, they were held on a grant from the emperor, in practice everyone knew that this was not so. Any title which implied that Shah Alam had any jurisdiction over British possessions was to be resisted, though Macpherson admitted that the emperor's title 'of King of the World certainly leaves me no retreat from the range of his imperial sovereignty'. Browne did not receive Macpherson's humour very well. He felt that he had been badly treated and so, too, did Shah Alam, for Browne was not to be replaced. James Anderson, the British agent at Sindia's court, was also to act as envoy to the emperor.

When Browne had an audience with Shah Alam to ask for permission to leave, he reported that the emperor protested that there were British agents with many Indian princes who were, in name anyway, still his subjects, while he was going to have to share an envoy with his own chief minister. 'Do not they [the British] perceive', he said, 'that this is declaring to the whole world that they have less respect for me than they do for my own servant?' There was also the question as to where, if the emperor were in Delhi and Sindia somewhere else, the agent would reside.

Browne's final interview with both the emperor and Sindia was not particularly friendly. Indeed—though it seems only to have been imaginary—Browne sensed a real threat in Sindia's manner. The emperor asked why the British had not sent the prince Jahander Shah back to

Delhi. The nawab-wazir of Oudh, he said, in whose territories the prince still lurked, took no notice of imperial
requests. Shah Alam was full of contempt for the nawab.
'Such is the wazir's character', he said, 'that even though he
is past the age of forty he spends his days and nights in
flying kites, watching cock fights, and roaming through the
bazaars of Lucknow'. Sindia agreed and suggested that
perhaps the prince was following the wazir's example. Then
he unexpectedly made a demand that the British should pay
their tribute, now many years in default, to the emperor.
Browne made no reply.

It is unlikely that Sindia expected a reply, but money was
always uppermost in the emperor's mind and a gentle
reminder that the British still owed tribute to the state
seemed a useful note on which to end Browne's mission.
Though Sindia had trusted Hastings just as Hastings had
trusted him, he did not feel the same about the new governor-
general. In the shifting policies of Indian rulers—and the
British were just as much a country power as Sindia himself
—there was always the possibility of a complete reversal. It
was therefore good policy to remind the emperor that the
British did not pay their debts either.

The new year of 1786 found Sindia still in very much the
same financial position as he had been the day he became
regent. There had been a great deal of military expenditure
and virtually no profit. Jaipur could wait no longer.

Taking the emperor with him—a safety precaution in the
still unsettled times, as well as a symbol of authority—
Sindia marched out in the direction of the Rajputana. He
hoped negotiations would result, and the approach of the
imperial forces did in fact produce them. The Jaipur envoys
included a Hindu priest who had some reputation as a holy
man and had once been spiritual adviser to the late raja.
Sindia, who was of low caste, greeted him by prostrating
himself and kissing the holy man's feet, but this extrava-
gance did not affect the hard bargaining when discussions
started in earnest. An agreement was finally reached on how
much was to be paid and, by the end of May 1786, the sum

of over one million rupees had actually been handed over. After this, both Sindia and the emperor left, the former for Mathura and the latter for Delhi, leaving a force behind to collect the next instalment.

This success had little lasting value. The million rupees disappeared into the always dry sand of the Mughal economy. The emperor was soon in financial distress again and sending envoys to Sindia demanding money. There was still no organized revenue and it seemed unlikely that there ever would be since fifteen years of anarchy and three of drought had ruined the countryside. The empire was bank-rupt and there seemed to be no way of putting it on its feet again. Constant and unremitting squeeze of reluctant rulers was the only expedient, and even that needed money before it could be exercised. Sindia's time was spent in small campaigns which cost more than they made. Even satis-factory expeditions such as that against Jaipur provided only the most temporary relief.

As soon as Sindia had departed, the two men he had left behind to ensure regular payment of the tribute proved to be lukewarm in his cause. One was Najaf Kuli Khan, as indolent as ever. The other was the raja of Macheri, who had his own ambitions—which did not coincide with Sindia's interests. The only man Sindia could really trust was one of his commanders who had been left behind with a force of 5,000 men. But these were not enough to enforce payment by Jaipur without the support of the other two leaders. At first, they all co-operated and had some success against vassals of Jaipur, but by the middle of 1787 it was clear to Sindia that only a really large army could overawe Jaipur and ensure payment of the tribute. Sindia also had an insult to avenge, for a suggested marriage between his daughter and the young raja had been rejected on the grounds that the high-caste Jaipur family could not allow itself to be polluted by the low-caste blood of the house of Sindia.

Sindia, however, remained reluctant to embark on a major campaign against Jaipur. The country north of Delhi was under continual threat from the Sikhs and the emperor was fearful for his own safety. If Sindia moved most of his forces to the south, he believed that a defenceless Delhi might be attacked by the British, who were ominously massing troops on the Oudh frontier. Sindia did not take the second threat too seriously, but he was concerned over the Sikhs. While preparing to attack Jaipur, he sent a force to deal with them.

Leaving Dig in the middle of March 1787, Sindia moved rapidly to a place some thirty miles east of Jaipur city. A few miles south of the city was the force that had been left behind to assist in collecting the tribute. As always, there was time for negotiation. Some of Sindia's principal advisers wanted him to accept a moderate amount of tribute so that he could avoid a hot-weather campaign in unfriendly territory, but the raja of Macheri managed to persuade him that, as he was now at the gates of Jaipur, it would do his prestige and dignity no good if he went off with only the same amount as had been promised to his subordinates. In effect, the raja enquired why Sindia had bothered to come at all if he had no intention of making an example of the Jaipur raja. In the disturbed condition of the empire, prestige was of the greatest importance; in any case, suggested the raja, Jaipur would probably give in without a fight now that Sindia had arrived.

Sindia hesitated, and his hesitation was exploited by those who hoped to place their own nominees on the throne of Jaipur. At last, exasperated by Jaipur's behaviour over the promised tribute, he decided to 'expel the defenders of the Jaipur capital and seize the city himself'. Negotiation—that war by subtler means—continued. The Jaipur envoys made an offer which they had no intention of fulfilling, as they were playing for time until allies arrived. On 7 April, the envoys left without taking formal leave of Sindia. At this, he moved his force to about thirteen miles from the city and brought up his other troops until they were outside the gates. Even this show of force had no effect. There was no alternative but to fight.

Unfortunately, Sindia had lost his numerical superiority. The Jaipur raja's vassals had assembled an army of some 20,000 men. The raja of Jodhpur had sent a contingent of 5,000 horse, and a mercenary force of the same number of infantry had been hired. The Jaipur forces now felt themselves strong enough to emerge from the fortified city and take up a position which would lock up Sindia's army between themselves and the capital. Seeing this manoeuvre, Sindia withdrew. Though he claimed that he did so only in order to draw the Jaipur forces away from their base and into a trap, it was obvious to all that he had been forced to retreat. This emboldened the defenders and a perpetual guerrilla war began against Sindia's columns. Nevertheless, Sindia kept moving, taking some of the smaller forts on his way. But he was losing parts of his army every day by desertion. Jaipur agents were hard at work suborning both men and officers from the imperial army and, though the numbers who deserted were not large, the steady stream of defections helped to undermine the morale of those who remained.

But worse was to come. Muhammad Beg, who had been given a command by Sindia because of his undoubted military talents, was bought by Jaipur. He and his nephew Ismail, with their contingents, left Sindia's army on 25 May. This was a major disaster. The Jaipur raja gave command of the defences of the capital to Muhammad Beg, and the knowledge that this formidable general was now on the other side sapped the courage of Sindia's own troops. It now became impossible to trust the imperial forces. Sindia could still retreat, but that would inevitably have led to the collapse of all that he had gained or hoped to gain. Urgent messages were sent to his other commanders in the north to come and reinforce him, and the emperor was asked to join him so that Sindia could have the prestige of his name and person. In the meantime he fell back. As he did so, the Jaipur army followed in the hope of encircling him and cutting him off from further retreat.

Sindia decided on a sudden offensive action against the

city of Jaipur, which was now, according to report, denuded
of troops. The problem was to avoid a battle on the way.
Though he still had imperial troops marching with him, they
had to be watched, and his own men believed that if it came
to an engagement they would immediately desert to the
other side. Sindia could do nothing until his reinforcements
arrived except move slowly and carefully towards Jaipur.
This he did until he came to the town of Lalsot, where a
Jaipur force threatened to cut his communications. Sindia
therefore made camp some miles south of the town, on
15 June.

A Maratha force under Ambaji Inglia was on its way
from the north but was finding the going difficult because
of the start of the rains. It did not arrive at Sindia's camp
until the middle of July. The second force, under Apa
Khande Rao, appeared at the end of June. In the meantime,
Sindia's position was less than comfortable. The countryside
was scarred by deep ravines, ideal for ambushes.

The Jaipur forces, however, were in little better state.
Their spies had reported that Apa Khande's force included
two battalions of disciplined infantry trained on European
lines by Benoit de Boigne, who was now in Sindia's employ.
There was also artillery commanded by Europeans. The
Jaipur forces had no such infantry and their artillery was
small in number and inefficient in handling. Their only
advantage was the character of the Jaipur cavalry, famous for
its courage and dash. The Jaipur generals decided that they
must choose a day for battle when rain would damp the
gunpowder of the opposing guns and make it difficult for
the infantry to operate. The very opposite was essential for
Sindia if he was to gain the victory.

On 23 June, with news that Apa Khande's force was near,
Sindia took the offensive. The vanguard moved off and kept
its distance two miles ahead of the second column which,
in turn, held place some three or four miles in front of the
main army of 7,000 men and ten guns, commanded by
Sindia in person. Next day there was a halt, and the commander of the second column, Rana Khan, went to Sindia's

camp. There, after prayers and prostrations before the family images, Sindia called him to his tent. The commander took a ritual bath and put on a fresh robe. Sindia smeared a mark of ash on Rana Khan's forehead and placed his own shield on his arm and his own sword in his hand. The one-time water-carrier, Rana Khan, now appointed supreme commander, then left to join his men. Next day he occupied the Lalsot pass. On 26 June Apa Khande rode into Sindia's camp and he and his men were sent up to join Rana Khan. As the supreme commander moved forward, Sindia followed, occupying his vacated position.

These movements brought Sindia's army to the place of battle. For some reason this has gone down in the history books as the battle of Lalsot, but the site was more than fourteen miles away. The whole terrain was particularly difficult, being surrounded on three sides by ranges of hills cut with deep ravines. The fourth side, to the south, was comparatively open. Sindia's forces, however, were not moving in this direction, but through the northern passes which gave on to level country and then, by way of two narrow ravines, to a wide plain. Sindia's forces proceeded without opposition. To the north lay the main Jaipur army.

There was no action for nearly a month. Sindia was waiting for Ambaji Inglia's arrival and still had hopes that he might be able to drive a wedge between the allies in the Jaipur army. Each move was taken with great caution. Rana Khan would go forward with his artillery while Sindia moved up behind him. The Jaipur raja, who was with his troops, was equally cautious, but his allies—the horsemen of the raja of Jodhpur, and the renegade Muhammad Beg—were not. Between them they persuaded the raja to send a challenge to Sindia to come out and fight. Both sides were waiting for reinforcements, Sindia for Ambaji, Jaipur for a contingent of musketeers from Sind, whom his advisers believed to be the equal of the European-trained infantry of de Boigne.

Inevitably, with two large armies so close together,

contacts were made. Skirmishes took place in which the participants were usually the Marathas, Muhammad Beg's contingent, and the Jodhpur horsemen. Sindia was suffering from a blockade of his supplies and was also unable to pay his men. His horses and elephants were dying for lack of fodder.

Sindia's camp was plunged into mourning at the death of his daughter, who, with his family, had accompanied him on the campaign, but the mourning was brought to an abrupt end when a letter from the Jaipur raja arrived. 'You are the Regent of the Empire', it said, 'and greatly experienced in war. If you dare, come out from behind the shelter of your guns and fight . . . We shall see then to whom God gives the victory'.

The battle began on 26 July with a cannonade. Muhammad Beg, directing his men from the back of an elephant, was killed when a cannonball, bounding off a tree, struck him in the body. His nephew Ismail took over the command. The Jodhpur cavalry concentrated on dealing with Sindia's infantry. These wild horsemen, inflamed with opium, had the reputation of being all-conquering. Now they took the last pulls at their pipes and mounted their horses. The watery sun gleamed on their plumed helmets and chain-mail cuirasses. Pennants flying from the ends of their lances, they formed and charged.

Sindia's infantry was in hollow square formation with the guns in the centre. As the cavalry approached, shouting 'Death! Death!', the front rank fell back and the guns opened up, hurling grapeshot into the waves of horsemen. But, though its lines were ripped apart, the cavalry kept on and managed to break through to the guns. Re-forming, the infantry opened fire again and again but were compelled to give way.

The initial advantage of the cavalry charge was not followed up. Jaipur had no infantry willing to face Sindia's men and the Jodhpur horse were too ravaged to press on convincingly. Muhammad Beg's men were so disheartened by their chief's death that they gave up fighting.

Sindia's imperial forces did not desert. The Maratha line held, and he decided to advance, but in the afternoon it began to rain and darkness came early. Each side fell back on its camp. The first round was over, and there was to be no second on that battlefield. Sindia's men were clamouring for pay and he had none to give them. Soon they began deserting to the other side. To attempt another attack would have been madness. Many of Sindia's troops stood by him only because of their European commanders. There was no saying how long these commanders could hold their men, especially as supplies were short; Sindia had moved the mass of his army with him, leaving not enough men to ensure the safety of the supply columns, of which few succeeded in getting through. The situation was so serious that all his generals advised a retreat, and the long line of the Maratha army began slowly to move back the way it had come. Rana Khan took the rearguard, and Sindia was in the middle with the main force, the baggage, and the families of the leaders. By making long marches, Sindia reached safety after a terrible journey of seven days on 9 August.

It had been a journey of constant alarms. At one place a powder chest exploded and nearly set off a battle between the imperial troops and the Marathas, who were convinced that they had opened fire on them. Rumour did its work. It was said that there had been another battle and that Sindia himself was dead. Men began to loot the baggage. When Sindia arrived on the scene the looting stopped, but a great deal of property had disappeared and many tents had been burned. Sindia ordered each man to load his supplies on to the camels carrying the swivel guns. With order restored, the columns moved on as rapidly as they could, pursued at a respectable distance by the Jaipur army. The rearguard, under Rana Khan, kept strict discipline, with its guns and muskets ready and primed for action. The main Jaipur force soon gave up the pursuit, for it too had been heavily mauled in the fighting. Ismail continued to harass the rear-guard but was always driven off. Finally he too gave up, and Sindia reached the safety of the fortress at Dig.

It was a sad return for the man who had held the empire in his hand. Now, in the darkness of his failures, he found himself surrounded by a world of enemies.

10

A world of enemies

BEFORE Sindia reached the fortress of Dig, his wife and family were sent off with the families of the other Maratha leaders to the safety of Sindia's great stronghold at Gwalior, under the escort of Apa Khande. Camp followers and other non-combatants were told to find their bread elsewhere, as Sindia had none to give them. He would be glad, too, to be rid of the soldiers of the imperial army who had caused him so much anxiety during the Jaipur campaign. After not having been paid for nearly a year, they were offered a small subsistence allowance and told that they would not receive the rest of the money due to them until there had been a successful campaign against Jaipur! Under the circumstances, it was hardly surprising that their commanders should have accepted grants of land instead. The only proviso attached to these grants was that the commanders should go and take the land themselves from the men who had usurped it. When it became obvious that Sindia genuinely had no money, and as the price of food steadily rose, most of the imperial troops left him.

There remained the question of Sindia's own men who, he now believed, were tired of their long stay in the north, away from their homeland. Reinforcements of fresh men were what he needed, men in whom the old Maratha fire had not been quenched by tiresome campaigns and treacherous allies. Sindia appealed to his nominal master, the Peshwa. For a while, the Peshwa seemed prepared to aid his deputy, but was at length persuaded not to by his minister, Nana Farnavis. The Nana pointed out that Sindia was of low caste and that no high-caste general would be prepared to serve under his orders, but his real reason was that he hoped

Sindia would wear himself out in an attempt to retrieve his
position in northern India and thus be no threat to the
minister's plans for his master.

Sindia also appealed to the British, his allies by the treaty
of Salbai. But from them, too, he received only the coldest
of responses. They intended, he was told, to remain neutral
and had no desire to interfere in the affairs of the Indian
states. Sindia's agents, however, did manage to raise a
number of men, and the two battalions commanded by de
Boigne remained loyal. The contingent commanded by
another mercenary, the Frenchman Lesteneau, also remained, though not for long. Lack of money slowed down
Sindia's recovery. His agents were out trying to raise
revenue and his bankers trying to raise loans, and money
did begin to come in, in time. But by then Sindia's enemies
had been busy.

The most important of these were Ismail Beg, who had
considerable support from the old Mughal nobility in the
capital, and Ghulam Kadir Khan, the son of Zabita Khan
(who had died in 1785) and grandson of the great Najib
Khan. Among the others who could be temporarily dis-
counted was Najaf Kuli Khan, who had departed to carve
out a state for himself. Sindia did not regard him as an
active enough enemy to cause him great concern. Najaf
Kuli did injure Sindia's ally, the raja of Macheri, however,
for it was out of his territory that Najaf Kuli constructed his
new principality. The Jaipur raja was content to leave the
Marathas alone if they did not trouble him for the remainder
of the tribute, and Sindia was therefore able to ignore him
for the time being. The raja of Macheri could not follow
Sindia's line; he had seized some Jaipur territory and the
Jaipur raja attacked him in order to win it back. Sindia was
unable to aid his ally, and the raja of Macheri was forced to
suffer alone.

Ismail Beg had soon become dissatisfied with his treatment in Jaipur. He had hoped to acquire lands for himself
but, while the Jaipur raja preferred to remain inside his own
state boundaries, there seemed unlikely to be any oppor-

tunities for this kind of enterprise. The cost of the campaign had, too, drained the Jaipur treasury and there was no money to pay Ismail. He decided to take advantage of Sindia's difficulties and attack the imperial forts. His first objective was the city of Agra.

Inside the fort there, Sindia's governor had a strong force as well as artillery. It was probable, however, that he could be starved out. All Sindia could spare to intercept Ismail was a party of light horse, without either infantry or guns. Ismail brushed it aside. Nevertheless, the small force continued to shadow Ismail up to the gates of Agra, harassing him as much as possible while keeping out of range of his guns. Arrived outside the city, Ismail had to meet an attack by the governor on his front while the Maratha horse attacked his rear. Unfortunately, the governor's force included Lesteneau's contingent which was so angry over its lack of pay that it turned its guns on its own side. This, not unnaturally, caused some confusion among the Marathas, which Ismail took advantage of. When he reached the city gate, discontented imperial troops opened it and let his men into the city, although the governor managed to regain the fort. With the characteristic aplomb of all mercenaries, Lesteneau took his men over to Ismail and accepted some grants of land instead of pay.

The fall of Agra city was a shattering blow to Sindia's prestige ; it was the Second City of the empire that had been lost. The imperial capital itself might be next to go. It was very little consolation that the fort was still holding out, as there was nothing Sindia could do. He had barely 15,000 men, mostly light cavalry. His infantry now consisted of only 1,000 men of de Boigne's battalions. Indeed, he could not even answer the emperor's frantic appeals to come and settle Ghulam Kadir, who was in the neighbourhood of Delhi with a much more intimidating force than Sindia could muster.

The emperor's position was extremely precarious. He had sent out appeals for help not only to Sindia but to the nawab-wazir of Oudh and to the British. He had even contemplated leaving the capital secretly and making for Oudh. But, in the event, Shah Alam clung to his illusive sovereignty and his defenceless capital. Perhaps he felt that, if ever he left Delhi to put himself once again under the protection of the British, he would never return. Perhaps, too, his experience of recent years made him feel that he would survive all the troubles, that he would one day emerge free and triumphant. In the opinion of the spies near to him, he lacked courage to leave the tarnished comforts of his palace for the hardships of exile. There may have been some truth in this. But he was to make one attempt to save himself.

In August 1787, he had been approached by Ghulam Kadir who, with Sindia's difficulties in mind, had decided that he would like to receive the appointment which had once been held by his father and, before that, by his grandfather. Sindia's representatives at court had tried to convince the emperor that Sindia was by no means crushed, and that he would certainly respond to the emperor's pleas in due time. But there was a faction at court—headed by the superintendent of the harem—who wanted to dispose of Hindu dominance at the Mughal court and believed that Ghulam Kadir might be the best tool for achieving this end. The reputation of the Rohillas still survived, and Ghulam Kadir's grandfather had not been forgotten.

If, in the imperial capital, there had been one man of courage, the city might have been able to repel Ghulam Kadir. The river by now was so swollen by floods that it was difficult for Ghulam's army to cross. The city's defences could soon have been put in order. But there was no one to lead. Sindia's agents were men who had no quality of mind or of military expertise. When one of them tried with a small contingent to attack Ghulam Kadir's force, he was simply driven back into the river. This useless sortie was observed from the ramparts by the emperor himself and most of the population. Afterwards, Shah Alam sent one of his personal slaves to open up talks with Ghulam Kadir. Sindia's two agents fled from the city and, as they were leaving, their baggage was set on and plundered by some of their own troops.

Now, there was nothing to keep Ghulam Kadir out of Delhi. On 5 September, he entered the city and received from the trembling hands of the emperor his father's title, as well as robes of honour. The appointment was a gesture of expediency, no more. The emperor still hoped that someone would come to his aid. In the meantime, he felt able to rely on the French-led force belonging to the widow of the mercenary Walter Reinhardt, who called herself the Begum Sumru. She had kept on her late husband's troops, primarily in order to defend the lands which had been given to Reinhardt by Najaf Khan. In Delhi, the widow had four battalions of well-trained infantry and eighty-five guns. Having refused to take orders from Ghulam Kadir, the new commander-in-chief, she had, in alliance with a Sikh chief, manned the walls with the obvious intention of keeping Ghulam Kadir out. The new commander-in-chief withdrew. So, however, did the Begum, anxious to return to her own domains in case they should be subject to attack in her absence.

In the following month, Ghulam Kadir returned to Delhi and turned his guns on the palace. Again, the emperor sent out frantic appeals. One, to Sindia, was countermanded by the superintendent of the harem, who was still a partisan of Ghulam Kadir. Soon Ghulam was pardoned his attack on the palace and left the city to take possession of the lands which went with his new title and which were mainly held by followers of Sindia.

There was another element in the swiftly changing equation of power. The heir-apparent, Jahandar Shah—who had also been appealed to by his father—arrived at Delhi in the first week of December. Since he, however, appeared to be devoting his time to arranging a conspiracy designed to overthrow the emperor, he was soon despatched to be governor of Agra—a city currently in the hands of Ismail Beg. He found that he was not welcome there and decided, as a result, to try his luck with Ghulam Kadir. But his welcome there was cool, too, and it was only by chance that he escaped being kidnapped by some of Ghulam Kadir's agents. After these rebuffs, the prince departed hurriedly for British territory. The expedition had not been altogether profitless, however, as he returned with his favourite wife and family, whom he had been forced to leave behind in Delhi at the time of his flight in 1784. A few months after his return to the British fold the prince died from what an English contemporary described as 'a putrid fever, occasioned by exposing himself for some hours to a burning sun on a visit of devotion to the tomb of a celebrated Muhammadan saint'. He was buried with some ceremony, the British resident at Benares attending the occasion with an escort of British soldiers. The prince's family, whom he had recommended to the care of the British, was given a pension and settled down at Benares.

The almost farcical interlude of the prince's return to Delhi promoted one real disaster. On his way to visit his father, the prince had passed through Agra, and Sindia wrongly assumed that he had made a pact with Ismail Beg and that he would seize the throne for himself and appoint Ismail as commander-in-chief of the empire. Sindia decided that he must make an attempt to relieve his garrison in the Agra fort.

Gathering together his small force, Sindia arrived outside Agra on 16 December 1787, to be met by Ismail Beg who had come out to face him. Wildly outnumbered, both in men and guns, Sindia stood firm ; but though the Maratha horse made repeated charges they could do nothing against Ismail's lines, heavily defended as they were by artillery. Soon the Marathas were in full retreat, de Boigne's men forming a protective screen around Sindia. An attempt to fight back at Dholpur ended in a rout and Sindia was forced to cross the Chambal river back into his own territories. Ismail, having plundered Sindia's supplies and baggage, left a detachment to see that he did not re-cross the river and made his way back to Agra and the siege of the fort. The last trace of Maratha authority had now been swept away from Hindustan. There was only one small gain for Sindia. While Ismail had been occupied in fighting him, the fort's defenders had been able to replenish their stocks of food.

While Sindia's enemies were consolidating their own individual gains and Sindia himself was building up his forces for another try, Shah Alam finally decided to take the initiative himself. His excuse was an invitation from the Jaipur raja to join him and other Rajput vassals of the empire in reconquering the imperial possessions! Again, it was a bid for control of the emperor's person, that talisman of legitimacy so potent that, though its holder could be treated in the most appalling way, other rulers would never give up trying to take possession of it. The emperor accepted the invitation, believing that he might be able to acquire a large portion of the Jaipur tribute for himself. This was an illusion —as might have been expected.

The emperor moved out of Delhi on 4 January, accompanied by a body of imperial troops and the mercenary army of the Begum Sumru. In the middle of February, the camps of the emperor and the Jaipur raja were side by side, and the raja made his submission in person to the emperor. Shah Alam automatically demanded the outstanding tribute, and was told that the campaign against Sindia had so diminished the Jaipur treasury that there was very little left. The emperor's financial position was so strained that he accepted the paltry sum of 25,000 rupees as a parting gift from the raja, though it did not help much. The unpaid troops were deserting every day, and only the Begum Sumru stood firm. If the imperial army were not to disappear altogether, there would have to be action.

Near at hand was a suitable object for the emperor's attention—Najaf Kuli Khan. While creating a principality for himself he had antagonized the Jaipur raja, who had hoped to use the emperor's presence as a lever for forcing him into submission. But though Najaf Kuli was a man who enjoyed soft living, he was prepared to fight if the need arose. Not only did he have more troops than the emperor;

he was also well aware that the Jaipur raja, anxious to escape the financial importunities of Shah Alam, was moving his troops out of the area. In response to a demand from the emperor that he give up his conquests and put in an appearance at the imperial camp, Najaf Kuli not only refused but demanded, in turn, that—as he was an adopted son of the late regent, Najaf Khan—the same title should be conferred upon him.

The emperor had trenches dug around his own camp and then sent a contingent of imperial troops to attack Najaf Kuli. Wisely, however, he kept the Begum Sumru's troops beside him. Though there was a shortage of food in the imperial camp, there seems to have been an adequate supply of liquor and drugs; it was the custom of the imperial troops to spend their nights drinking. Najaf Kuli therefore mounted a night attack on the imperial camp, killing many of the officers and putting the rest of the contingent to a somewhat alcoholic flight. Some Sikh allies of Najaf Kuli almost reached the emperor's tent, and Shah Alam only saved himself by riding off to seek the protection of a square formed by the Begum Sumru's troops. A section of those troops, under the command of an Irish mercenary, George Thomas, managed to throw back the attackers, and the rest of the force—under the personal command of the Begum, who directed them from a palanquin—was able to retake the emperor's camp.

Both sides now requested the Begum to mediate on their behalf. Najaf Kuli realized that he could not win while her disciplined troops continued to protect the emperor, and the emperor was conscious that the Begum was not strong enough to crush Najaf Kuli by herself. A charade was arranged to cover the bargaining. On 19 March the Begum led Najaf Kuli into the emperor's presence, his wrists tied together with a piece of silk as if he were a captive. The emperor removed the silk, gave him a robe of honour as a symbol of pardon, and then conferred on Najaf Kuli the territories the latter had refused to surrender to their rightful owner! So this ludicrous affair ended, and the

emperor, accompanied by the Begum—now bearer of the
title of 'Most Beloved Daughter', returned to Delhi.

Ismail Beg was still at Agra, vainly trying to reduce the
fort. Ghulam Kadir was besieging the great fortress of
Alighur. Sindia, after gathering his forces and blooding
them in a campaign against his own rebellious tributaries,
was preparing to cross the Chambal river and take up the
fight once again.

Sindia's only major ally was now the Jat raja, whose house
had now been somewhat restored by Sindia's return of its
ancestral stronghold of Dig; Sindia had promised to help
revive its one-time glory, which had been lost after the death
of raja Suraj Mal. With Sindia's support, the present raja,
Ranjit Singh, had been building up his forces by recruiting
among the many deserters from the imperial army, as well
as from mercenaries who, in the confused state of the
times, could not find an employer. An alliance between
Ismail Beg and Ghulam Kadir drove a number of the
former's supporters into the Jat raja's camp, because they
had earlier been plundered and deprived of their lands by
Ghulam Kadir. The French mercenary, Lesteneau, also
took his two battalions and artillery over to what he believed
would once again be the winning side.

Fearing a revival of Jat power and apprehensive at the
daily desertions from his army, Ismail Beg came to an
agreement with Ghulam Kadir that they should divide the
Jat possessions up between them. When Ranjit Singh
heard of this, he called on Sindia to come and assist him.
Sindia at first sent only a small force across the Chambal,
and it was driven back again by an advance party of Ismail
Beg's. He then sent a larger force commanded by Rana
Khan. Moving rapidly, this force outflanked Ismail,
attacked the small garrison of besiegers left behind at Agra,
and inflicted a serious defeat. Ismail immediately turned
back on Agra, calling on Ghulam Kadir to join him, but the
Marathas left Agra and fell back on a place some miles
away.

When Ismail and Ghulam Kadir met, they exchanged

turbans as a sign of friendship and agreed on a plan of campaign. Leaving a body of men to continue the siege of Agra fort, they moved off to attack the main Jat stronghold at Bharatpur. Between them, the allies had an army of some 24,000 infantry, 12,000 horse, and 100 guns of various sizes. The combined Jat and Maratha forces amounted to roughly the same numbers.

The Maratha commander, unwilling to risk a direct engagement, devoted his energies to harassing the advancing army, but the Jats were caught in a direct confrontation on 19 April and forced to retreat on Bharatpur. There was now no possibility of avoiding a battle. When it took place, the casualties on both sides were so heavy that neither could take advantage of the situation. Ismail Beg and Ghulam Kadir removed themselves from the vicinity of Bharatpur and laid siege to some less well-defended forts instead, taking that at Kumbher on 3 May with large stores of ammunition, muskets, and swords.

The allies next turned towards Dig, where Ismail ordered his men to make a direct attack on the walls. An eyewitness reported that the scene was like the Day of Judgement. The attackers had no cover and were stretched out in line under the walls. Artillery and small-arms fire opened up, cutting great holes in the ranks. Led by Ismail in person, the assailants managed to reach the ditch surrounding the walls. There they met a hail of shot, rockets, balls filled with gunpowder, burning naphtha, even heavy lumps of wood studded with nails. The casualties were frightful, and the survivors fled. This catastrophe was compounded by the arrival of Rana Khan and a Jat force, which set upon Ismail's camp and chased his and Ghulam Kadir's men as far as Fathpur Sikri. Ismail stayed there a week and then returned to Agra.

In the meantime a Maratha force was plundering Ghulam Kadir's home lands in the hope of separating him from Ismail. The Maratha horse kept up a running fight with Ghulam Kadir's force, but the moment there was any attempt at a stand they vanished. Sindia and his ally were now strongly on the offensive. Leaving Agra and the main enemy armies to strictly guerrilla harassment, they concentrated on attacking their outposts. Very soon these tactics paid off. Ghulam Kadir could no longer tolerate the bad news of what was happening in his home lands and, despite appeals from Ismail Beg, set off with the bulk of his army to regain his possessions.

Ismail was now in a serious position. His communications were constantly being cut by Maratha guerrillas and very little food was getting in to Agra. Starving soldiers were deserting him in ever-increasing numbers. There was disease in his camp, and treachery, too. Both helped to undermine his position. He had no allies. There was little chance that Ghulam Kadir would return in time to help him against the combined force of Marathas and Jats that was reported to be on its way to Agra.

Sindia's armies arrived outside the city two days after Ghulam Kadir had left. Fast couriers had been despatched to the commanders of the Maratha detachments who were plundering his lands, instructing them to rejoin the main force. Sindia had managed to gather together enough money to make a small payment to his troops, and his agents had accepted an offer from one of Ismail's most powerful mercenaries to go over to Sindia's side. In Sindia's camp there was a feeling of victory in the air, that strange revival of spirits that sometimes comes upon a despairing army.

It was hardly the right time of year for a major battle. It was the height of the hot season, that terrible period just before the breaking of the rains when the sun burns implacably and the air is like the draught of a furnace, a time when men and animals seek shade, not battle. But necessity knows no leisure. The opposing armies drew up opposite each other on a large plain outside the city of Agra and waited. Ismail Beg had the river Jumna at his back, and it was even now slowly swelling as the snow melted in the far Himalayas. In the bright sun, the domes and minarets of the city showed no sign of decay. Behind the great red sandstone battlements of the fort, Sindia's governor watched anxiously through his English telescope to see what went on in the plain below.

Rana Khan had placed his European-led infantry in the centre of his line, with guns in front. At either end was a strong body of horse, and there was another in the rear. The line moved slowly forward towards Ismail's camp, guns firing, but because Sindia's guns had to stop for firing and reloading, Ismail's artillery caused more damage. When it became clear to Ismail that this was no common sortie, to be shrugged off with artillery fire, he did not wait to arrange plans with his commanders but personally led a cavalry charge against the approaching infantry. The infantry halted and opened heavy musket fire, while the two wings of Maratha cavalry moved inward and cut Ismail off from his rear. As hand-to-hand fighting developed, the third body of Sindia's cavalry moved round to attack Ismail's base camp, setting fire to his tents and blowing up his ammunition reserves. Ismail's position was hopeless. Though he tried to rally his men for what would have been a suicidal charge, his nephew grasped the bridle of his horse and dragged him away towards Agra. There Ismail and a few troopers crossed the river, Ismail carrying his favourite mistress on his own horse.

Others were less fortunate. Ismail's wife was drowned while fording the swollen river on an elephant, and many of his soldiers suffered the same end. His army had ceased to exist. But Ghulam Kadir's remained. When he had realized Sindia's strategy, Ghulam Kadir had returned towards Agra but had taken no part in the battle because he had been unable to get the bulk of his men across the river. Next morning, Sindia's artillery began to shell Ghulam Kadir's camp and his advance guard began to attempt a crossing of the river some distance above the camp. Ghulam Kadir withdrew, while Ismail Beg—having first made an effort to reach Oudh—doubled back and headed for Delhi. There he was refused entry by the emperor and returned to join Ghulam Kadir who was by then moving towards the city.

Sindia had won a splendid victory against his two most important enemies, but he had not crushed Ghulam Kadir. Nor was he able to go to the aid of the emperor and the imperial city. He was still surrounded by other enemies who might well destroy him if they decided to join forces. Sindia's only supporter remained the Jat raja, and it would take time before the waverers could decide whether the victory over Ismail Beg was the result of a revived Maratha spirit or merely of rashness on Ismail's part.

Shah Alam was anxious for Sindia to go to his aid, for he had lost the protection of the Begum Sumru who had taken her troops back to her own lands in order to discourage the many predators who would have taken advantage of her prolonged absence. But Sindia dared not go to Delhi with only a small force; his enemies there occupied positions of influence and would have disdained no expedient which might prevent him from resuming power over the emperor.

Whatever Sindia's inclinations might have been—and Shah Alam was now completely at the mercy of the super-intendent of the harem and his supporters, who were intriguing with Ghulam Kadir—he had to wait, consolidate his position at Agra, conciliate old enemies, and make new friends. He paused for two months. During that time, Shah Alam was struck the bitterest blow in a lifetime of bitterness, and the dreams he had left Allahabad to realize sixteen years before were shattered forever.

11
The scourge of God

GHULAM KADIR, accompanied by Ismail Beg, arrived on the outskirts of Delhi on 1 July and began plundering the surrounding countryside of whatever was to be found. The gates of the city had been closed on the instructions of Shah Alam, who still hoped that Sindia would come to his aid. Sindia did, in fact, send two agents to put the defences in order but they received no encouragement either from the emperor or from the superintendent of the harem, who was now active on Ghulam Kadir's behalf and even went so far as to have a supply of shot and gunpowder delivered to him from one of the imperial magazines.

The imperial forces, stiffened by the small body of Maratha soldiers which had escorted Sindia's envoys to the capital, ventured out of the city in an attempt to stop Ghulam Kadir's activities, but the imperial troops had been suborned in favour of Ghulam and went over to the enemy. As a result, during the night of 14 July, the Maratha commanders withdrew leaving the capital defenceless.

Four days later Ghulam Kadir entered the city. The fort itself could still have held out if there had not been a conspiracy in favour of the invader. The superintendent persuaded the emperor to grant an audience to Ghulam, who gave assurances of his loyalty and friendship. While the audience was in progress, Ghulam Kadir's men took possession of the fort.

Now began nine weeks of terror and nightmare. Ghulam Kadir had never forgotten that the emperor had allowed Zabita Khan, his father, to be persecuted and deprived of his office as regent. Now, he saw himself not only as an avenger, but as his father's successor. His hatred of Shah Alam was

198

equalled only by the religious fervour of his desire to rid the empire of the Hindu domination of Sindia. He saw visions of himself as the sword of his faith, and frequently referred to himself as 'the scourge of God'. First, he demanded money with which to begin his holy war against the unbelievers. The money was found somewhere, and the emperor's son Sulaiman was sent to Ghulam's camp as a hostage to the emperor's good faith. But the funds that had been produced were not enough ; and Ghulam was sure that the emperor had secret hoards hidden away in the palace.

In the meantime, Ghulam remembered his revenge. He was reminded partly by others who had waited a long time for theirs. When Ahmad Shah had been deposed, to be replaced by Shah Alam's father, Alamgir, the members of his branch of the imperial family had been kept in confinement as state prisoners. Forgetful, perhaps, of his own experiences in a similar situation, Shah Alam had made no attempt to mitigate the sufferings of those involved. To them, Ghulam Kadir appeared as a saviour who would release them from their misery into the light. Anxious to take revenge not only for their treatment but for the dispossession of their line from the imperial throne, they were quick to catch Ghulam's ear.

Most active among the conspirators, however, were not the prisoners in the fort but two old women who lived in comparative comfort in their own mansions. Both were widows of the emperor Muhammad Shah. They approached Ghulam Kadir with an offer of over 1,000,000 rupees if he would put their husband's grandson on the throne. The offer was accepted instantly. The widows did not make clear that the money was to be paid out of the imperial treasury after the new emperor's installation, nor did they seem to realize that Ghulam Kadir intended, whatever the situation, to take everything that could be found.

On 30 July, Ismail and Ghulam appeared at the gates of the palace and asked permission to visit the emperor in order to swear their loyalty to him upon the Koran. The commander of the palace guards tried to persuade the emperor not to allow the two men beyond the fortifications. But Shah Alam, under pressure from some of his advisers, said that their entry was not to be opposed.

Once the gates had been opened, it was not only Ismail Beg and Ghulam Kadir who entered. Two thousand soldiers swarmed into the palace and expelled the guard.

The noise of this skirmish reached the emperor and his sons, waiting in the Hall of Private Audience. His officers of state had all deserted him and there was no one he could send to find out what was happening. His son and heir, Akbar, turned to him and said: 'We have only one thing left that we can do. If you will allow us, we will go and throw ourselves on the traitors. Martyrdom is better than surrender'. But the emperor replied: 'No one can resist the ways of destiny and the decrees of God. The power has now gone from me into the hands of others'. At this, Akbar drew his sword and placed the point at his throat, intending to kill himself, but the emperor snatched the sword from his son's hand and placed it at his own throat. Such was the outcry among those present that it was heard by Ghulam and Ismail, then on their way to the audience hall. They hastened ahead.

Shah Alam received them with ironic politeness. To Ghulam he said: 'The money you required has been paid. Is it necessary that, instead of marching against Sindia, you humiliate me?' Ghulam replied with threats to kill the emperor, and demands that he disclose the hiding places of the imperial treasure. When the emperor refused, he was taken away with his sons and confined in the private mosque of the palace. Ghulam and Ismail then took over the emperor's private apartments for themselves which, not unnaturally, produced a wave of apprehension in the harem. But, for the time being, the women were safe.

Next morning Ghulam and Ismail visited the emperor again. Ghulam was polite. The emperor said that he had relied on Ghulam's oath of loyalty, taken as it had been on the holy Koran. As far as the imperial treasure was concerned the emperor said he had nothing more to give than had already been given. At that moment, one of Ghulam's captains brought forward the eldest surviving son of the former emperor, Ahmad Shah. Ghulam leaned forward and took Shah Alam's dagger from his girdle while others seized the princes' swords. The emperor, with nineteen of his sons and all his attendants, was taken away and confined in that part of the palace reserved for state prisoners. Meanwhile, Ahmad Shah's son was taken to the audience hall and placed on the throne. The drums were sounded, and he was proclaimed emperor under the title of Jahan Shah. When the priests of the city mosque asked in the name of which emperor the daily prayers should be read, Ghulam told them: 'In the name of God and his prophet'.

Muhammad Shah's two widows were invited to the palace and told by Ghulam that they were now to consider themselves in charge of the deposed emperor's harem. They immediately set about searching the private apartments of Shah Alam's wives and concubines, and handed over such jewels and money as they found to Ghulam Kadir. Everywhere in the vast palace, Ghulam's men were engaged in ripping up floorboards and tapping walls for hidden treasure. Additional women were sent into the harem to make a more thorough search than before.

The next days were punctuated by the screams of the tortured. Servants were held over fires to make them disclose the whereabouts of hidden jewels. Others had boiling oil poured into the palms of their hands. Eunuchs were beaten to death. Shah Alam himself was brought out of his prison and subjected to less extreme torture. He was made to sit in the burning sun without food or drink. He was continually threatened, and Ghulam would—without warning—fling his arm round the ex-emperor's neck and blow a cloud of acrid smoke from the hookah into his face. To all the demands for money, Shah Alam replied that everything he possessed had been in the storerooms rifled by Ghulam's men. 'Do you think I have treasure hidden in my belly?'

To which Ghulam replied that it was easy enough to search out truth with a dagger.

Ghulam seems soon to have slipped over the edge of madness. On 10 August, tired of Shah Alam's constant complaints, Ghulam turned to his bodyguard. 'Throw this babbler down and blind him!' The ex-emperor was instantly struck to the ground and needles were driven into his eyes. Ghulam asked the moaning Shah Alam whether he could see anything, and he replied: 'Nothing but the holy Koran between you and me'.

Next day, Ghulam sent for a court painter and ordered him to record the scene as he and one of his commanders extracted Shah Alam's eyeballs with a dagger.

Shah Alam, half dead, was taken back to his prison and left without food or water. When one of his servants tried to take him some the servant was killed on the spot, as were two others and a water-carrier who took pity on their former master.

Ghulam now also denied food and drink to the rest of the imperial family, including the wives of the new emperor. Within a short time, a number of the children and some of the older women died. By Ghulam's order, their bodies were left to rot in the place where they had fallen. The private apartments began to stink like some terrible charnel house.

All this pressure produced no more plunder because there was no more to find. The royal library, which had still retained some of its treasures, was completely gutted. Part of the silver roof which still remained in the Hall of Private Audience was ripped out. Even the semi-precious stones in the mural decorations of some of the apartments were gouged from their marble settings.

From the torture of servants, Ghulam had gone on to members of the imperial family. The two widows of Muhammad Shah were the first to attract his attention. One of them was foolish enough to ask Ghulam to hand over the palace to her; the amount promised him for deposing Shah Alam and placing Jahan Shah on the throne had now been paid, she said. Ghulam replied that the wealth he had so far appropriated represented only what had been taken from his father. The widows therefore still owed him the money they had promised. Both women were ejected from their mansions, which were immediately pillaged, and they were then placed on one of the terraces facing the river and kept there in the public view and without water for several hours. The princes were beaten, and so, too, was a sister of Shah Alam.

Inside the palace, few were spared humiliation at the very least. Even those who had conspired to give Ghulam control of the empire, and might have been thought to have some claim on him, suffered. The superintendent of the harem was taunted. 'Everyone, even maid-servants, is revealing the places where gold and jewels were hidden, yet you who have been superintendent of the emperor's household for so many years did not know of them?' When the superintendent begged Ghulam to spare him and, hoping to soften him, recounted the tale of how he had saved Ghulam's life and treated him as a son, Ghulam replied: 'Are you not acquainted with the old saying that it is not wise to kill a snake and spare its young?' The superintendent was ordered to produce 700,000 rupees as a fine for lack of memory, dragged into one of the palace privies, and threatened that, if he did not pay up, he would be suffocated in excrement.

Most of Ghulam's commanders approved of his attempts to lay hands on as much treasure as possible, for they expected to gain some profit for themselves. But they became restless at the treatment of the imperial princesses. The peculiar respect in which the Mughal name was held in India might permit the blinding of one emperor and his replacement by another. That was a matter of politics. Public humiliation of the women of the imperial family, on the other hand, was an act which brought dishonour not only on the women but on those who abused them. No previous conqueror, not even Nadir Shah or Ahmad Shah Abdali, had plundered the imperial harem or molested the imperial princesses. Even professional bandits in the greatest extremity would not have attacked a party which included a member of the imperial seraglio. Ghulam Kadir, 'the scourge of God', was the exception.

One day he had brought to him two young princesses whom he had been told were very beautiful. When they arrived, suitably veiled, he had them stripped and fondled their breasts and thighs, to the accompaniment of obscene remarks from his companions. Before matters could go any further, the princesses were rescued by one of Ghulam's Sikh supporters, who threatened to leave Delhi, taking his troops with him, if the princesses were molested again. Though Ghulam shouted that he would tell his men to take *all* the princesses, without the formality of marriage, 'so that from their seed a manlier race might be born', he allowed them to be taken away.

Despite constant warnings that his treatment of the imperial family was losing him the support of many of his chiefs, Ghulam persisted. He had Shah Alam's sons brought to the private apartments and ordered them to dance. This was an insult, as dancing was considered to be only for women, and professional women at that. When they protested, Ghulam told his guard to cut off the noses of any who refused. None did. Prince Akbar was forced to drink spirits and then, when he was drunk, to dance again. After this, Ghulam ordered his attendants out of the room, and then went to sleep with his head in one of the princes' laps. In Ghulam's girdle was a large dagger, and by his side a sword. When he woke up, he exclaimed: 'What cowards you all are! How can you hope to rule when you had not enough courage to try and kill me?'

The reign of terror in the palace had shown some profit for Ghulam. Shah Alam had always claimed to be without enough money even to feed the members of his household. But much of this was exaggeration. The emperor's family itself seldom went without. It was the hundreds of lesser members of the imperial house—the 'emperors' grandsons' and their wives and children—who suffered. So, too, did the thousands of palace servants. Inside the vast congeries of buildings that made up the palace there was an infinity of hiding-places where gold and jewels had been placed for safe keeping by many earlier rulers. Much of this treasure had been left undiscovered and untouched before Ghulam arrived. A great deal of what Ghulam plundered was neither gold nor jewels, but costly cloth and fine furniture for which there was no ready sale. Estimates based on the amount of cash and jewels vary from 250,000,000 rupees to as little as 1,500,000 rupees. But whatever the truth of the sum involved, the pillaging was almost complete. It was not only the palace that suffered. The mansions of the great Mughal nobles were sacked, and Ghulam even ordered his men to remove the gold leaf from the domes of the great Jama Masjid mosque. One dome was stripped and the gold sold, but the work was stopped after the same Sikh commander who had saved the imperial princesses warned Ghulam that it would outrage the people and that they might well rise against him.

While Ghulam Kadir and his men were stripping the palace of its wealth, Ismail Beg was sulking in his camp. Though the two men had agreed to share the spoils, Ismail had received nothing but small sums—perhaps because he had protested against the deposition of Shah Alam. The city was virtually divided up between the armies of the two one-time allies, which often came to blows in the streets; Ismail's men frequently had the support of the inhabitants. But Ismail's army was deserting for want of pay. Finally, there seemed to be nothing for it but for Ismail to come to an arrangement with Sindia, whose forces, a little belatedly, were approaching the city.

Though Sindia had been slow to move to the aid of the emperor, he had not been entirely inactive. His cavalry had interrupted communications with Delhi and had prevented grain convoys from reaching the capital, while on 14 September a large force commanded by Rana Khan was sent off towards Delhi. The men, still without their long arrears of pay, were only with difficulty persuaded to move.

Another force followed soon after. On the outskirts of the city, Ismail Beg joined them. Together the two armies occupied the old city on 28 September. They met with no opposition. The palace was the next target. Guns were brought up and opened fire on the walls. Seeing the size of the force assembled against them—which now included the Begum Sumru's contingent—Ghulam's men surrendered after no more than a few minor skirmishes.

Ghulam Kadir decided that he could not hold the fort and withdrew across the river with his treasure train, carrying with him as hostages some of Shah Alam's sons, and the new emperor Jahan Shah. His departure followed an explosion in the fort's powder magazine which blew down some of the outer defences. This Ghulam took as a bad omen. 'The fort itself has turned against me', he said. During his withdrawal and retreat a great deal of his treasure was looted by Sikhs and others.

When Rana Khan's scouts reached the fort, they heard shouting from some of the rooms near the wall. From these voices they learned that the fort was empty of defenders. Taking possession of it, they released some of the imperial family who had been left behind there. Inside the palace, Shah Alam had barricaded himself inside the room in which he had been confined by Ghulam Kadir. It was only with difficulty that Rana Kahn persuaded him to come out. The emperor was treated with great respect by the Maratha commander, one of whose first acts—after ordering food and water to be taken into the palace, where everyone was starving—had been to send in a number of barbers to trim the hair and beards of the emperor and his sons. The former water-carrier was apparently well acquainted with the psychology of self-respect.

The Maratha commander was so busy rounding up Ghulam Kadir's partisans in the city and trying to regain some of the spoils that Ghulam had been unable to take away with him that it was some days before he could wait on the emperor in person. On 16 October, in the ruined but cleaned hall of audience, Rana Khan and the other leaders waited on the sightless emperor. It was a meeting of some poignancy, for none of the usual protocol was abandoned. The emperor wished to know what was to happen to him. It was usual for blindness to disqualify a man from holding the throne. Rana Khan's instructions from Sindia were vague on this point, and he said that this was a matter for the regent himself. In the meantime, Rana Khan had the prayers in the Jama Masjid read in the name of Shah Alam.

One favour Shah Alam could demand, for it was one which coincided with Sindia's own interests. This was the hunting down of Ghulam Kadir Khan.

The 'scourge of God', in his retreat from Delhi, had been harassed by bands of Maratha horse. These he was easily able to keep at bay by means of superior firepower. But though Ghulam closed the ferries across the river Jumna after him by the simple expedient of destroying the boats, the Marathas were still able to get across and he found himself being pursued by Rana Khan and the Begum Sumru's contingent. The battalions commanded by de Boigne remained behind in the imperial city to garrison the citadel.

The hunt began in earnest. Rana Khan was reinforced by a contingent from the Jat raja and another of Marathas, which had been sent by the Peshwa in delayed reply to Sindia's previous appeals for help. Ghulam at first made for the fortress at Alighur where he had a vast store of ammunition and supplies. But the news that his commander there had given in without a fight destroyed Ghulam's hopes of being able to make a stand for long enough to permit the delicate negotiations that would be necessary if he were to make a deal with Sindia. Ghulam now moved northwards without any fixed plan of campaign, suffering continually from guerrilla attacks, until he reached the town of Meerut on 4 November. There he managed to defend the fort against a Maratha siege, but the blockade of supplies was so successful that very soon his men and animals were dying. As there was no place to bury the corpses, and as the Muslim faith does not approve of cremation, Ghulam soon had disease as an additional enemy inside his own gates.

Under a flag of truce, Ghulam sent out an offer to surrender the captive imperial princes in return for a guarantee of his lands and a free pardon. Negotiations broke down. In a rage, he threatened to murder the hostages and was only prevented from doing so by the same Sikh commander who had taken a firm line on earlier occasions. Conditions inside the fort soon became unbearable and, leaving his Sikh commander to cover his escape, Ghulam slipped out at dead of night. With a small escort of 500 horse—of whom he lost half in a skirmish—he managed to break through the Maratha patrols. In the confusion and the darkness, Ghulam and the remnant of his escort became separated. He tried to find them, but the country was difficult, overgrown with thorny acacia, the ground full of holes. In one of these his horse caught its foot and fell, breaking a leg. Ghulam went on, on foot, until first light came and he saw that he was near a small village. There he found that he had covered some forty miles during the night, but in a direction that had taken him away from his own country.

Going up to the most substantial house, Ghulam knocked and asked for shelter. The owner was a high-caste Hindu and suspicious, especially when the ragged visitor offered him a costly diamond ring from his finger if he would keep him hidden during the day and then find him a horse and a guide to take him to Gausgarh. At this point the owner of the house realized who his visitor was and secretly sent off a messenger to find someone to whom the information would be welcome. The messenger found the commander of the Peshwa's contingent, who sent a body of horse to surround the house and take Ghulam Kadir—who had been locked in by the owner—prisoner. It was 19 December 1788.

Two days earlier, when the news of Ghulam's flight had become known to the besiegers at Meerut, they had entered the fort and released the prisoners. They also found there the superintendent of the harem and a number of Ghulam's

Hindu partisans. These were put under arrest, as was the Sikh commander of the rearguard. When Ghulam Kadir was brought back, Rana Khan had chains hung on his legs and an iron collar placed around his neck. He was then put in an open bullock cart and, surrounded by an escort of two regiments of infantry and 1,000 horse, sent to Sindia at his headquarters at Mathura.

When Ghulam reached Sindia's camp he was received with unexpected courtesy. New clothes were produced, and fine food set before him. It was suggested that much might be forgiven if he would be prepared to disclose where he had hidden the plunder of Delhi; little had been found in Meerut and, though his treasure train had been attacked by bandits, all had presumably not been lost. Ghulam replied that he did not know what had happened to it. (In fact, a substantial hoard of jewels had fallen into the hands of the French mercenary, Lesteneau, who took the opportunity of this unexpected though often hoped-for windfall to leave for British territory and later for Europe.)

Sindia would probably have preferred to keep Ghulam Kadir alive, at least until some of the treasure was recovered, but on 28 February he received a letter from Shah Alam who had heard of the delay in taking vengeance on the man who had blinded him. In it, the emperor threatened to abdicate and leave on a pilgrimage to Mecca if Ghulam was allowed to live. So Sindia ordered that Ghulam and the former superintendent of the imperial harem were to be tortured to death. Ghulam's ears were cut off and hung round his neck. With his face blackened, he was paraded round the city in a bullock-cart. Next day, his nose and lips were cut off and again he was shown to the city. The following day, his eyeballs were torn out and yet again he was placed in a cart and trundled slowly through the streets. His eyes were followed by his hands, and then by his feet. Finally his head was cut off and the corpse was hung upside down from a tree.

There was to be a strange climax, a suitable embroidery of fantasy to the horrors of the last few months. Ghulam

KING OF THE WORLD

Kadir's ears, lips and eyeballs were placed in a casket and sent to Shah Alam in Delhi as a grisly proof that the right kind of vengeance had been exacted. It was intended that Ghulam's body should be sent too, so that it could be displayed in the streets as a proof and a warning. But first, for three days, it hung on the tree at Mathura. Below it, a large black dog with white rings round its eyes lapped up the dripping blood. Though stones were thrown at it, it would not go away. On the fourth day both the dog and the corpse had disappeared. The 'scourge of God', went the rumour, had been claimed by his true master, the devil.

PART THREE

A Mere Pageant

The Dominion of the House of Timur no longer exists, but is a mere pageant held up to preserve appearances and delude the prejudices of mankind.

1
A lampless desolation

WHEN SINDIA liberated Shah Alam from the madness of
Ghulam Kadir, it was rescue from a nightmare. But it also
brought about, as William Palmer, the British Resident at
Sindia's court, wrote to the governor-general, the extinction
of the 'Dominion of the House of Timur'. In return for
security, the emperor gave up any independence he ever
had.

Shah Alam's gratitude to Sindia was profound. The
emperor had appealed for help to the nawab-wazir of Oudh,
still nominally the first minister of the empire. To this
appeal there had been no reply. Nor had there been any from
the nawab's real masters, the British. The governor-general,
claiming that he was debarred by a British Act of Parliament
from interfering in the affairs of Indian states, with great
politeness refused his aid. Only Sindia had come to the
rescue, even if he had been too late to save the emperor's
sight. According to the usual custom of Eastern royalty,
Shah Alam should have been disqualified from restoration
to the throne by his blindness. Indeed, when he was released
he suggested abdicating in favour of his son, Akbar Shah,
who made it quite clear that he would welcome the opportunity. For a time, Sindia thought that such a solution
would be in his own best interests. There was much to be
done in settling the country after the upheavals of the
preceding years, and it would have made settlement easier
if the emperor were able to travel about with Sindia, lending
his prestige whenever circumstances required it. An old
man, in poor health and blind as well, could not possibly
have withstood the rigours of campaigning. A young man
was in every way to be preferred on that account.

When the proposition was put seriously to Shah Alam, however, he changed his mind. He had begun to recover from the shock of Ghulam Kadir's treatment, and his gratitude to Sindia had begun to regain a sense of proportion. William Palmer reported to the governor-general that the old emperor 'was as tenacious of royalty as if it was attended by all the power and renown of Akbar and, Aurangzeb'.

When Sindia consulted the British, they were against a change, and there were better arguments even than that. A young man could quite easily turn out to be less than docile—though this seemed unlikely in the case of Akbar Shah, who appeared to be no more than an honest and worthy cipher. Ghulam Kadir had placed another candidate on the throne, Jahan Shah, and had displaced him again because he had gone into the bazaar to fly a kite! It was in Shah Alam's favour that he had held the imperial throne almost unchallenged for thirty years, and the barbarity of his treatment by Ghulam Kadir had given him something of an aura of martyrdom. Old and blind, he seemed less likely to become the focus of intrigues than another man. A factor which also carried weight was that the court of an emperor who did not have all his faculties would be cheaper to maintain.

The problem of the emperor's maintenance arose immediately after the liberation of Delhi. Ghulam Kadir had taken away most of the imperial treasure. Sindia arranged for an allowance of 600,000 rupees a year to be made to the emperor, but it was said that only 17,000 rupees a month actually reached him. In June 1789, Palmer, who was also the governor-general's agent at the court of Delhi, wrote: 'It is very discreditable to Sindia to leave the Shah and his family so long without any settled provision, or any person in proper authority to transact the cash business of the court and the city. You can hardly imagine how indigent and degrading the king's position is'. A year later, Shah Alam's position seems to have been no better.

The blame for this was not directly Sindia's. His visits to

the imperial capital were infrequent, and the city was left in the hands of his representatives. Unfortunately, the men he chose were unintelligent, cowardly, and not particularly honest. Shah Alam suffered a great deal from them. They frequently did not even show him the respect which good diplomacy, if nothing else, required. One, who was Sindia's envoy from 1780 until 1789, was particularly offensive. During the Hindu festival of Holi, a kind of bacchanalia which heralds the coming of spring, he had a man dressed up to look like the emperor in fine but tattered clothes and a false beard. This man took his place on an old bedstead with a young boy in his arms dressed in woman's clothes, to represent the emperor's daughter who always accompanied him when he went out. This ensemble was paraded through the city streets preceded by a number of beggars carrying ragged versions of the royal insignia. For this comment on the emperor's poverty the envoy was at last removed.

In August 1789, Sindia appointed Shah Nizam-ud-din—popularly known as Shahji—as his governor of the Delhi territory. Shahji was a Muslim, a descendant of saints, and it was thought that his appointment would help to reconcile the people of Delhi to Sindia's domination. More important, Shah Alam had a weakness for holy men and had at one time used Shahji in diplomatic negotiations with Sindia's envoys at his court. Sindia believed that Shahji's spiritual influence over the emperor would be of value. But he was careful to give only civil and administrative powers to his governor. The command of the military forces and of the fort was held by a Hindu who was completely independent of the governor.

Shahji, descended from saints and with a reputation for holiness himself, affected to despise money. This did not prevent him from misappropriating the emperor's allowances. He was reported to give the emperor every day a meagre ration of a pound of pilau—a dish made with chicken, rice and spices—four pounds of meat, and two loaves of bread. This was for the emperor, his doctor, his son Prince Akbar, his favourite daughter, and one of his two hundred women. The rest of the household, princes, princesses and servants without distinction, received a pound of barley flour among three persons, which they had to bake themselves. Though this report was probably exaggerated, there is no doubt of Shahji's miserly treatment of the imperial family. If the emperor's immediate family suffered, others inside the palace were much worse off. So too were his subjects outside the palace, scraping a living from a land devastated by famine and the passage of plundering armies. There was little food, and other necessaries such as oil for lighting were so scarce that one chronicler described the state of the country as 'a lampless desolation'.

The careful and efficient system of local administration had long collapsed as invader and marauder followed on each other's heels. The once fertile land had gone back to dust as the irrigation canals, once famous for their efficiency, had been left to fall into ruins. No water entered Delhi after 1761, and the waterways had become stagnant pools heavy with the deadly curtain of breeding mosquitoes. In 1785, a great famine had killed off more people than all the wars put together; between one-third and one-half of the rural population had died. The soil had become dust and out of the clouds thrown up by their horses came men who stole and burned such crops as grew. Those villages that were not abandoned became little republics, surrounded by mud walls to keep out marauders and tax collectors. Over the village wells would be built protective towers, sometimes over fifty feet high. Inside, men with matchlocks stood guard, and the only way in was by rope ladder. Some villagers might occupy and repair a ruined mansion or a large mosque and turn it into a fort. Occasionally, a number of villages banded together to form a confederacy and hire some of the many unemployed mercenaries left behind by the armies of the great chiefs. The rural population resisted authority of any kind and contributed to the endemic anarchy by themselves turning to banditry and cattle-lifting. Every village headman had become a robber baron.

If the revenues of the state were to be restored, all these little republics had to be brought to order. But Mahadaji Sindia had other problems of a more pressing nature. After the defeat and execution of Ghulam Kadir, Sindia remained at Mathura. He had been ordered by the Peshwa to have the area round the town assigned directly to him. Mathura was the centre of an area of great holiness in Hindu eyes, for it was the scene of many of the escapades of that most popular of Hindu gods, the divine cowherd Krishna. There were many shrines and objects of pilgrimage which remained crowded by the devout even in times of anarchy. The settlement of the area took time, the grant of it from the emperor even longer. It was a matter which Sindia might well have left to his subordinates, but there was an important personal reason for his remaining in this sanctuary of the gods. He wanted a son. He gave large sums of money to the priests for the adornment of temples and images; he spent his time moving from shrine to shrine, worshipping the gods by means of hymns he composed himself. The gods ignored him.

They also failed—or so it was widely believed—to protect him against the curse put upon him by Ghulam Kadir's mother. Soon after her son had been killed, Sindia went down with a mild fever. Its effects were so slight that he continued his round of hopeful visits to the sacred places. But soon an inflammation appeared on his face, and then a swelling which spread to the neck and chest. No medicine seemed to have any effect. By the first week of June 1789 his condition was so serious that he considered sending for a European doctor, his own Hindu and Arab physicians having failed. The British Resident at his court offered the services of the Residency surgeon, but they were refused, for Sindia's ministers believed that a foreigner might attempt to poison their master.

The swellings continued to erupt as boils, which sup-purated and burst, causing Sindia great pain. But still nothing that the doctors tried brought relief. They decided that, as their medicine could do nothing, the source of the disease must be supernatural. Astrologers were consulted and, of course, confirmed the doctors' diagnosis. Instructed to seek out the source of the witchcraft, they had no difficulty in finding evidence. Spies reported that a woman had been overheard at the sacred shrine at Brindaban boasting that she had cast a spell on Sindia. She was immediately seized and brought before him.

The woman admitted that she had practised witchcraft in order to kill Sindia, and that she had done it at the request of the warrior-monk Himmat Bahadur, a man who sold his services indiscriminately to anyone he believed to be on the edge of power. He had once been attached to Najaf Khan, and later to Afrasiyab. While Sindia had been preoccupied with the Jaipur raja, Himmat Bahadur and his brother had taken advantage of the situation to seize some lands. Though they were chased off into exile in Oudh, Himmat Bahadur had seized the opportunity of Ghulam Kadir's emergence to return and attack the Marathas when they were at their weakest. Unwilling to move against a high-caste priest, Sindia had granted him certain lands. But now things had gone altogether too far. While the witch cast new spells to counteract her evil ones, men were sent off to arrest Himmat Bahadur.

Sindia began to improve after the saying of the magical rites—a sure proof of Himmat Bahadur's guilt. The warrior-monk, however, was warned and managed to escape. The sanctuary he chose was the headquarters of Ali Bahadur, commander of the contingent that had been sent by the Peshwa to aid Sindia against Ghulam Kadir. When Ali Bahadur was asked to give up the monk, he replied insolently that Himmat had neither been invited there by him, nor was he kept there. If Sindia wanted the monk, he could send for him. When Sindia's men arrived they found Ali Bahadur's army standing to and apparently ready to fight. Sindia backed down, losing some of the prestige he had regained. Himmat Bahadur managed to survive all Sindia's attempts to take him, and lived long enough to become a vassal of the British after they defeated him in 1803.

The attitude of Ali Bahadur and Sindia's weakness towards him brought another enemy into the field. When the Peshwa had finally agreed to send men to support Sindia, Ali Bahadur's force had been accompanied for part of the way by a contingent under Sindia's old antagonist, Tukoji Holkar. Tukoji had deliberately dawdled in the hope that Sindia would be defeated, and had spent a year in the Rajputana putting pressure on the rulers there and collecting tribute from them. At the time of Himmat Bahadur's flight, he had been camped for some time about eighty miles from Mathura. Now, he visited Sindia and demanded half of all Sindia's gains from the recent campaign. Sindia swore that there had been no real gains at all, and that all the money acquired had gone to pay his troops. Tukoji refused to accept this and left to join Ali Bahadur, encouraging the Peshwa's representative in his hostility towards Sindia. The Marathas were once again divided amongst themselves and, as always, there were plenty of ambitious men ready to profit from the fact.

One who tried was Ismail Beg. After going over to Sindia's side before the fall of Delhi, Ismail had been sent away to settle matters with Najaf Kuli Khan, now the sole remaining heir of the dead regent, Najaf Khan. After Shah Alam's futile attempt to crush him, Najaf Kuli had reinforced his position. Sindia was determined to suppress him. The task seemed an excellent method of neutralizing Ismail Beg, perhaps the most dangerous ally, as he had been the most persistent enemy, of Sindia's reviving power. Ismail had moved rapidly towards Najaf Kuli's stronghold of Kanud. As he came near, Najaf Kuli emerged from the fort to give battle. After two days of fighting, he was driven back into the fort. Ismail made no attempt to attack him, but set about taking control of Najaf Kuli's possessions and collecting the revenue for himself.

Both sides increased the numbers of their soldiers, but as they were unable to pay them there were constant mutinies and desertions. This put the war into a position of stalemate. Finally, in March 1789, Ismail had begun to besiege the fort of Kanud after defeating an attempt by an ally of Najaf Kuli's to relieve the town. For capturing the town, Ismail received a robe of honour from Shah Alam. The siege of the fort went on until November, when it was finally abandoned.

Instead of sending money to Ismail to pay his troops, Sindia demanded that the revenue from Najaf Kuli's former conquests should be delivered to the emperor. This was too much for Ismail, who had not even received the bribe promised him in return for deserting Ghulam Kadir. Like every other general of the time, Ismail was in considerable difficulty with his troops. Desertion resulting from lack of pay seemed likely to reach such levels that Ismail would soon have no army at all and would be entirely at Sindia's mercy. Sindia, he knew, had no liking for him. Money had to be found, and Ismail did not have far to look for a source.

At one time, Ismail had been in the employ of the raja of Jaipur. The raja, and the ruler of Jodhpur, were now looking for allies. Sindia had not forgotten his virtual defeat at Lalsot; spies had reported that, as he moved away from the battlefield, he had sworn: 'If I live, I shall reduce Jaipur and Jodhpur to ashes'. When the news of Ghulam Kadir's death reached Jaipur, the allies began to make preparations for the battle they were certain could not be far off. In March 1790, they offered Ismail a payment of over 1,000,000 rupees—with 200,000 on account. Ismail accepted. As proof of his goodwill, he sent his family to Jaipur as hostages.

Against Ismail, now reinforced by troops from Jaipur and Jodhpur, Sindia sent his French general, Benoit de Boigne.

2

The French General

BENOIT DE BOIGNE was about to become the most powerful man in Hindustan. In 1790 he was thirty-nine years of
age. De Boigne had been born plain Leborgne, and though
he was known as a Frenchman his actual place of birth had
been Chambéry in Savoy. He had gained his first military
experience in the service of the king of France, though not
in a French regiment. He belonged to one of the Irish
brigades originally raised by partisans of the exiled James II
of England in 1689. De Boigne had also served in the army
of Catherine the Great of Russia, and was rumoured to have
been her lover. Further adventures at last led him to India,
where he won a commission in the East India Company's
army at Madras. Leaving the army, he had made friends of
many men in high places—with the governor-general,
Warren Hastings, and with Claud Martin, the Frenchman
who had made himself virtually purveyor-general to the
nawab-wazir of Oudh. In 1783, de Boigne set off from
Lucknow in the party accompanying Major Browne on his
way to Delhi, and though he had intended to make his
way overland to Russia he accepted instead an offer of
employment as a mercenary in the army of Mahadaji
Sindia.

This appointment was unofficially approved of by the
British. De Boigne was known to be a friend, and a friend in
the right place was worth having. In fact, de Boigne had
been introduced to Sindia (unofficially) by the British envoy
at his court. De Boigne showed what a disciplined corps of
men trained on European lines and led by European officers
could do at Lalsot, and later at Agra, but after the defeat of
Ghulam Kadir he left Sindia's service and returned to

Lucknow. The reason was partly professional. Like everyone else, he lacked money to pay his men. But the jealousy
of Sindia's generals also had its effect. When de Boigne had
asked Sindia to expand his two battalions into a brigade of
10,000 men, Sindia had felt compelled to refuse so as not
to antagonize them. He and de Boigne parted amicably. It
was later suggested that Sindia had guaranteed to recall him
as soon as it was possible to persuade the other generals.

The time came more quickly than de Boigne had expected. In the middle of August 1789, convinced that he
would soon have to fight Ismail Beg, Sindia sent an envoy to
Lucknow to ask de Boigne to return and raise a brigade.
There would be no quarrel about terms. De Boigne left
immediately for Mathura, where he met Sindia and they
reached agreement. De Boigne was to have the rank of
general and the pay to go with it. He would have a free hand
to raise his brigade and train it as he thought fit, and the
money would be provided by a grant of lands which would
be under his direct control. His friend, Claud Martin, wrote
prophetically when he heard the news : 'The balance of
power will be held by you. What glory to see at your feet
emperors, princes and princesses seeking your friendship
and God knows what else !'

There was very little time for de Boigne to assemble his
brigade. His old battalions had mutinied after the defection
of Lesteneau and had become such a menace that Sindia was
considering sending his cavalry against them. But de Boigne
persuaded them to parade before him, officially disbanded
them, and then re-enlisted those who had not been ringleaders in the mutiny. Messages went out along that tele-
graph of rumour that seemed to reach out to every unemployed
soldier, wherever he might be. Recruits flocked in, new
battalions were formed with experienced men from the old
battalions divided amongst them. European officers were
appointed. George Sangster, a Scot who had commanded
part of René Madec's force, was put in charge of the
ordnance and immediately began casting cannon and laying
in supplies of powder. A Dutchman, John Hessing, who

had been an officer in the old force, and Robert Sutherland, who had been cashiered from a Scots regiment but was a fine soldier, were also appointed. There were a couple of English officers; and Captain Drugeon, who was a native of Savoy, like de Boigne; and a Frenchman, Pierre Cuiller who, under the pseudonym of Perron, was ultimately to succeed de Boigne. None of them were men of genius, but most were competent and some rather more than that. The genius was to be de Boigne's contribution.

The provisioning of his brigade was left to de Boigne's friend, Martin, in Lucknow. Uniforms were designed and ordered. An English bandmaster soon arrived, but Martin was able to recruit only one European musician and could not find a French-horn player anywhere. Apparently, however, this problem had been overcome by the end of 1789 when de Boigne paraded his men before Sindia. It was to the sound of French horns that 5,000 infantry dressed in scarlet with black leather accoutrements and blue turbans entered the parade ground. Behind the infantry, in green, with red turbans and cummerbunds, came the cavalry, well mounted on small wiry ponies. Then followed the heavy guns drawn by bullocks; the light artillery; then the supply train, with great carts full of shells and shot, and a team of bullocks for each. Behind came camels drawing lighter loads, and—unprecedented in a native army—a field hospital with a doctor and surgeon. At the end of March 1790, the new force made its way from Mathura to Sindia's capital of Gwalior. The time of testing was almost at hand.

The campaign against Ismail Beg and his Rajput allies opened in May. As usual with Indian chiefs, there was little or no trust between them, even though Ismail's family was safe in Jaipur city. Ismail had not been reinforced by armies from either Jaipur or Jodhpur, though the former had supplied some cavalry, but he had at his command some 30,000 infantry, 13,000 cavalry, and 130 guns. Many of his men knew the country intimately. There was, however, very little discipline. Ismail Beg had not paid his troops for some time, and his arrogant manner had offended many of his captains—at least one of whom he had had murdered. Tensions ran so high that at one time only the presence of the Jaipur cavalry, lying between two parts of the army, prevented them from attacking each other.

Sindia's army caught up with Ismail at Patan, about eighty miles north of Jaipur, on 22 May, but an attempt to break into his lines failed because the Maratha guns could not reach Ismail's position.

Neither side seemed anxious to join battle. De Boigne, whose men were in the van of Sindia's army, decided to try to force an action. He moved his men up close to Ismail's trenches and bombarded them with grapeshot. Sindia's commanding general then sent forward a body of horse to try to provoke Ismail's men into pursuing them when they were forced to retreat before the fire of his guns. The provocation succeeded. Ismail's men left their trenches only to be decimated by de Boigne's artillery, and the rest of the battle was a rout. On all sides Sindia's cavalry advanced. In the centre, the artillery moved forward covering the infantry. Ismail's lines were quickly stormed and the defenders driven to flight. Only night stopped the advance and the slaughter.

Ismail's cavalry fled as far as they could. His infantry made for the town of Patan, but surrendered the next day. It was triumph for de Boigne and his men. His losses amounted to 129 killed and 472 wounded; the spoils were 107 guns, 6,000 stands of arms, 252 colours, 15 elephants (including five of Ismail's own), 200 camels, 513 horses, and more than 3,000 bullocks. 'All their camp was burnt and destroyed', wrote de Boigne to a friend in Calcutta. 'They have saved nothing but their lives'.

When news of the victory reached Sindia, he sent off a letter to de Boigne beginning 'My Valiant Sir'. The only criticism he had to make was that de Boigne had insisted on his soldiers returning their plunder, 'which has irritated the men and in all probability they will lodge complaints against you to us'. But Sindia assured de Boigne that no allegations would be heeded. 'Believe', he ended, 'that our admiration and kindness towards you is daily on the ascendancy'.

It was a pity that the victory had not put an end to Ismail Beg. He had escaped when the battle was obviously lost, and was now collecting troops in the territory of the raja of Jodhpur. But first an attempt was made to negotiate. Jaipur asked de Boigne to go and see him. De Boigne was prepared to go, but Sindia told him not to. Treachery, he said, was the usual practice of Jaipur. An agent might be sent, but de Boigne was not to risk his own life. 'Remember you occupy one of the highest ranks in the empire'. Apparently, de Boigne had never thought of this. He took Sindia's advice. Next the raja of Jodhpur tried to buy the Savoyard off with an offer of the great fortress of Ajmir and lands to go with it. By this time de Boigne had learned his lesson and replied that, as he had already been promised the whole of Jodhpur and Jaipur, he could hardly be bought for less.

A confrontation was unavoidable. Sindia insisted, de Boigne approved, and Rajput honour demanded it. The defeat at Patan had humiliated the two rajas and their over-weening pride demanded revenge. In an attempt to satisfy their various emotions, the two sides met at the town of Merta, some forty miles north-west of Ajmir, and the result was the complete defeat of the Rajputs and their allies.

Merta was a large, mud-walled city standing on high ground in the centre of a grassy plain. The armies of Jaipur and Jodhpur consisted of tribal levies, raw soldiers but fine horsemen. Their infantry was undisciplined and badly armed. Patan had convinced both rulers that they should not face de Boigne's force without trained infantrymen and gunners, and they intended to wait for the arrival of Ismail Beg. De Boigne, however, was determined to attack before Ismail appeared.

The weather was unusually hot, as the monsoon had failed. A dry river-bed made it difficult for de Boigne to manoeuvre his artillery into position. The troops were tired after the long march from Ajmir, and a rest was ordered.

The Rajput forces, told to avoid battle until Ismail arrived to reinforce them, settled down in their camps and, as was their usual custom, smoked opium and went to sleep. Just before daybreak on 10 September, de Boigne's guns opened on the Rajput left wing and were followed by an immediate infantry assault. Caught wholly by surprise, the Rajputs broke and ran.

But this initial success for de Boigne almost turned into disaster. The commander of three of his battalions, a Frenchman named Rohan, lost touch with the main body and left a gap between his own men and those under de Boigne. Into this gap flooded the Rajput cavalry. They wheeled against Rohan's men and overran them. Then they turned against de Boigne. Ignoring the fire from his artillery they swept down on him, broke through and killed the gunners. Two wings of the Rajput horse now turned in an attempt to attack the line from the rear. But there was no rear. As soon as de Boigne had seen the attack on Rohan's battalions, he had turned his force into hollow square, so that the cavalry found themselves facing concentrated musket fire instead of a strung-out and exposed line.

The cavalry found it impossible to break the square and turned instead to face Sindia's cavalry, which had remained inactive, hamstrung by the belief that de Boigne's force had been crushed. Now attacked by the Rajput cavalry, they fled, leaving the other wings of Sindia's army unprotected. There was a period of confused hand-to-hand fighting until Ali Bahadur, who commanded the Maratha right wing, rallied his cavalry and set upon the now exhausted men and blown horses of the Rajputs and pushed them back.

All was by no means over yet. A number of Rajput chiefs who had promised their ruler that they would return with victory or die, took a last pipe of opium together and donned saffron-coloured robes—the dress of a bridegroom but also, in Rajput chivalry, the sign of preparation for death. Three thousand mounted men formed up behind their chiefs on the western end of the plain and prepared to attack de

Boigne's square. The ground began to shudder as the cavalry gained speed, shouting 'Kill! Kill!' The sun glittered from bayonets and flashed on the brass of de Boigne's cannon. In the centre of de Boigne's square flew the pennant of Savoy, a white cross on a blue background. The Rajputs carried pennants of many colours. The dust rose, the noise intensified, and suddenly there came the swift sharp crash of the guns. The Rajput line broke, re-formed, and broke again. 'I have seen', wrote one of de Boigne's officers, 'fifteen or twenty men return to charge one thousand infantry and advance within ten or fifteen paces of our line, before they were all shot'. Two men almost won through to de Boigne himself, but were cut down by his bodyguard.

The Rajput chiefs found death, not victory. The plain in front of the town was strewn with corpses of men and horses, and against the parched yellow of the grass they stood out— the brown of the horses, the white cotton of the soldiers, the saffron of the Rajput chiefs, the dark crimson of drying blood everywhere. Across the plain now moved the Maratha army. There was still some opposition. A troop of gunners operated a device called an 'Organ', made up of thirty-six musket barrels joined together to fire simultaneously. But it was soon abandoned in the flight. The town of Merta opened its gates and was given over to three days of pillage. The spoils were few, though in one building a large quantity of raw opium was found. But there were compensations. 'The ladies at first seemed displeased with our coming abruptly into the town but at length grew more kind, acknowledging with good grace that none but the brave deserve the fair'.

Though Merta was a great victory, and a disaster which shattered Jaipur and Jodhpur, it was by no means decisive. In India, there was always another day, another grouping of one-time enemies turned into hostile friends. Ismail Beg, who had arrived too late to help his Rajput allies, left the battlefield as quickly as he could and continued to cause trouble to Sindia until he surrendered to de Boigne's deputy, Colonel Perron, in April 1792. Shah Alam demanded that he be put to death for his part in the emperor's humiliation by Ghulam Kadir, but de Boigne refused. De Boigne had taken Ismail under his protection, as well as the family of Najaf Kuli Kahn, who had died in 1791. De Boigne also took one of Najaf Kuli's daughters into his harem. Ismail Beg was later moved to Agra fort. When Mahadaji Sindia died, Shah Alam ordered Ismail's jailer to kill him and the man acted before de Boigne could stop him. So the emperor's vengeance was at last complete.

In the case of Jodhpur and Jaipur, upheavals continued, not because the two rajas tried to resist Sindia after their defeat at Merta, but because Tukoji Holkar—who had been present at the battle with Ali Bahadur—insisted once again on division of the spoils. Naturally, there was conflict, and Holkar stirred up as much trouble for Sindia as he could. Spies reported that he was actually financing Ismail Beg, and it became certain that at some time he and Sindia must openly clash.

The antagonism between Sindia and Holkar was kept hot by the Peshwa's minister, the real ruler, Nana Farnavis. Holkar was encouraged to milk one Rajput state so dry that when Sindia's men arrived there was nothing left at all. Both sides had their peace parties, and Sindia was always unwilling to go to war with another of the Peshwa's officials, but when Holkar occupied territories which were part of the empire of which Sindia was deputy regent, he felt forced to take them back. Holkar began to intrigue with the Jaipur raja in the hope of forming a Rajput coalition against Sindia. In October 1792, a force of Sindia's captured Holkar's camp in Jaipur, seizing not only his baggage but his personal standard. This was an insult to Holkar's honour. The Holkar family began to raise more troops, including some trained on European lines and commanded by a Frenchman, the Chevalier Dudrenec. But Tukoji's youngest son, Malahar Rao, insisted that he be sent to command the force in the Rajputana. Malahar Rao had no faith in the military expertise of the Europeans and put his trust—as did some later generals in other countries—in the use of cavalry. Against the advice of Holkar's more experienced commanders, he was sent to put in motion an aggressive policy towards Sindia.

At this stage both the Peshwa and Nana Farnavis tried to interfere. They had no objection to keeping Holkar and Sindia in a state of mutual tension, but they knew that if it came to a fight de Boigne's battalions would probably swing the balance in Sindia's favour. Holkar at first resisted any attempt at compromise but, under pressure, at last agreed to negotiate. Terms were accepted by both sides. This angered Malahar Rao who, when he arrived at his ageing father's camp, taxed him with spending money uselessly on raising an army only to sacrifice his honour for a bit of paper. 'This', he shouted, 'has destroyed even the little prestige that was still left to us. You stay here with your peace. I will go to battle'.

Again it was to be **won** by that European expertise Malahar Rao so foolishly despised. The two armies fought at the end of May 1793 near the town of Lakheri on the way to Ajmir, in broken ravine-split scrubby country. Dudrenec's force was no match for de Boigne's. Malahar Rao's cavalry attacks were utterly routed, and Malahar Rao himself, the potential saviour, was found drunk in a waterhole by his retreating men. Only Dudrenec stood his ground, fighting to the last, and saved his own life only by pretending to be dead. In the retreat, Sindia's town of Ujjain was sacked, but it was only a gesture.

When the news reached Sindia, then at the Peshwa's capital of Poona negotiating with Nana Farnavis, it could not have come at a more welcome time. An agreement between the two had been delayed while Nana Farnavis and the Peshwa awaited the outcome of the clash with Holkar. They now agreed to Sindia's terms without question. To de Boigne, Sindia wrote: 'In truth you are the support of my right arm ... By the intervention of the gods, the long-cherished desire of my heart to punish the Holkars has been accomplished'.

There were also side effects. The raja of Jaipur immediately surrendered to de Boigne and offered him a grant of
land which, with Sindia's permission, he accepted on behalf
of his small son. Sindia ordered him to raise another brigade,
and lands were granted for their upkeep. De Boigne was
becoming a power in his own right, and there were many
who recognized the fact. The emperor's mother wrote to
him of the imperial family's ill-treatment at the hands of
Shahji, and de Boigne promised to take the matter up with
Sindia, whom he believed to be unaware of what was going
on. 'When I shall mention full particulars to him, then his
eyes will be opened'. When Nana Farnavis thought of
attacking Sindia—which seemed to him the only way of
preventing Sindia from taking over the Peshwa as well as the
emperor—de Boigne sent a contingent under Perron to
overawe him.

In his own territories, de Boigne was virtually a king. 'I
have seen him daily', wrote one of his officers, 'rise with the
sun, survey his arsenal, review his troops, enlist recruits,
direct the vast movements of three brigades, raise resources
and encourage manufacturers for their arms, ammunition
and stores ... give audience to ambassadors, administer
justice'. His men were always promptly and well paid. There
were payments for the wounded and pensions for the
invalid. The peasants on de Boigne's lands were well
treated, the soil well irrigated, and the crops carefully
reaped and stored. In the anarchy of northern India, it was
rumoured to resemble paradise.

Sindia's triumph did not last for long. On 12 February he
died in Poona of what was described as 'a feverish com-
plaint'. The usual rumours circulated. He had been poisoned ;
Nana Farnavis had had him murdered by an armed gang.
But Mahadaji Sindia genuinely had died of a fever. He had
no son, despite all his efforts at the shrines of Mathura, and
he had nominated his nephew Daulat Rao Sindia as his
successor. There was no opposition, as de Boigne early
declared his support for his dead master's chosen heir. The
death of Mahadaji Sindia was followed in 1795 by that of

the Peshwa; in October of that year he was killed in an accident and his death was followed by a series of revolutions which were to lead to the end of Maratha hegemony in northern India.

For de Boigne there were no more great battles. With his army, he might have taken over control of the emperor and of Hindustan. But his ambition was to return home and live the life of a gentleman. By October 1795, he had decided to retire. His health was bad after the rigours of the previous few years. Daulat Rao did not want him to go, but there was little he could do to stop him.

On Christmas Day 1795 de Boigne held his last parade and took the salute on the plain outside the city of Agra, where he had gained his first major victory for Sindia seven years before. Next day he left for British territory. He was accompanied by an escort of cavalry; his baggage filled 150 bullock carts; and his fortune was estimated at over £400,000. De Boigne's last advice to Daulat Rao Sindia was simple. He warned him 'never to excite the jealousy of the British government by increasing his battalions and rather to discharge them than risk a war'.

3

An English visitor

WITH THE triumph of Sindia over Ghulam Kadir, great
events in northern India had seemed to bypass Delhi and the
emperor. With the rise of de Boigne, the capital of the
empire had seemed to move to the French general's great
fortress at Alighur. But in sentiment, Delhi remained the
centre of the world. Within the limitations imposed by his
own miserliness and the embezzlements of Sindia's
governor, Shah Alam maintained his royal state.

On 29 November 1794 there appeared outside one of the
gates of Delhi a small cortège of armed men accompanying
a palanquin. Inside was Mr Thomas Twining, a member of
the East India Company's civil service. He had approached
the city through a countryside strewn with ruins. 'Houses,
palaces, tombs, in different stages of dilapidation, composed
this striking scene. The desert we had passed was cheerful
compared with the view of desolation now before us'. But
there had been one delight, for, after 'traversing ruined
streets without a single inhabitant for a mile', he had come
to an elegant tomb of sandstone topped by a dome of white
marble, almost as beautiful, he thought, as the Taj Mahal.
It was the tomb of Humayun, the second emperor of the
Mughal dynasty and 'one of the most virtuous but most
unfortunate princes of his race'. Turning aside, the little
column had continued on its way until it was stopped at the
city gate by an officer of the guard, who would not let it
enter without a pass from the governor, who lived outside the
city. Nineteen-year-old Mr Twining was not pleased at
being kept waiting in the hot sun but, as he carried a friendly
message from the British commander-in-chief in Bengal to
the emperor, he sent his head servant—'whose diplomatic

address I had so often proved'— to the governor, accompanied by the captain of the escort and two servants in livery and wearing the badge of the East India Company.

The time dragged by, but at last Twining's 'embassy' returned accompanied by one of the governor's officers with orders to conduct him into the city, where he would be lodged in one of the palaces. Twining was impressed by the magnificence of this building, and, consequently, by the diplomatic talents of his head servant. From the great court of the palace, he was ushered into 'a fine garden, at the extremity of which, and adjoining the principal building, was a handsome pavilion, consisting of a splendid hall, with a deep verandah towards the garden, and numerous rooms of smaller dimensions'. Finding this very much to his taste, he settled in the pavilion. 'The situation was most pleasant and, as said of another garden, seemed to make Hesperian fables true'.

The following morning, after breakfast, Twining was visited by the agent of the British Resident at Sindia's court, who was also agent at the palace. Arrangements had to be made for Mr Twining to visit the emperor, but before these could be set in motion a messenger from the governor arrived to inquire whether he was well lodged. He replied that he was most comfortable and, with the governor's permission, would call upon him next day.

Early the next morning, Twining took a ride through part of the city. The streets were long but not particularly spacious. The inhabitants, he noticed, had 'a lofty, military air' but were 'perfectly civil, the curiosity I excited being attended rather by an endeavour to conceal than by any marked notice or vulgar stare'. At ten o'clock he was ready to visit the governor. The British agent had found a *munshi* for him, 'a learned native of Delhi for the purpose of accompanying me in my excursions about the city, and of giving dignity to my appearance before the great Mogul'. With the munshi and part of his guard, armed with shields and swords, he left the city and, after marching across a plain inevitably strewn with ruins, reached the governor's mansion.

This was the home of the ascetic Shahji, though it hardly looked like it. There were numerous courts full of armed men, leading into a beautiful garden. Near the centre, in a handsome open pavilion before which was a pool of water, was the governor, surrounded by attendants. As Twining approached, the governor rose and came down the steps to meet him and lead him back into the pavilion. There was some desultory conversation. Did the king of England not have elephants in his train? The admission that he did not made it difficult for Twining to convey that his sovereign was, nevertheless, magnificent. As conversation seemed to flag, the governor asked whether Mr Twining would like to see round the mansion, 'an unusual honour, as I afterwards understood'. It was large, with many stairways and narrow corridors, but very sparsely furnished. Twining saw nothing of the governor's family. 'Whether the Cashmirian beauties who formed, doubtless, the principal ornaments of the palace had an opportunity of gratifying *their* curiosity, I could not say; but I had none of satisfying *mine*, although I dared to glance a look down some of the passages leading apparently to the seraglio, as I passed them at the governor's side'.

After their tour, Twining and the governor returned to the pavilion in the garden. Servants came forward with trays of betel nut, attar of roses, oranges, and other fruits. The perfume was poured on to the palms of Mr Twining's hands and then wiped off with a handkerchief. Rose-water was sprinkled from an elegant silver vessel with a long neck perforated with holes at the end. A piece of fruit was eaten and, after what Twining described as 'the usual compliments', he took his leave.

Instead of returning directly to his quarters, the young Englishman went off to have a look at the great cathedral mosque of Delhi, the Jama Masjid. He removed his shoes, according to custom, and wandered inside admiring the fine marble and mounting the 128 steps to the top of one of the minarets. When he returned to his palace, he found that on the following day he was to have an audience of the emperor. 'The rest of this afternoon was principally spent in preparing for my visit the next morning ; in learning the customary forms ; the amount of the *nuzzur* [gift] to be presented, the way of offering it, the language to be used, and other matters prescribed by etiquette. Being told that it would be necessary to take off my shoes before His Majesty, I said that I had not the least objection to that or any other established usage'.

On 1 December, preparations for the visit began early, though the time fixed was not until midday. Twining's escort had made themselves as presentable as possible after the exigencies of the long journey to the capital, 'and made a very respectable appearance'. Mr Twining himself had dressed in white, 'and was enveloped in a very long orange-coloured shawl'. In the bazaar he had bought a magnificent pair of sandals worked in gold : 'The end or toe advanced very considerably, and having gradually diminished almost to a point, curled back over the foot, with a high sweep, like a Dutch skate'.

Soon after eleven the party moved off, accompanied by some of the imperial guard. The procession was strung out in a long line, with Twining on his little charger at the centre and the munshi and the British agent, mounted, on either side. Behind was carried his palanquin. 'The people salaamed as I moved gently through the streets'.

After passing through several courts of the imperial palace to the audience hall, Twining dismounted from his horse and was welcomed by finely-dressed court officials. First he was shown into the Hall of Public Audience, 'a fine building which formed with its numerous accessory apart-ments one entire side of a spacious square. It was so extensive as to seem itself a palace'. Next he was conducted to the Hall of Private Audience, which, though it bore 'more marks of modern spoliation' than the other, still looked splendid with its white marble pillars. While Twining was admiring 'these beautiful specimens of oriental magnificence', he was approached by some court officials 'sumptuously dressed in shawls' who told him that the emperor had taken his seat in a side hall and was waiting to receive him.

On a large carpet spread on an open terrace were lines of

richly-clothed men. At the edge of the carpet Twining took off his slippers and 'advanced alone a little beyond the first line of persons sitting, and turning to my right, when half way between the two lines I saw the emperor immediately before me at the further extremity of the lines'. Shah Alam was sitting on a low throne covered with crimson silk.

Twining made three low bows as he had been instructed and then, raising himself, looked around. He noticed that the lines of men nearest him were composed of young men, and those furthest away of older men. These were the princes of the imperial family. Twining advanced and made three more low bows, then moved forward again until he was near the throne. He now had a clear view of the emperor. 'Though prepared to see him blind, as he was, the appearance of the Great Mogul upon his throne in such a situation was an extraordinary and most distressing spectacle ... There was, however, nothing repulsive in the emperor's appearance, nothing being perceptible but a depression of the eyelids'. By the emperor's side were his son, Akbar, and the governor of Delhi, Shahji.

Twining's munshi, who had followed him to the throne, placed a piece of fine muslin, folded to about six inches square, on Twining's right hand and placed five gold coins on it. Twining extended this to the emperor, 'who being informed of what I had done, stretched out his right hand, and laid it upon my offering'. A court official then came forward and took the coins. The munshi next placed three gold coins on the cloth, and these were presented to Prince Akbar, who took them himself. Some smaller sums were then offered to others in the same way. After the ceremony was over, Shah Alam expressed his pleasure at Twining's visit. 'I returned my acknowledgements for this con-descension, adding that the fame of His Majesty and of his imperial house had reached the distant parts from which I came. The celebrity of his virtues had inclined me to approach the seat of empire, where my reception into the august presence would ever be a source of satisfaction to me in my own country'.

The young civil servant then presented the commander-in-chief's letter, which was written 'in the Persian language upon highly varnished paper, spotted with gold'. Its contents were read out by an official, the emperor enquired after the general's health, and Twining replied, promising that he would communicate 'His Majesty's condescension to the general, to whom it would be more pleasing than victory'.

It was now time for the presentation of a dress of honour, which Twining accepted with suitable expressions of gratitude. He left the emperor's presence temporarily, 'retreating backwards between the two lines' of courtiers. He reached the edge of the carpet safely enough, though not, he was sure, 'in a very straight line', and was conducted to another apartment where he could put on the dress of honour. There was 'a long splendid robe of muslin, richly bespangled and embroidered with gold. It covered me entirely, and reached down to my golden sandals. A turban of fine gold muslin, many yards in length, was wound round my head. A handsome scarf of white muslin, worked with gold, and ending with deep fringes of gold, was placed over my shoulders, and reached almost to the ground. Another long piece of muslin, also embroidered with gold, was wound round my waist, forming a broad thick girdle over the robe and under the scarf'. There was also a handsome green shawl for the munshi.

Suitably dressed, Twining returned to the emperor, and after the ritual bows was told by Shah Alam that he was welcome to tour the palace. A meal would be provided for him from the emperor's own table and he hoped that Twining would stay a few days so that he might be properly entertained. Twining replied: 'May your Majesty be blessed with years, prosperity and health', and then withdrew, 'backwards as before'.

The pavilions and the gardens of the imperial palace turned out to be very beautiful. Twining was impressed 'by a succession of marble rooms susceptible of different degrees of heat from stoves, of which there was no exterior appearance'. These were the baths. 'The bather proceeds at intervals of a few seconds from one room to another—perspiration being thus gradually produced'. There was little sign here of Ghulam Kadir's search for plunder, but it was not so in the empty magazines and arsenals. Twining, however, was still feeling a little overwhelmed by his audience with the emperor, and told his guides that he would retire. Reaching the gate, he mounted his horse 'and adopting the same order of procession as before, returned gently through the city with all my imperial honours thick upon me'.

In the evening, the chief of the emperor's kitchen arrived at Twining's pavilion with twenty men, each carrying two dishes slung from a bamboo pole. These were placed on a large carpet and the qualities of each dish were explained to Twining as he ate. Twining had allowed his attendants to come into the hall to watch him eat the imperial repast, but he was sure they were better pleased by what followed—a 'numerous set of handsome and richly-dressed nautch or dancing girls, who came in pursuance of orders from the palace'. They were accompanied by musicians and immediately began to perform. They danced in a row, one or two shuffling forward occasionally and then returning. After 'they had exhibited nearly two hours, conceiving they must be tired, and beginning to feel so myself, I allowed them to retire, and finally closed the ceremonies of this important day by making the customary presents to the officers and servants of the imperial establishment, and to others who had contributed to my amusement'.

Twining spent the remainder of his stay in the imperial city sightseeing, commenting in his journal on the mortality of human fame as he marched from one ruined tomb to another. He was warned to be careful in his excursions outside the city, for the ruins were the haunts of robbers who would not hesitate to fire on him. He therefore avoided, as far as possible, 'such old walls and broken masses as seemed favourable to such an attack', and went about armed with a pistol and sword. His munshi 'on these occasions wore a handsome scimitar'. In fact, everyone carried arms, 'generally a scimitar, or convex blade, enclosed in a black scabbard, and a round black shield with four or five small bosses in the centre'. Even tradesmen went armed about their affairs, an indication of the insecurity of life.

After buying some souvenirs, hookah bowls for which Delhi was famous, a strange gun set in the handle of an axe, and a coat of chain-mail, it was time for Twining to leave. He sent a message to the emperor announcing his departure, and asked the agent of the British Resident who had smoothed his way at court to find an opportunity to tell the emperor that Twining hoped 'the time might perhaps come when I might be in a situation to prove the interest I should ever feel in the prosperity of His Majesty's affairs'. As he noted in his journal, 'surrounded as the imperial throne now was by the vaqueels [agents] of native powers, jealous and watchful of all foreign influence, and particularly of the powerful influence of the East India Company, these communications required some circumspection. But having succeeded in arriving so far, and witnessed the personal affliction of the old emperor, I was extremely desirous of conveying to him information which might shed a ray of light upon his *mind*, at least by opening the prospect of more prosperous days'.

His respects paid to the emperor and to the governor, Twining prepared to leave for the south, though he had been strongly advised that the road was dangerous. 'But', he noted, 'I had found that in travelling, as in other situations, when embarrassments occur, the means of overcoming them generally present themselves ; and I was unwilling to return ... without seeing, if it were possible, General De Boigne, whose fame was spread through Hindostan'.

Before he left, Twining received from the emperor 'His Majesty's permission to wear a seal or ornament, inscribed with his name and the date of my visit to the Presence'. The governor, rather more practically, sent 'twenty-one fine sepoys, armed with matchlocks and sabres' to escort him.

4
The Irish raja

THE PREOCCUPATION of the Maratha leaders with their own internecine quarrels intensified after the death of Mahadaji Sindia in 1794. Two years before his death, when he left northern India himself, Sindia had divided the administration of what were in theory provinces of Shah Alam's empire, but in practice Maratha dependencies, into six regions. The first was Delhi city and an undefined area around it. The second area was that of Panipat, which was fluid to the north and west and under constant pressure from the Sikhs. Then came the district known as Hariana, the country to the north and west of the imperial city. The fourth district was centred on the towns of Meerut and Saharanpur, and the fifth on Alighur, around which lay the lands assigned to de Boigne's force. The sixth region was not considered as part of Hindustan proper, because it contained Sindia's official capital of Ujjain. None of these districts had any precise boundary, nor was the administration secure or settled. Invasion, internal rebellion, endemic brigandage, all sustained a state of permanent anarchy, and Sindia's governors were constantly at war. The doors of opportunity remained always open for any military adventurer to pass through.

One who accepted the invitation was George Thomas, who, as an officer in the Begum Sumru's contingent, had helped to save the emperor during his farcical campaign against Najaf Kuli Khan. Thomas was an Irishman, born in Tipperary about 1756. He had arrived at Madras as a common sailor in 1782, then, deserting his ship, had begun a career of adventure which led, for a short time at least, to the creation of a principality of his own.

Thomas was a man of presence, tall and handsome, with an air of wildness which did not affect his military efficiency or his generosity. The Begum, who enjoyed more than military service from some of her European officers, was attracted to Thomas, and his rise in her army was assured. He was appointed revenue-collector for one of the districts of her state, and not only ruled with firmness but drove off the Sikh raiders who always lurked around its margins. As a further reward, the Begum married him to one of her adopted daughters. But his unexpected success as a revenue raiser—a success based on organization rather than oppression—made Thomas enemies among the less efficient of the Begum's European mercenaries. Some of her French officers, one of whom was her current lover, persuaded the Begum that Thomas was growing too powerful and intended to cut a state for himself out of the Begum's dominions. While Thomas was away pursuing Sikh raiders, his wife and family were seized as hostages. Thomas returned to rescue his family, and they left for his headquarters at Tappal, where he proclaimed himself independent.

His sovereignty did not last for long, for the Begum sent her entire army against him—a tribute, at least—and captured him in September 1791. His release was obtained by Sindia's governor of Delhi, Shahji. Not wishing to offend the Marathas, the Begum reluctantly had Thomas and his family conducted to the border of British territory at Anupshahar, and gave it out that he had been dismissed her service for seducing female members of her household!

Thomas was not prepared for idleness. With the small sum of money he had managed to hold on to, he bought weapons and, arming a small band of desperate men—of whom there were plenty to choose from—turned himself into a bandit. With the profits, he then formed a small contingent of 250 men, cast some cannon from the brass utensils taken in his many raids, and offered his services to Sindia's general, Apa Khande Rao, in about October 1793. Apa Khande Rao was at that time one of Sindia's district governors.

With his contingent enlarged to 500 men, Thomas spent two years successfully collecting the revenue from refractory chiefs. Impressed by his work, Apa Khande sent him with his men, in November 1795, to drive off a force of 5,000 Sikh raiders who were besieging a fort in the Saharanpur district. Apa Khande next decided that Thomas should increase the size of his contingent, and assigned a piece of land, with villages, for its maintenance. As the area had never paid taxes to Apa Khande, it seemed to be an economical move. Thomas set off for this territory and, on the way, plundered some of the lands of the Begum Sumru, as a small gesture of revenge.

When he arrived at his allotted lands, bandits stole Thomas's horses during a night halt. This was too much. Thomas was prepared for a peaceful occupation but ready for a bloody one, if necessary. After some hard fighting, the area was pacified. Unfortunately, Thomas was so pleased with his success that he began to plunder some of the surrounding countryside, and had to be driven off by the Begum's troops.

Before he could settle down, Thomas received an urgent appeal from Apa Khande, who was besieged by his own troops, demanding, as usual, their arrears of pay. Making a rapid march of forty miles, Thomas appeared outside the fort in which Apa Khande had taken refuge and managed to persuade the mutineers to accept a payment on account. As a reward, he was told to raise a force of 2,000 infantry, 200 cavalry, and 16 guns, and was assigned more land for their upkeep. His role was now to keep the Sikhs from crossing the upper Jumna river.

In 1796, Thomas was instructed to co-operate with Daulat Rao Sindia's European force, now commanded by General Perron, in an attack on a rebel town. The contingent sent by Perron was commanded by two ex-British officers who believed that they were more experienced and better soldiers than Thomas. They insisted that the town was too strongly defended for an immediate assault and that it would need a regular siege to take it. Thomas disagreed and was overruled. He then made a personal reconnaissance and decided not only that the town could be taken by a sudden attack, but that he could do it himself without the help of Perron's men.

Early in the morning he attacked and occupied the town and the fort, before his allies realized what was happening. When they arrived and demanded their share of the loot, Thomas refused. He had taken the town by himself and the reward was his and his alone. He then took himself and his men off, just in time to throw back an attack on his lands by the Begum Sumru.

Apa Khande continued to use Thomas in various campaigns. In one, he gave his protection to a chief who Apa Khande wished to hang. When Thomas refused to break his word to the chief, the Maratha general arranged for a robber band to ambush Thomas and kill him. An expedition was arranged for Thomas, and the band assembled at a place he would be forced to pass, but spies at Apa Khande's headquarters warned Thomas. The Irishman set off as agreed but, by doubling his daily marches, surprised the robbers on the night before he was expected and killed most of them. Two of the wounded men were sent back to Apa Khande with a note from Thomas informing him that the plot had failed. Apa Khande denied that he had been aware of any plot, and reinforced his denial with the most potent of proofs, a large sum of money. He also appealed to Thomas to come once more to his aid, as he had been attacked by a Sikh force and his troops were not trustworthy. Thomas answered the appeal, drove off the attackers, and departed for his own possessions, only to find they were being attacked by another force of Sikhs. Driving them off, he pursued them into the territory of the raja of Patiala and extracted an indemnity from him.

The next appeal for aid came from an unexpected quarter. The Begum Sumru had made the mistake of marrying one of her officers, a Frenchman named Le Vasseau. The delicate balance maintained by equal opportunity for all to sleep with the Begum, but no lasting favourites, was broken.

As soon as the marriage became known, her troops rebelled and put in her place a son of her former husband, Walter Reinhardt, by another wife. The Begum and Le Vasseau fled from their capital of Sardhana in the direction of British territory, that only sure asylum, but were caught before they could reach it. Le Vasseau killed himself, but the Begum was taken back to Sardhana and kept chained between two guns in the open air. Occasionally, when the sun had warmed the barrels so that they became almost too hot to touch, she was set astride one for a while.

How long she would have lasted under this torture was fortunately never discovered. One of her officers sent a message to George Thomas appealing for help. Thomas took his time in responding—almost six months, in fact—though he spent part of that period in bribing the Begum's troops with money supplied by the Marathas. Then, in July 1796, he marched secretly to Sardhana and, with the aid of the men he had bought in the Begum's army, surprised the ringleaders and replaced the somewhat worn Begum on her throne. For this he received her immediate thanks, but not her friendship.

After this, Thomas's position deteriorated, even though his now barely disguised enemy, Apa Khande, died in 1797. After his death, the Maratha administration fell to pieces and Thomas could not get supplies or payment out of his superiors. The income from his lands was insufficient to maintain his troops, and Thomas was forced to become, like many others before him, a bandit constantly raiding other rulers' territories adjoining his own. In 1798, however, he was offered a subsidy of 50,000 rupees a month to join Apa Khande's successor in an attack on Jaipur, which was still managing to avoid paying its annual subsidy. As the Marathas had repudiated their agreement with Thomas and had almost driven him out of his possessions in the previous year, it was surprising that he agreed to the new proposition. But in India, a mercenary's relationships were strictly businesslike. Thomas, virtually pushed out of his former lands, had moved into the almost desert area of

Hariana and had set up his headquarters at the derelict town of Hansi. There, he had set about establishing an adminis- tration, building arsenals, and even striking his own coins, but he was not yet fully established nor was the land— constantly ravaged by marauders—in a fit state to provide revenue. His banditry continued, and the expedition to Jaipur was merely a more formal application of the same system.

Thomas therefore joined forces with the Marathas and entered Jaipur. After severe fighting, he took the town and fort of Fathpur, though attempts were made by a large Jaipur army to dislodge him. Thomas moved out and, because there was no co-ordination between the Jaipur commanders, was able to beat back repeated attacks. Then the Jaipur general ordered a frontal assault by a body of 6,000 picked troops, but, as Thomas's biographer laconic- ally recorded, 'this main body had by this time become a confused mass, without order, regularity or method . . . Mr Thomas perceiving them at a stand, commenced a heavy fire of grapeshot, when after sustaining much loss the enemy retreated'. Unexpectedly, the Jaipur cavalry re-formed and rode down on Thomas's line. The Maratha cavalry which was supposedly supporting Thomas fled, and the Jaipur horse broke his left wing. 'The moment was critical . . . Mr Thomas with the only gun that remained, which he loaded up to the muzzle, and about 150 of his followers, waited the event with fortitude. After permitting the enemy to approach within forty yards, he gave them three discharges of his gun accompanied by three volleys of musketry'. This was all that was needed to put the un- disciplined cavalry to flight.

Thomas now left Jaipur territory to re-form his men, who had been badly mauled in the engagement at Fathpur. But he threatened soon to return. The Jaipur raja sent him a sum of money. Thomas accepted and turned his attention to another Rajput state. There, too, he was bought off. Next he accepted an offer from the Maratha general Ambaji Inglia to join in an attack on Udaipur, the terms agreed being 50,000 rupees down and a share of the plunder. A force of Perron's army was sent to co-operate with him, but it was commanded by one of the English officers he had earlier humiliated, and this officer withdrew his men at the Udaipur frontier. Nevertheless, Thomas's reputation had preceded him and the ruler tried to buy him off. Thomas, however, had a peculiar sense of honour. Whoever was paying him at the time was entitled to his loyalty. He refused the offer, but did not attempt to attack without the support of Perron's detachment.

Thomas was now a power to be feared. His little state was beginning to produce revenue, and the people were co-operating with a ruler who, for the first time, protected them not only from invaders but from the depredations of his own men. His assessments for tax were always reasonable. His collectors were not allowed to coerce. His justice, though rough, was equitable. Soon the deserted area attracted settlers and their families from the insecurity that was commonplace outside it. But Thomas's power was relative. Against the undisciplined rabble of native rulers he was usually successful. But against determined enemies he was forced to give way. His generalship was based on a quick appreciation of tactics and personal bravery. Against a force trained and disciplined on European lines and led by European officers he did not stand a chance. In his own force, the only Europeans were himself and an Englishman named Morris.

In 1799 he found himself drawn into the struggle between a widow of Mahadaji Sindia, and his successor, Daulat Rao Sindia. But by one of those unpredictable quirks of fortune, he found himself on the losing side although he himself did not lose by it and continued with his profitable raids. In January 1800 he entered the Sikh State of Patiala at the request of the raja's sister, who had been thrown into prison by her brother. The next year, he joined her again. Before doing so, he wrote to the British governor-general, Lord Wellesley, in Calcutta, asking for his approval of an attempt to conquer the Punjab. In his letter, Thomas said : 'I have no other design in view than the glory of my King and country and do not wish to see my conquests fall to those at enmity with them'. By 'those at enmity' Thomas meant the French, whom he—and Wellesley—believed were planning a blow against the British in India. Thomas's hopes of conquering the Punjab, which seem to have been genuine, were a fantasy. Though he had some initial success against the divided Sikh chiefs, as soon as they came together they forced him into a hurried retreat to his own dominions. But if Thomas's plan to conquer the Punjab was a dream, his fear of the French was not.

For symbolic images, Thomas had the kind of unreasoning hatred that is often to be found among the illiterate. He had been told often enough, when he was a sailor in the English service, that the French were England's most bitter enemies. All Frenchmen were therefore Thomas's enemies. At the head of the most powerful military force in northern India, as Daulat Rao's viceroy of the north, was a Frenchman, General Perron.

Lord Wellesley believed that Perron was a French agent, the advance guard of a French conquest which would throw the British out of India. Wellesley was about to embark on a campaign with the primary intention of destroying French pretensions in India. Thomas, too, saw his coming conflict with Perron as a small episode in a patriotic war. Nothing could have been further from the truth. Perron was certainly out to consolidate his position in northern India, and in the course of this aim Thomas would have to be crushed. But it was a strictly personal ambition. Perron was a mercenary, and no different from other mercenaries.

Thomas had no friends, but there were men who respected him. One was Perron. If Thomas could be bought all the better. An attempt to arrange terms took place during a meeting between the two men near Delhi in October 1801. The offer was liberal. Thomas was to join Daulat Rao's army with his force, and would receive in return a substantial monthly subsidy. But Thomas's hatred of the French came between him and this sensible offer.

His excuse to a friend was : 'Mr Perron and myself being subjects of nations in a state of hostility, could not possibly act together in concert, and I was convinced that he being a Frenchman and I an Englishman, Mr Perron would always be prepared to misinterpret my actions'. Whatever the truth, Thomas—to use his own words—'marched away in disgust'.

Early in 1801 Perron sent a force under the command of another Frenchman, Major Bourquin, to crush Thomas, then away from his own possessions on a plundering expedition. Bourquin's force was made up of ten battalions of infantry, and 3,000 cavalry—some 12,000 men in all. In command were a number of European and Eurasian officers. Thomas's force at the time numbered about 10,000, of whom only 500 were cavalry. His officers had been increased by two Eurasians, and he seems to have had some European sergeants, probably deserters from the East India Company's army.

A detachment of Bourquin's force was sent to attack the fort at Georgegarh (which Thomas had named after himself). It stood some sixty miles north of Hansi. Thomas advanced to the relief of the fort and defeated Bourquin's detachment. On his way back to Hansi, however, he was intercepted by Bourquin with his main force and severely mauled. Bourquin's casualties were also high, as he had been led by Thomas into a sandy area where his guns could not manoeuvre easily. But Thomas lost his second-in-command and made no attempt to take advantage of Bourquin's difficulties. According to one of Bourquin's officers, Thomas instead, 'oppressed by the loss of his only friend and worn out by the strain of so many years constant fighting, together with his present anxiety ... abandoned himself to one of those prolonged debauches to which he was unfortunately addicted'.

Drunk or not, Thomas allowed the opportunity to slip and was finally forced to make for his capital of Hansi. Before he left, he told his infantry to make the best terms they could with Bourquin and, abandoning his baggage, made off accompanied by some of his cavalry. But his position at Hansi was impossible. He had been closely pursued by Bourquin's cavalry and had lost many of his men. Though he held out against attack for as long as he could, there was no alternative but to surrender to overwhelming force. After Bourquin's English officers insisted that Thomas should be granted a safe conduct, Hansi surrendered, and on 1 January 1802 Thomas and his tattered men marched out. Thomas became a guest of the victors while arrangements were made for him to leave for British territory. This he did in a few days.

Thomas's dreams still followed him. At Benares he met Lord Wellesley and was shown a map with red shading on it. When he asked what the shading meant, he was told that it marked British territory. Putting his hand over the whole of the Punjab, he said sorrowfully : 'Had I been left alone I would have made all this red with this hand'. Thomas was sick and worn, though when his affairs had been settled there was a small fortune to take home with him. But he never reached home. He died at Berhampur in Bengal on 22 August 1802, at the age of forty-six.

General Perron was now the unquestioned master of northern India. Every threat had been eliminated, except one that was over the horizon. The British were about to sweep the Marathas out of northern India and take the aged emperor into their own indifferent care.

5

An insolent declaration

WHILE PERRON was engaged in destroying George
Thomas, events were on the move elsewhere. The emperor,
neglected in his great palace, still had ears in all the courts
of India, and the news he received was not altogether
welcome. Most of it was concerned with the British. During
their first war with Tipu, sultan of Mysore, the great
menace to their rule in south India, the British had persuaded the Marathas to help them. The Marathas had
agreed reluctantly, for they were conscious of the growing
power of the British and would probably have preferred
them to be defeated. But the main reason for the Marathas'
reluctance had been the confusion at the Peshwa's court.
The struggle for the succession had ended with the elevation
of Baji Rao, and the return of Nana Farnavis from a self-
imposed exile. But the hostility between the houses of
Sindia and Holkar, and between both and the Peshwa, had
not ceased even after the deaths of Mahadaji Sindia and
Tukoji Holkar.

It was a situation ripe for outside intervention, and Lord
Wellesley, who was appointed British governor-general in
1798, had every intention of profiting from it. He arrived in
India with all the hatred of Bonaparte that so dominated the
English ruling class at this time. The French revolution had
been an outrageous attack against the established order, and
all who knew themselves to be part of that order or who
profited from it looked on Jacobinism with all the loathing
of a twentieth-century American millionaire for com-
munism. Wellesley was convinced that Bonaparte had
designs on India, and though he may have been right, it was
unlikely that Bonaparte could have found the means. Never-

theless, this fear was to be the excuse for Wellesley's empire-building, for his aggressive policy towards the Maratha chiefs.

A revived threat from Tipu of Mysore had to be dealt with first. It was known that Tipu was in touch with Bonaparte and that he called himself Citizen Tipu, in the hope of extracting some real aid from the French envoys who came to his court and did nothing except make promises. Tipu was disposed of in a bitter war, and killed in his capital in 1799. Wellesley was now able to turn his attention to the north. His purpose was not only to crush the Marathas, who were known to employ French mercenaries —and whose real purpose, Wellesley believed, was to seize control of Hindustan for France—but to ensure that Shah Alam should not fall into the hands of the French. As Wellesley later said in explanation of his actions, 'the person and authority of His Majesty ... might form a dangerous instrument' in the hands of some ambitious person. Despite Shah Alam's 'total deprivation of real power, dominion and authority, almost every state and every class of people in India continue to acknowledge his nominal sovereignty'. The real prizes were dominion, and the person of the old blind emperor in Delhi.

There is no doubt that Shah Alam was aware of what was going on, but he could do nothing positive. He was entirely in the hands of Daulat Rao Sindia's agent, Perron, and could only await the outcome while, in the meantime, taking out an insurance policy with both sides. When it came to the clash he would, of course, openly support Sindia and the Peshwa, for the latter was his nominal regent and the former held the power. But he would also maintain secret contact with the British. Perhaps out of the conflict he might be able to pluck real rather than nominal sovereignty.

In 1798, the Peshwa, dissatisfied with the subordinate role he found himself playing in relation to his minister, Nana Farnavis, encouraged Sindia to act against him. A body of Sindia's troops under the command of a Neapolitan mercenary arrested the Nana and confined him in the fortress of Ahmadnagar. In theory at least, the Peshwa and Sindia were now allies—but not for long. Sindia released the Nana after he had paid a large bribe. The Peshwa, beginning to fear Sindia's intentions, invited the minister to resume his office but, unfortunately for the Peshwa, the Nana died in March 1800. This removed from the scene the one Maratha of real talent and foresight, and left the feeble Peshwa unarmed against the diplomacy of pressure which Wellesley now proposed to exercise.

Before the British could persuade the hesitant Peshwa to turn openly against Sindia, his own foolishness preci-pitated a crisis. Tukoji Holkar's successor was Jaswant Rao Holkar. In April 1801, the Peshwa captured Jaswant Rao's brother and, pleased at the opportunity of asserting his supremacy over one of the warring factions of the Maratha confederacy, had him sentenced to two hundred lashes and then watched him trampled to death by an elephant. This ruthlessness seemed to work, for Jaswant Rao submitted to the Peshwa's authority, though not in person. The Peshwa's spies reported that he was deeply angry.

A few months later, Holkar emerged to attack not the Peshwa but Sindia. He defeated a detachment of Sindia's troops, trained and led by Europeans, and forced another to surrender. This victory—though it was by no means complete, for another European-led contingent both man-aged to save itself and to defend Sindia's artillery park—convinced Holkar that the old-fashioned Maratha methods of warfare still had an advantage over the new-fangled European style of force which Jaswant Rao Holkar, unlike his father, despised.

Holkar's attack roused Sindia to action. Extracting a large sum of money from the Peshwa, he set out from the Peshwa's territory. Behind him he left his father-in-law, Sarji Rao Ghatke, with five battalions of infantry and 10,000 horse. With Sindia out of the way, the Peshwa tried to have Ghatke assassinated, but the plot was bungled and Ghatke moved his troops to the outskirts of the Peshwa's capital, Poona, and threatened to burn the city. The Peshwa was forced to ask the British agent to mediate, but he was in fact saved by Sindia calling on Ghatke to leave Poona and come to his aid against Holkar.

Sindia's force caught up with and defeated Holkar in October 1801. His capital of Indore was savagely plundered, but Sindia did not follow up his victory. He claimed loftily that he had no more to fear from Holkar. But his defeated enemy refused to lie down. Holkar, who was rather more of a bandit at heart than most of the Maratha leaders, began to ravage the countryside so successfully that he was soon able to attract deserters from Sindia's army. This was partly due to his own immense personal attraction. Holkar's name became synonymous with skill and personal courage, while his temper and his cruelties were accepted as marks of genius. He had the bravery which inspires hero-worship and conceals faults. At the beginning of his campaign against Sindia and the Peshwa, he told his troops that he had no money to pay them with and that they must find their own profit in plunder. They accepted these conditions with alacrity, because of the honour of following him. Even in retreat, he could still attract men from the armies that were pursuing him.

Holkar's success and Sindia's apparent indifference decided the Peshwa to open up negotiations with Holkar, and Holkar said he would come to Poona to claim, in person, the Peshwa's support against Sindia. He went about this in a way which frightened the Peshwa more than it did Sindia. Holkar's forces swept the countryside for plunder— defeating, in passing, two of the Peshwa's own generals. To Baji Rao, Sindia soon began to appear the lesser of the two evils. But Sindia was slow to move, and when he finally decided to go to the aid of the Peshwa his troops refused to march until they had received arrears of pay.

On 23 October 1802, Holkar was encamped within sight of the Peshwa's capital. Two days of negotiation achieved no agreement between them, but in the meantime Sindia's forces joined with those of the Peshwa.

Finally, the two armies met at a place near the British

Residency in Poona, which, surmounted by a vast Union Jack, was carefully respected by both sides. Both armies included European-led infantry, but it was Holkar's wild cavalry that gave him the victory. After capturing all Sindia's baggage, stores and guns, Holkar offered to negotiate with the Peshwa. He ordered his men not to enter the city, though the gates had been opened to him, and even turned guns on to some of his own troops who wanted to plunder it. Later, when he heard that the Peshwa had fled, he allowed his men to have their way.

As soon as he learned of Sindia's defeat, the Peshwa had departed, and it was the British Resident who went to Holkar's camp to discuss terms. While the talks were in progress, the Peshwa sent a message to the Resident accepting British protection. Holkar heard of this—nothing could be kept secret for long—and sent men after the Peshwa, who thereupon begged the British to send him a ship so that he could leave by sea for Bombay. On 6 December 1802 he landed in British territory, safe from Holkar at least.

With the Peshwa in British hands, it seemed as if the first part of Wellesley's plan to bring the Marathas into the British empire was almost achieved. Earlier, he had come close to resigning his appointment and returning home, because his superiors in London had not only refused to support his policies but had ordered him to reduce his military expenditure immediately. After the Peshwa's flight, however, Wellesley decided to ignore his instructions. This event, he wrote on 24 December 1802, had brought about 'a conjuncture of affairs which appears to present the most advantageous opportunity that has ever occurred of improving the British interests in that quarter'.

On 31 December at Bassein, the British concluded a treaty with the Peshwa by which he became a dependant of the Company. Wellesley was convinced that Sindia would be bound to associate himself with the treaty of Bassein, but that 'unprincipled chieftain' refused to do so. The situation facing the governor-general was one of considerable complexity. Holkar was openly hostile to Sindia. Sindia was more concerned with his position as overlord of the Mughal emperor than with fighting Holkar or treating with the British. Another Maratha leader, the ruler of Baroda, had relapsed into lukewarm friendship with the British; while the raja of Nagpur could not make up his mind whether to support Sindia or the Peshwa.

Wellesley was even more convinced than he had been before that the Maratha 'empire', as he insisted on calling it, was about to form an alliance with the French. Certainly, there were French agents moving about northern India, and of course there was General Perron, that almost independent ruler at Alighur. Enmeshed in this conviction, Wellesley tried to press all the Maratha chiefs to accept 'the benefits of the defensive alliance' which the anguished Peshwa had been bullied into signing at Bassein—regretting it immediately afterwards. Wellesley believed that he could gain everything he wanted by persuading the Maratha chiefs to agree *voluntarily* to accept terms which could, in fact, do nothing other than put an end to their independence.

The governor-general's brother, Major-General Arthur Wellesley—recently embarked on the road that was to lead to the victory of Waterloo—was ordered to escort the Peshwa back to his capital at Poona and see him established there. The city was shattered by Holkar's plundering, and the countryside, too, had been devastated. The general recorded that there was not 'a stick standing at the distance of 150 miles from Poonah; they [Holkar's troops] have eaten the forage and grain; they have pulled down the houses, and have used the materials as firewood'. Cultivation of the land had ceased, most of the people had fled, and those who remained were starving. Packs of jackals feasted on the bodies of the dead. But at least the Peshwa was back in his own capital, with a force of British troops to protect him against both Sindia and Holkar. But who was to protect him against the British? For the moment at least, he had nothing to fear from them. Their attention was turned elsewhere.

As far as the other Maratha leaders were concerned, Wellesley would have been satisfied if Sindia had dismissed his French officers and given up the Ganges and Jumna valley; if the raja of Nagpur had given up Orissa, a piece of territory which Wellesley believed rightly belonged to the British; and if both had accepted a tributary relationship with the British.

Wellesley was, however, determined not only to achieve 'the complete consolidation of the British empire in India' but to strike a telling blow at France, with whom Britain was once again on the edge of war in Europe. In the latter aim he had the fullest support of the British government, who shared his illusions about the French threat in India. Though many of his compatriots close to the realities of central India did not share Wellesley's view of the French menace, most of them shared his excitement at the thought of being *able* to strike a blow at the French. There were Indians, too, who looked forward to a British victory.

In the Maratha territories, the persecuted and oppressed began to anticipate an end to their sufferings.

The British were particularly anxious to bring Sindia and the Nagpur raja to heel. Holkar appeared to them to be no more than a bandit, while the ruler of Baroda was an ally of sorts. It was Sindia who appeared as the key to peace or war. The British Resident at Sindia's court was instructed to press that ruler to sign the treaty of Bassein, but his arguments had no effect. When he warned Sindia not to try to form an alliance with the ruler of Nagpur, Sindia replied that he would consult the raja—if he so chose—and then inform the Resident whether he favoured peace or war.

On 27 June 1803, the governor-general—offended by Sindia's 'insolent and hostile declaration' to the British Resident—ordered his brother who now commanded the southern army to drive Sindia and the Nagpur raja back into 'their respective territories'. The governor-general still thought that actual war would be unnecessary but, as Major-General Wellesley moved towards them, Sindia and the raja stood fast. War was inevitable. The Resident handed Sindia General Wellesley's ultimatum—'I offered peace on terms of equality and honourable to all parties. You have chosen war, and are responsible for all consequences'. Then the Resident, with his retinue, left Sindia's camp on 3 August 1803.

6

The tattered canopy

SHAH ALAM knew that the time of decision had now come. He could do very little about his own position. Perron's army held the city, and the commander of the palace was one of Perron's deputies, Major Drugeon. As well as news from spies and newswriters, which arrived constantly at the palace and was discussed and discussed again in the secrecy of the emperor's private apartments, Shah Alam had received a personal letter from Lord Wellesley. This arrived late in July, when the British were massing troops ready to move into Hindustan.

In his instructions to the commander-in-chief, General Lake, Wellesley had made it clear that 'the point of most urgent importance connected with the destruction of M. Perron's force is in my opinion the security of the person of the Moghul [emperor] and of the heir apparent, and it is therefore my earnest wish that early measures should be taken for that purpose'. His letter to the emperor reminded Shah Alam, rather falsely, of 'the sentiments of respect and attachment which the British government had invariably entertained towards your royal person and family'—a version of the truth which must have been received with some cynicism by Shah Alam who had, if little else, a long memory.

Wellesley went on to regret that 'the circumstances of the times have hitherto precluded the interposition of the British power for the purpose of affording to your Majesty effectual relief from the oppressive control of injustice, rapacity, and inhumanity. Nevertheless,' he said, 'in the present crisis of affairs it is probable that your Majesty may have the opportunity of again placing yourself under the protection of the British government, and I shall avail myself with cordial satisfaction of any event which may enable me to obey the dictates of my sincere respect and attachment to your royal house. 'If', continued Wellesley, 'your Majesty should be disposed to accept the asylum, which, in the contemplation of such an event, I have directed his Excellency the commander-in-chief of the British forces in Oudh to offer to your Majesty, in the name of the British government, your Majesty may be assured that every demonstration of respect and every degree of attention which can contribute to the ease and comfort of your Majesty and the royal family, will be manifested on the part of the British government, and that adequate provision will be made for the support of your Majesty and of your family and household'.

This letter was delivered in the 'strictest secrecy' by Syed Reza Khan, the agent of the British Resident at Sindia's court who had been so helpful to young Mr Twining. Secrecy was essential but by no means complete, for Major Drugeon heard about the letter and it was probably he who was responsible for the emperor's reply, received by Lake on 1 September. This announced 'his Majesty's intention of taking the field in person', and required the governor-general 'to prohibit the further prosecution of military operations'.

The emperor's reply was taken for what it appeared to be, a statement of defiance made under duress. Not that it mattered greatly what the emperor's reply was. Wellesley's instructions to Lake had been precise. He was to treat Shah Alam with due respect, but that was all. The governor-general had no doubts about the outcome of Lake's campaign. The emperor would ultimately find himself in British hands, and it would be the British who decided his future.

Shah Alam had undoubtedly recognized the realities of the situation even before he wrote his reply to Wellesley. By then, the British had taken the great fortress of Alighur and General Perron had departed with the profits of his tenure as the emperor's keeper—into British territory! All this had come about quite simply, because regardless of what Wellesley might think Perron had had no intention of fighting the British.

Lake had left his base at Cawnpore, about 185 miles from Alighur, on 7 August 1803. The East India Company's forces had not fought a European enemy for twenty years, but this did not worry Lake who, at over sixty years of age, was a veteran of wars in Germany, America, and Holland. Against his force of 10,000, he knew there to be Perron's army of at least 15,000, as well as another 4,000 irregulars based on the fortified cities of Alighur and Agra. In favour of an English victory, however, was Perron's determination to get out while he could. After a skirmish near Aligurh on the morning of 29 August, Perron retired. The commandant of Aligurh, another Frenchman, opened up negotiations with Lake but was arrested by his own second-in-command, a Maratha. Lake finished up by storming the fort, taking it at a cost of 260 men. The defenders lost 2,000. The fort was afterwards relieved of a great deal of loot.

The fall of Aligurh convinced the rest of Sindia's French mercenaries that they should quit before it was too late. Wellesley had already requested British mercenaries commanding the Maratha's forces to leave Sindia's employ, and they had agreed, though some of them made it a condition that they should not be asked to fight against their former employer. After the capture of Aligurh, Perron himself appeared in Lake's camp announcing that he had resigned from Sindia's service (though he had, in fact, fallen to the intrigues of another French officer). He was given an escort to British territory and treated with fulsome ceremony. In 1806 he sailed for Europe, carrying with him a substantial fortune.

Lake now turned to the capture of Delhi. It was reported that a large body of Sindia's troops, under a French commander, was marching to meet the British. Lake's army, setting out at 3 a.m. on the morning of 11 September, covered eighteen miles in eight hours. When they halted to make camp, Lake went out in person on a reconnaissance and discovered a large body of the enemy drawn up on a section of rising ground flanked by marshes. He immediately ordered up his artillery and infantry, while the cavalry occupied themselves in drawing the Marathas' fire. As soon as the infantry and artillery arrived, Lake began a pretended withdrawal. The Maratha infantry left their trenches in pursuit, only to find themselves face to face with the major part of the British infantry, concealed in the long grass. Lake himself headed the charge, and the Marathas fled across the river Jumna while the British artillery tore them to pieces. The defeat was complete, and Lake's losses amounted only to 461.

The battle had been watched from the ramparts of the palace by the imperial family, and each episode was retailed to the blind Shah Alam who sat on the terrace. At the news of the fall of Alighur and Lake's approach to Delhi, there had broken out there what was virtually a civil war between Perron's officers. Before Perron had decided that the time had come to go over to the British, he had sent tents and baggage animals to Delhi so that the emperor and his family could be removed to Mathura, where Perron's main force was concentrated. The orders had been sent to Bourquin but, on 4 September, this officer set himself up as an independent agent of Sindia's and repudiated Perron's authority. Next day, he attacked the emperor's baggage train and, lowering the imperial standard, replaced it with that of Sindia. Bourquin then set his men to the pleasurable task of plundering Delhi and threw Perron's envoy and another Frenchman into jail.

In the city Lake's agents were doing what they could to suborn the European officers in Bourquin's force and were meeting with some success. Realizing that he might be overthrown by his own force, Bourquin decided to make as much profit as possible before he retired. It was therefore necessary to take control of the palace, where the treasure was held. Bourquin demanded that Drugeon surrender the palace. Drugeon refused. Bourquin then brought up a battery of six guns and began to bombard the palace. At this stage, Shah Alam sent a messenger to Lake appealing for protection and aid.

Lake's approach brought indescribable confusion to the city. Bourquin's men were deserting. Bourquin himself, denied entry to the fort, decided that the best way to save himself and his fortune was to go over to the British. This he did by crossing the river Jumna, ostensibly to attack them ; instead, he joined them.

On 14 September the British force crossed the river by a bridge of boats which Bourquin had deliberately left intact, so as to ingratiate himself with the British commander. From the emperor, Lake received a message of congratulations on his victory and a request that he might come and deliver the imperial family from Maratha control. Lake had accompanied Wellesley's letter of July with one of his own, in which he informed the emperor that he was 'cordially disposed to render your Majesty every demonstration of my loyalty'. It was a gesture of courtesy which had a purpose while the outcome of the war remained undecided. Afterwards it had no meaning. Yet Lake's instructions from Wellesley were to treat the emperor with 'every demonstration of respect'. So the charade was maintained.

On 16 September, Lake set out for an audience with Shah Alam. According to the arrangements, Prince Akbar was to go to Lake's camp outside the walls at noon, but because of some delay it was three hours later before the prince arrived. After a number of ceremonies, the prince remounted his elephant and the cavalcade moved off, reaching the palace only at sunset. The streets outside the palace were crowded with people, which made passage difficult, but finally the commander-in-chief was led into the Hall of Private Audience. It was lit by flickering torches. And there, as one of Lake's party wrote later, the emperor, 'the descendant of the great Akbar and the victorious Aurangzeb, was found, an object of pity, blind and aged, stripped of authority, and reduced to poverty, seated under a tattered canopy, the fragment of regal state, and the mockery of human pride'.

The flickering torches, the poverty, even the tattered

canopy may have been a carefully considered pretence, the stage-set of a drama which had been enacted many times before. But it was, in fact, the last scene in the last act of the Mughal empire, which thereafter disappeared into the shadows.

Epilogue
An empire of shadows

THOUGH THE British had captured Delhi and taken the emperor under their protection, the war against the Marathas was not yet over. Lake had more battles to fight and win. So, too, had Arthur Wellesley. But in the end Sindia and the Nagpur raja accepted defeat and negotiated their surrender. Only the 'bandit' Holkar stood out. In 1804 he even threatened the British garrison in the imperial capital. Yet he, too, was beaten off, and though the conflict between the British and the Marathas was not finally settled for another fifteen years, Delhi and its nominal ruler remained firmly in the keeping of the British.

Wellesley had wanted to remove Shah Alam and his heir from the imperial city and offer them a new residence within the British dominions. He was not, however, prepared to use force and Shah Alam had no intention of leaving Delhi—that would have been tantamount to a denial of his imperial authority. To this he clung for the three years before his death in 1806 with the same tenacity as he had held on to life itself. He had tried his usual strategy, when faced with overwhelming power in the past, of retaining his nominal authority by making his master a great officer of state. The Marathas had accepted the subterfuge because it did not interfere with their interests. But the British were different. Wellesley had no intention of making a show of submission to the emperor, whatever the British commander-in-chief might choose to do. Lake had accepted from the emperor a range of high-sounding titles—Sword of the State, Hero of the Land, Lord of the Age, and Victorious in War. All these titles were, however, inferior to those held by Sindia, who had not, at that time, been defeated. It was one of Shah Alam's axioms never to close down an option.

The British were at least prepared to arrange for regular payment of the emperor's maintenance, though Lake seized a large sum which Drugeon had kept in the palace and which Shah Alam insisted was meant for him. Wellesley ordered that it be returned to the emperor, and soon afterwards a regular source of income was arranged. But the British signed no treaty with Shah Alam, nor would they accept that their position relative to him was anything other than overlords to pensioner. Unlike previous conquerors, they did not treat the emperor as a puppet. Instead, they regarded him as an idol which they did not worship themselves but which they thought it unwise to remove in case the faithful should be offended.

British policy was really a product of the particular British view of political reality. They regarded the emperor, whom they now called 'king of Delhi', as merely a pensioner, maintained out of sentiment and ignored out of policy. Such an attitude was, however, quite alien to the Indian political consciousness. As long as the king remained in his palace—pensioner or not, with or without real power—the dignity of his position somehow remained untarnished. However nominal his authority, the authority of his name could not be denied.

Because of what can best be described as an attack of romanticism, the British decided to act out what they thought was only a charade, a courteous and well-meaning exercise in make-believe designed to soften the blow that their victory had dealt to the Mughal dynasty. In certain circumstances, too, they believed that the Mughal name was politically valuable, especially that of Shah Alam. For thirty years after his death they continued to issue coinage bearing his name, as if it were a talisman. But it was no charade for the king and his family, nor for others who resented British power. The king, they said, was still king. Even the British admitted as much and acted in his name. It was a situation quivering with danger, a danger which was compounded over the years until it finally made the court of Delhi the focus of rebellion in the Mutiny of 1857.

While Shah Alam lived, there was some excuse for the British and for the charade. Afterwards there was none, for with him died the last link with the empire's unconquered past. Within the walls of his palace, the king was permitted to exercise ruling powers. The inhabitants, servants, retainers, tradesmen, were his direct subjects, and members of the imperial family had immunity from British law. The ceremonial of the court was maintained. Officials still bore the high-sounding titles of their predecessors and the formal rituals of court etiquette were rigidly adhered to. When the British Resident, the real ruler, went to visit the king, he too followed traditional protocol, dismounting in an inner courtyard and standing respectfully in the royal presence.

The financial arrangements were not ungenerous. For Shah Alam they were ample. In fact, he was even able to save money; at his death there was over a million rupees in his treasury. So, in comparative affluence, and certainly in a kind of security he had never known, the old blind emperor lived out the last years of his life. There is no record of what he thought, but his mind must often have wandered over the past. As a boy, he had seen the imperial city drown in blood when the Persian conqueror, Nadir Shah, had ridden into Delhi. When Afghan and Maratha had met in the holocaust of Panipat, he had been a wanderer without a home. He had once fought those same British who now controlled the world outside his palace, at Buxar, and had escaped them for a while by his flight from Allahabad. There had been the horror of Ghulam Kadir. And there had been moments of hope. Because of them he had survived. Blind, he could not see that, all the time, he had been only a shadow in an empire of shadows.

Bibliography

RECORDS AND DOCUMENTS, UNPUBLISHED
Persian
Rhaguvir Library, Sitamau. Collection of *Akhbarata*
Marathi
Poona Records Office. *Menavli Daftar*
English
British Museum, London. *Warren Hastings Correspondence*
Foreign and Commonwealth Office (late India Office),
    London. *Home Miscellaneous Series* vols. 336, 485, 492,
    708, 765

RECORDS AND DOCUMENTS, PUBLISHED
Persian
Calendar of Persian Correspondence vols. I—X (1911–)
Persian Records of Maratha History vol. 1 *Delhi Affairs.* Ed.
    J. Sarkar (1953)
Marathi
Aitihasik Lek Sangraha 12 vols. (1897–). Ed. V. V. Khare
Delhi Yethil Marathyanchin Raj-Karanen vols. 1 and 2, and
    suppl. (1913–14). Ed. D. B. Parasnis
Historical Papers of the Sindhias of Gwalior 2 vols. (1934,
    1940)
Holkar-Shahichaya Itahasachi Sadhanen 2 vols. (1944–45).
    Ed. B. B. Thakur
Marathanchya Itihasachin Sadhanen 21 vols. (1898–). Ed.
    V. K. Rajwade et al.
Selections from the Peshwa's Daftar 45 vols. (1918–). Ed.
    G. S. Sardesai
English
Browne Correspondence. (1960). Ed. K. D. Bhargava

Despatches, Minutes and Correspondence of Marquess Wellesley 5 vols. (1836)

Mahadaji Sindhia and North Indian Affairs vol. 1 Poona Residency Correspondence. (1936). Ed. J. Sarkar

Selections from the Letters, Despatches and other State Papers preserved in the Foreign Department of the Government of India vols. I–III. (1890). Ed. G. W. Forrest

Selections from the State Papers of the Governors-General of India. Warren Hastings vols. I–III. (1910). Ed. G. W. Forrest

Selections from the Unpublished Records of Government 1748–1767. (1869). Ed. J. Long

CONTEMPORARY OR NEAR CONTEMPORARY WORKS, UNPUBLISHED

British Museum, London :
  Anon. *Tarikh-i-Ahmad Shahi*
  Anon. *Tarikh-i-Alamgir Sani*
  Miskin (pseud. of Tahmasp Khan) *Memoirs*
Oriental Public Library, Patna :
  Khair-ud-din *Ibratnamah*
  Munalal *Tarikh-i-Shah Alam*
India Office Library, London :
  Wendel, F. X. *Account of the Jat Kingdom*

CONTEMPORARY OR NEAR CONTEMPORARY WORKS, PUBLISHED

Duff, James Grant *History of the Mahrattas* (1826)

Elliot, H. M. and Dowson, J. *The History of India as told by its own Historians* vol. VIII (1877)

Francklin, W. *History of the Reign of Shah Aulum* (1798)

Francklin, W. *Military Memoirs of George Thomas* (1805)

Fraser, J. B. *Military Memoirs of Colonel James Skinner* 2 vols. (1851)

Gentil, M. *Mémoires sur l'Indoustan* (1822)

Ghulam Husain Tabatabhai *Siyar-ul-mutakherin* (Calcutta edn. 1833)

Hodges, W. *Travels in India* (1793)

Law, Jean *Mémoire sur quelques affaires de l'Empire Mogol* (1913). Ed. Martineau

Orme, R. *Historical Fragments of the Mogul Empire* (1805)

Polier A. L. H. *Shah Alam II and his Court* (1947). Ed. P. C. Gupta

Scott, J. *History of the Dekkan* vol. II (1794)

Thorn, W. *Memoir of the War in India* (1818)

SECONDARY WORKS

Chatterji, N. L. *Mir Kasim* (1935)

Compton, H. *A Particular Account of European Adventurers of Hindustan* (1892)

Datta, K. K. *Shah Alam II and the East India Company* (1965)

Edwardes, Michael *Glorious Sahibs* (1968)

Edwardes, Michael *Plassey: The Founding of an Empire* (1969)

Grey, C. and Garrett, H. L. C. *European Adventurers of Northern India* (1929)

Gupta, H. R. *History of the Sikhs* 3 vols. (1939–44)

Irvine, W. *Later Mughals* (1922). Ed. J. Sarkar

Sardesai, G. S. *New History of the Marathas* 3 vols. (1948)

Sarkar, J. *Fall of the Moghal Empire* 4 vols. (1932–50)

Sen, S. P. *The French in India* (1958)

The sources of the quotations on the part titles are as follows:

One: Edward Thornton: *The History of the British Empire in India* (1842) vol. 1 p. 410

Two: Lines from a translation of a poem written by Shah Alam on his blindness. From William Francklin *History of the Reign of Shah Aulum* (1798)

Three: William Palmer, Resident at the court of Sindia, to the governor-general, Lord Cornwallis, 4 August 1788

Index

Personal names are shown in the index in SMALL CAPITALS